A Medieval Woman's Mirror of Honor
THE TREASURY OF THE CITY OF LADIES

A Medieval Woman's Mirror of Honor

THE TREASURY OF THE CITY OF LADIES

Christine de Pizan

Translated, with an introduction by
Charity Cannon Willard

Edited, with an introduction by
Madeleine Pelner Cosman

BARD HALL PRESS / PERSEA BOOKS

For information, address the publishers:

Persea Books, Inc.   Bard Hall Press
60 Madison Avenue   32 Knickerbocker at Oak
New York, New York 10010   Tenafly, New Jersey 07670

Library of Congress Cataloging-in-Publication Data

Christine, de Pizan, ca. 1364–ca. 1431.
   [Livre des trois vertues. English]
   A medieval woman's mirror of honor : the treasury of the city of ladies /
Christine de Pizan ; translated, with an introduction by Charity Cannon Willard ;
edited, with an introduction by Madeleine Pelner Cosman.
      p.   cm.
   Translation of: Le Livre des trois vertues.
   Bibliography: p.
   ISBN 0-89255-144-5 : $22.50. —ISBN 0-89255-135-6 (pbk.) : $11.95
   1. Imaginary conversations. 2. Women—Conduct of life—Early works to
1800. 3. Women—History—Early works to 1800. 4. Feminism—Early works
to 1800. I. Willard, Charity Cannon. II. Cosman, Madeleine Pelner. III. Title.
PQ1575.L6913   1989
248.8'43—dc19   89-150

Designed by Peter St. John Ginna

Typeset in Garamond by Keystrokes, Lenox, Massachusetts

Manufactured in the United States of America

First Edition

ACKNOWLEDGMENTS

A book so long in the making as this one has many talented people to honor. Many women and men have made specific contributions. Charles Garth, Sirvart Kevorkian, and Gladys Seitel spent hours at the computer processing the text. Gretchen Limper helped copyedit the finished manuscript, and Steven Glaser, Charla Powell, and Johanna Ginsberg ably checked and rechecked galleys and page proofs.

Special thanks and appreciation are due to Marin Cosman who crafted the leaf and vine decorations for the chapter heads and whose inspiration it was to create a glossary, an invaluable addition.

We acknowledge, with particular gratitude the many acts of scholarly graciousness of Dr. Laura Monti, Keeper of Rare Books and Manuscripts; Dr. Guiseppe Bisaccia, Curator of Manuscripts; and Dr. Zoltan Haraszti, former Keeper of Rare Books at the Boston Public Library.

CONTENTS

A Medieval Woman's Mirror of Honor:
The Treasury of the City of Ladies

CHRISTINE DE PIZAN'S
WELL-TEMPERED FEMINISM

Madeleine Pelner Cosman

Long ago, on a rugged mountain, I learned to climb and scale rock faces. After gaining competence and confidence with grappling tools and rope, I was tested on a high precipice. Not precisely pushed, I was encouraged to fall over the edge, with only the rope between myself and the chasm below. As I dangled, my father shouted down from the rim: "What do you do when you come to the end of your rope?" The correct answer had three parts: 1) Tie a knot and hang on. 2) Look around. The view never will have been so piercingly clear. 3) Climb back up and exult.

I often thought of that affirmation of self-reliant pragmatism when years later I first encountered the well-tempered feminism of Christine de Pizan, a professional author living in the late fourteenth and early fifteenth centuries. Christine demanded assertive courage of intelligent women so they might thrive in adversity. To prepare them for exigencies, she gave explicit instructions which, like my childhood mountain training, indirectly taught the philosophy: what must be done can be done. Furthermore, what must be known can be learned. Experience and books will teach. Christine, superb pedagogue of practical morality, suggested that reading her advice would encourage a woman to endure the slings and arrows of outrageous fortune and of some men's inhumanity to women.

In 1977 I had the happy obligation to reread all of Christine's work while preparing lectures for a series I was giving at the Metropolitan Museum of Art in New York called "Medieval Women at Work." Dr. Charity Cannon Willard graciously lent me her translation of *Mirror of Honor (Le Livre des Trois Vertus)*, which Christine had written in 1405. For my talk on "Women Writers and Artists," and another on "Lady Bosses, Rulers of Manors and Monasteries," I welcomed this book enthusiastically.

So did the 709 devoted, eager members of my lecture audience. Christine's *Mirror of Honor* depicted the likely reality of the intelligent, powerful, professional woman's life in the fifteenth century. This book, after all, was written for the woman whose vocation was ruling. Better than literary works, this mirror of conduct presented a practical ideal for a princess, duchess, or baroness, as well as for a lady, tradeswoman, or whore. The medieval woman looking into this book should have seen herself reflected as if in a mirror. The medieval "mirror" instruction books—there were mirrors for princes, mirrors for magistrates—created double reflection: reality imitated art, just as art mimicked reality.

Christine's *Mirror of Honor* is an astonishingly important document for the study of medieval culture and for the perception of medieval women's place, achievements, perils, and pleasures. The translator's task has been formidable: truth to word must balance truth to spirit. Charity Cannon Willard's translation is the first completed (although not the first published) English translation of Christine de Pizan's *Mirror of Honor*. Also, she has prepared an edition of the original French *Livre des Trois Vertus,* which will be published this year (1989) in Switzerland.

Dr. Willard's half century as a literary scholar in faithful appreciation of Christine's life and work often resembles the archaeologist's life, with its rewards and risks. Tantalizing fragments newly dug up must be pieced together with previously discovered vestiges of a once-complete work of imagination to recreate today an approximation of the original glory. Aspects of Christine's life history, for example, are only partially known with certainty. Some evidence is incomplete; some pieces of information conflict with others; the origin and validity of certain manuscript translations are suspect. Similar uncertainties nag the meanings of Christine's own words and concepts and the interpretations of her works by her medieval contemporaries. All these factors enter into this translation, as they did into the writing of *Christine de Pizan: Her Life and Works,* Dr. Willard's respected biography.

This translation of *The Mirror of Honor* is superbly close to

Christine's original word and spirit. It is sound, sagacious, respectful of both subject and reader, and is presented with a good-natured high-seriousness derived from a mind constantly and intimately conversant with Christine de Pizan. Indisputable readings of Christine's words are presented straightforwardly and speculations, when necessary, are clever. Despite the ever-present possibility of a great potential tragedy of scholarship—the slaying of a beautiful hypothesis by an ugly fact (as T.H. Huxley reminds us)—if Charity Cannon Willard suggests an idea as "most likely," it is. Until some radiant new manuscript of Christine's *Mirror of Honor* lights our understanding, we must be grateful for the warm glow of Charity Cannon Willard's informed, affectionate knowledge in translation.

Charity Cannon Willard and Christine de Pizan have served one another well. More than half a millenium ago, Christine de Pizan voiced her faith and hope that in a later age her life and works would be treated with high regard and benevolent appreciation, that is, with *caritas* or Charity. Fortunately, some fifty years ago, the two intellectual women joined minds.

Christine de Pizan as Professional Writer

Modern critics dare not forget the literary habits of Christine's time, which she indulged, adapted, or ignored. Perceiving what was typical of her age, modern readers will more fully appreciate her genius. For although most of Christine's ideas seem universal and variously applicable to the modern condition, it is dangerous to forget that she wrote when fashionable ladies wore tall, pointed hats called hennins and tossed their diaphanous, long veils down their backs before eating roast peacock for dinner. It is imperative, therefore, to remind ourselves of the fifteenth-century context surrounding aspects of her art that her audience handsomely paid her to provide: stylistic devices such as quotation from authority, allegory, humility formulae, and character exaggeration.

Christine was a practical professional writer who wrote for money. No matter that she desired fame and immortality; she did. However, she also had creature requirements for the cash, goods, and preferments for herself and her children that patronage provided. As every Christinophile knows, the twenty-five-year-old widow supported her three children, her mother, and assorted relatives by that one powerful instrument—her pen—that was not in court litigation after her husband's death, and thus not subject to takeover by litigious local vultures who preyed, then as now, on the newly grieving.

Her facility in writing what the noble patrons commissioned or were likely to reward does not reduce the originality or the virtuosity of her poetry and prose. But critics who discuss Christine's artistic balance or subject emphases or authorial peculiarities are perilously close to being preposterous if they forget that context of patronage in which she wrote.

Christine's contemporaries, as well as her followers later in the fifteenth century, appreciated her learned style, effervescent with quotations from the classics and the Bible, which pleased patrons because it flattered their own knowledge while adding legitimacy to the ideas presented. Medieval audiences did not welcome something new as enthusiastically as they did something traditional rediscovered or reaffirmed. A novel idea allied to the best of the past (a classical or Biblical golden age) delighted them far more than an idea unattributable to great forebears. So a medieval writer wanting immediate reception placed herself in the company of past luminaries. This was not arrogant conceit, nor pomposity, nor padding a text to extend it, but rather, routine professional writing procedure. Given the choice between the spider—which spins out a gorgeous filament from its gut—and the bee—which collects nectar from many flowers to produce the sweetness and light of honey and candle wax—the medieval audience would select the bee.

So, Christine emulated the bee. William Caxton, the earliest English printer and publisher, translated one of Christine's books and made it one of the first to roll from his press, soon after the Bible; he called her "the mistress and mirror of intelligence." The poet Deschamps lauded her learning. Martin le Franc insisted Christine was the equal of Cicero for eloquence and Cato for wisdom.

An international cultural force, Christine affected the attitudes of both women and men in France, Portugal, and England by arguing cogently and convincingly, as well as by utilizing the literary conventions her audience loved. Daughter of her time, she wrote allegories. She pleased her market with those precious "mind battles," the *psychomachias,* which personified abstract ideas. Today, out of context, allegory seems slightly ludicrous. Yet, it is simply out of conscious fashion, but remains potent in the modern subconscious. In modern language we allegorize constantly, and it is not difficult to train ourselves to enjoy allegories in the medieval manner. For example: my colleague looked at an exquisite, rich chocolate cake for dessert, salivated, and said, "My desire for this is tremendously powerful, but my discretion is holding me back." We need only capitalize the initials of those abstractions; clothe, arm, and horse Desire in flaming red while similarly garbing Discretion as a warrior in sedate royal blue; then allow them to lunge and fight furiously on the battlefield of the Undecided Mind. If Desire emerges victorious, the prize cake is sensually devoured. If Discretion prevails, caloric temptation is overthrown and the cake is untouched.

Imaginative medieval battles between opposites, questions of conscience, or choices between extremes routinely were personified within medieval literature and literate conversation. The more cleverly detailed the transference of qualities from level to level of meaning, the more the audience praised. Modern readers will have to make a greater effort than Christine's contemporaries, who were more experienced at this, literally to see her *Vision,* in which Truth, Justice, and Chivalry languish in prison, while Voluptuousness, Fraud, and Avarice frolic at court. Modern readers expecting character development will be surprised that the best medieval allegories have only linear consistency with each upper or lower parallel stratum. The educated medieval mind perceived the literal, the allegorical, and other implied levels of meaning (such as the anagogical or inspirational; tropological or dogmatic; and the historical) simultaneously, allowing for the intellectual delight of discovering hidden meanings and (as Spenser later called his own allegories) dark conceits.

When taken out of context, another of Christine's stylistic devices usually generates amusing, if ridiculous, psychoanalysis. She often refers to herself as wishing to be a man, as metamorphosed from a woman to a man, or as a woman required to "take on a man's heart." These are rhetorical or literary ploys for introducing predictable dramatic action. For example, in *The City of Ladies* her desire to be a man "so I will be thought as wonderful as men think themselves to be," sets up the dramatic occasion for the three allegorical Virtues to enter to convince her, regally though loquaciously, that she is better off being a woman. Similarly, in *The Mirror of Honor,* when she advises a widow to "take on a man's heart" and be constant, strong, wise, and aggressive in pursuing her own advantage, Christine is maintaining a consistent dramatic analogy and certainly not penis envy.

Similarly, Christine's effacing "I am a mere woman" is no more self-deprecatory than the customary medieval male writer's disclaimer. Geoffrey Chaucer also uses such words as "I present this book which my meager human wit has produced." This is a typical medieval humility formula, tracing inspiration from God and crediting divine wisdom as having bestowed the gift of literary creation. The human author is mere conduit for a higher idea and a more perfect expression. Humility formulae, therefore, as well as allegory, traditional quotations, and statements of negatives to invoke their positives, are all fifteenth-century literary conventions that intelligent women and men of authority and wealth expected from the writers they paid to please them.

To be vested with enormous authority is a fine thing; but, as Mark Twain said, to have the onlooking world consent to it is even finer. Powerful, dominant medieval women had both authority and consent, and were co-rulers with their husbands, or regents for their young sons, or surrogates for their husbands away at war or on crusade. Or they were widows of dead lords, whose lands they ruled. Or they controlled their own vast inheritances.

Running the medieval noble household was comparable to directing a small town. The lady boss was responsible for the huge supplies necessary for the care, feeding, and daily life of hundreds, sometimes thousands of people. Superintending the kitchen meant not only guiding food preparation for courtiers, servants, and workers, but controlling the farms, forests, hunting preserves, fishing lakes, and herb gardens that provided the raw materials. The bake houses, wine cellars, larders, pantries, and spiceries were under her jurisdiction, as were the farm laborers, hunters, kitchen workers, banquet servitors, musicians, dancers, and jugglers. Fabric and making clothing for the whole household were her responsibility, from sheep-shearing to spinning, from weaving to tailoring. Hiring, firing, paying, directing, adjudicating, she supervised all the personnel and activities pertaining to kitchen, hall, and home. She assumed the same responsibilities with regard to the education of her young children, obtaining their tutors, chaplains, and chamberlains.

Whether ruling alone or with her husband, the lady boss often had responsibility for the court cultural life, selecting the poet-propagandists, the manuscript makers, scribes, and illuminators, the sculptors and artists who decorated chapel and hall. Although these were not necessarily permanent members of the household, nevertheless during their tenure of months or years, the lady might be their patron.

For everyone under her supervision, the medieval woman leader served as the quasi-legal arbitrator of disputes, often holding court, handing down judgments, and assigning punishment. She was also the quasi-official health officer responsible for the care of her staff in illness. Literally laying on the hands of healing, the lady boss was trained in practical medicine, expected to be facile in diagnosis and traditional treatment. Moreover, she was responsible for the security of her domain; many women successfully held their manors and castles against armed attack, vigorously protecting their property and people from assault.

The work schedule for such a medieval lady boss was formidable. Here is a typical day's activity.

The woman vested with enormous authority—princess, baroness, or country lady—works excruciatingly hard, performing at least twenty-seven activities in any twenty-four hour day. After a few hours of sleep, the lady boss awakens early, often before dawn. Dressing, breakfasting, and then attending chapel, she prays as much for political as for religious responsibility. According to Christine, the lady ruler need not spend as much time in lengthy prayers as those who have greater leisure, for the ruler derives heavenly merit from attending to the public good and the welfare of those in her power. Leaving the chapel, she must give alms and listen to requests from poor petitioners, granting promptly and generously whatever she can, not only for charity but for enhancing her reputation. If unable to hear all the pleas, she must delegate the job to an honorable and efficient surrogate, for whose actions she is responsible.

On the days her government council meets in the morning, she must conduct herself with such bearing and countenance that, seated on the high throne of authority, she not only appears to rule but does. Authority requires acknowledgment by the ruled. To be revered as a wise mistress of great power she must listen diligently to all proposals and opinions, weighing carefully the best advice and replying cogently and sagely. If possible, she should have had advance briefings by her counsellors on all important matters. She also ought to consult with her fool—an intelligent courtier hired for his impertinent statements of truth. Jokingly serious, he will be earnest in jest. Among the flatterers, he is paid to tell the truth.

Thereafter, she must preside at a noontime feast. The guests, all seated according to social protocol, are served different foods according to their rank. Entertainments in the hall include music, dance, dramatic readings of poems on valiant deeds, and plays both edifying and delightful. As the feasting progresses, the lady boss holds audience for those who have come from afar to seek her counsel or her money. Receiving each graciously and with due honor, she speaks seriously to the elderly, and more gayly to the young. After sharing digestive spices to adjourn the feast, she goes to her apartment for a brief rest, some useful handwork such as embroidery or weaving, dictating to her secretary, and simple talk and amusement with her ladies-in-waiting. Politics here is as important as friendship. The lady boss, laughing and talking informally, is encouraging her women to faithfulness and discretion, so that they will protect her against slander and injury and, as Christine counsels, "love her with great devotion."

Next she must visit the sick in hospitals or, if members of her own manor (gentlemen, stewards, or farmers) are ill, she must go to their quarters, touching with her hands of healing.

Then she must do the financial books. A medieval lady maintains five classes of expense accounts for appropriately distributing her income. The first category is gifts to the poor. Second is the money for her household: hundreds of men and women are fed and paid from her own revenues, namely, the rents and taxes paid directly to her. The third account pays her officers and court ladies, counselors, and ambassadors to distant holdings or foreign courts. A fourth amount of money is reserved for gifts to strangers or to her subjects who evidence particular merit; this patronage allows the lady boss to encourage art, science, and technology within her domain, and to be celebrated for generosity. A final personal treasury is for purchasing her own jewels, gowns, and apparel.

This same afternoon, she must visit her children—not only for maternal pleasure but for political necessity. Carefully having arranged their proper tutoring, the lady boss who is a mother must consistently guide her offsprings' activities, regularly checking on their progress. As Christine says, "the greatest protection and ornament she can have is her children, for, as often happens, someone who might wish to harm the mother will refrain from doing so for fear of the children."

The lady boss will hear crop reports from her head fieldmen and gardeners. As a successful manager, she earlier will have watched farm activities from a window, intentionally allowing the workers to be aware of her scrutiny. The cloaked face gazing into the distance was asserting her primacy over laborers' tendency to sloth. Christine correctly warns that many in the field will stop raking the ground beyond scratching the surface or will sleep in the shade of a willow if they think no one is watching. Indifference reigns where supervision does not.

Then the chief shepherd will relay news about the vigor of the sheep. If the lady boss fears laziness of the shepherds, she will soon wisely walk up to the castle roof ramparts, as Christine recommends, to reconnoiter, appraising the flock from afar. Watching her, the untutored eye would see only an elegant lady and her attendant strolling for pleasure; the knowing eye perceives her protecting her wool income.

Below in the hall, she will supervise purchase of foodstuffs from merchants (some of whom are women), obtaining their imported delicacies, spices, and herbs. Maintaining good relationships with merchants by paying promptly for goods and services, she keeps her credit rating respectable. She also must supervise the cooks' menus, providing great varieties and quantities of food for all classes eating within the great hall, and tasting the wines and ales whose quality asserts "power bought this."

The sun now setting toward Vespers time, the lady boss will say prayers in chapel or chamber before exercising in the garden in advance of supper. She will not wander alone, for she must hold a late afternoon audience with her subjects who need her. She may have to indulge in "discreet dissimulation" with her enemies lest she appear in any way to be weak in her control over people or purses. This twilight stroll thus is as political as it is healthful.

This afternoon she also might ride horseback on a hunt, or boat on the river, or dance, or play backgammon or billiards or chess. All of these public entertainments serve purposes of policy. Certainly the lady boss must not allow herself to be checkmated.

Supper, again a public meal, includes entertainments such as dancers, minstrels, jugglers, jongleurs, jesters, and poets reading aloud or chanting dramatic story. In these preprinting days, news and propaganda are transmitted quickly to large numbers by reciting rather than reading.

And so to prayers and bed. Extraordinarily busy dawn-light through candle-light, the responsible lady boss must briefly sleep before the next day's significant activity.

Far from boring, merely ceremonial activities, the vocation of the woman in power required physical stamina as well as exemplary control over emotions and deeds. Scrutinized by a public that might either wish her well or desire her death, the medieval lady leader constantly exercised authority so that her power was acknowledged and reaffirmed.

To such a vigorous daily schedule, medieval women leaders added the occasional rigors of riding to crusade; the arduous yet ceremonial voyages, called progresses, to visit landholdings; the political travels to new acquisitions got by diplomacy or war; the visits to markets, fairs, and banking houses; and the defense of their establishments by the sword.

Women committed to guarding their properties with their lives did so. Margaret Paston, for example, while her husband was journeying on business or when he became a political prisoner in the Tower of London, found enemies attacking the Paston manors. She valiantly defended their property while the bombarded walls crumbled and her household retainers fell dead at her feet. In one letter to her husband, Sir John Paston, in late 1449, she requests that he send to her at Gresham various armaments such as crossbows, grappling irons, and "quarrels," or iron shooting bolts, as well as short poleaxes for protecting the doors, to enable her and twelve retainers to protect the house against Lord Molyns' aggression. A few paragraphs later, she also asks him to send almonds, sugar, and fabric for the children's clothes; the defense arrangements were simply part of the usual dangerous duties of the medieval woman at work. Years later (in October 1465), she reports to her husband another act of violence against their property; this time the Duke of Norfolk sent three hundred men against them in Hellesdon, ransacking, pillaging, and destroying the castle, the tenant houses, even the church. Margaret dealt with the aftermath of that attack and the assaults upon the lives of their devotees. As a widow four years later, she writes to her son about yet another siege against Paston property, in October 1469, counselling him to protect Caister Castle against the Duke of Norfolk's three thousand men who surrounded, then seized it.

Other Englishwomen also dramatically guarded their domains, such as the Countess of Buchan, who defended Berwick Castle against the attack of King Edward I. He later hung her up in a cage on the ramparts of her own castle for his soldiers to mock. Lady Alice Knyvet in 1461 refused to give up Bokenham Castle to the king who had ordered ten commissioners and a justice of the peace to claim it on the spot by legal proceedings. When they arrived, however, they found the drawbridge up and Alice and her fifty men armed with swords, glaives, and bows and arrows. From a tower Alice shouted, "Mister Twyer, you are a justice of the peace. I require you to keep the peace. I will not leave possession of this castle. If you make war to take this place from me, I shall defend myself, for I prefer in such wise to die. For my husband charged me to keep this place." She kept it.

Hiring help was another major activity of medieval women's work, requiring intelligent decision paired with trained intuition.

Certainly for rulers the faithfulness and expertise of servitors might make the difference between monarchy or anarchy in parts of the realm. The same held true for the wealthy but untitled lady boss, such as the fifteen-year-old wife of the kindly, aged Goodman of Paris, a rich fourteenth century merchant. She learned how to hire both temporary workmen and permanent servants, carefully checking their recent references and observing their actions and manners. Flatterers were to be avoided, and dependable workers found, for well-chosen servants were public representatives of their master's and mistress's virtues. Not only reputation but life itself might depend upon faithful employees. As the Goodman says, "If you engage a maid or man of high and prideful answers, know that when such servant leaves he will slander you if he can; contrariwise, if he is all flattery and blandishments, trust not such servant, for he is doubtlessly in league with someone else to trick you." And when you find the perfect servant, love him or her as your child.

Numerous women in authority were actually young teenagers. Life was far too short to spend too long in childhood. Though many women lived until their eighties, an average age at death was thirty-three. Arranged marriages for children allowed young noble husbands and wives to play ball and hoop and read Latin and dance together before consummation of their union at puberty. Though benevolent parents were unlikely to make arbitrary or cruel unions, nevertheless they frequently betrothed children to unite large landholdings or resolve disputes between warring families, making pledges for purely dynastic purposes.

Once reaching puberty, or the usual age of consent—fourteen for boys, twelve for girls—young spouses could request annulment if either did not willingly agree to the union. Though such ecclesiastical figures as the great canon lawyer Gracian insisted upon consent, families sometimes pushed unwilling children into union, but not always successfully. Making her recalcitrant daughter an offer difficult to refuse, Margaret Paston locked the daughter up in a tower, permitting neither visitors nor food until she would consent to marry an old, rich man whom Margaret had selected. Slimmer and stubborner for her ordeal, the young lady ultimately triumphed with the young lover of her choice, who was a faithful family servitor. Astonishing fourteenth century documents consecrated the engagement of noble children *in utero*—the unborn daughter still in the womb of a pregnant noblewoman being promised to the equally unborn son of another noblewoman. A safety clause held that the agreement would continue in force even if the sexes of the two children were the opposite of those expected, and abrogated the contract if the sexes were identical.

Christine's advice to young widows becomes more poignant when we consider these women's ages. An early medieval example is the family of Euginia Picot. Associated with the twelfth-century court of King Henry II and Queen Eleanor in England, Euginia was the daughter of Ralf Picot, from whom she inherited lands in Wilton, Kent. By age twenty-nine, she had been married and widowed twice. Her first husband was William Malet, a member of the royal household, who died in 1170, leaving Euginia an inheritance in Cambridgeshire. Subsequently married to Thomas Fitz Bernard, chief forester for the king and queen, she produced one daughter and three sons, who were ten, eight, five, and three at their father's death in 1185. King Henry had given Euginia's daughter Maude in marriage to an infant boy, the heir of John de Bidun. However, the baby-boy groom died, leaving Maude a widow at age ten. She then lived in custody of her mother, who controlled her marriage-inherited lands. Mother Euginia also held yet another child's dowry, for her eldest son, also age ten, was already married to an heiress who brought her land, a large Essex manor, with her at the age of five.

To give clue to the vastness of such inheritances, consider the following awesome list of properties and income allocated in 1376 to Elizabeth, a knight's wife, at the death of her husband Edward le Despenser. For all the castles, forests, rental properties, towns, churches, abbeys, and priories on this list, she swore homage and fealty to King Edward III and promised him her service as a knight, pledging not to marry without the king's license. "Her right and heritage" of properties both in England and the border of Wales included: the castle and town of Kerfilly, the "country" of Sengh above and below Caugh, the hamlet of Rothery, Enysuaylgoun, the manor of Whytechurch, the manor and country of Talvan, the town of Coubrugge, the castle and manor of Lanblethian, the country of Ruthyr, the manor of Tuekesbury in Gloucester, the manor of Faireford, the "foreign court" of Bristol, the castle and manor of Haneleye in Worcester, the manor of Bischley, the manor of Stanford in Berkes, the manor of Yelvertoft in Northampton, the "hundred" of Chadlynton in Oxford, as well as other castles, towns, manors, and lands.

Christine's book permits us to comprehend the practical meaning of such responsibility: the personal requirements for stamina, perseverance, perceptiveness, courage, diplomacy, judgment; plus the planning, staffing, directing, coordinating, reporting, budgeting, and other classical functions of organization required of the chief executive. Nothing in such a woman leader's day or night could be without political implication.

This emphasis upon the political nature of the commonplace is one of Christine's many virtues. Her book forces us to see anew the familiar fifteenth century portraiture of magnificently garbed women hunting, hawking, and dancing as being of women not simply at play, but of women at work. The exquisitely poised ladies of the *Belles Heures* and the *Très Riches Heures* of Jean, Duc de Berry were politically resilient public figures deftly wielding power at the instant they let fly the hawk from the wrist. The woman at the window, needlework in hand, is not busy-fingered and mind-vacant. She is watching her workers and posing for her people as the watcher watched. Enormous power is the severest form of public servitude. Every common act, each gesture, frown, or sneeze is critically observed and interpreted. "My lady enjoys this." "My lady squints in disbelief." "My lady must not be permitted to lose this quarry," or "this game of chess."

Medieval women vested with enormous authority and with

their realm's or king's consent labored powerfully during their long day's journey into night. Their sons and daughters could inherit their vast holdings at the final nighttime. Adventures of medieval women in authority depict the ambivalent position of one in power: it is a perilous pleasure and pleasureable peril. Christine de Pizan analyzed this ambivalence accurately, pragmatically, and humanely. Her feminism in *Mirror of Honor*, as well as in her previous work, *The City of Ladies*, was three ways "well-tempered": she was perfectly tuned to the emotional pitches of both women and men of her time. She was thoroughly good-natured. She balanced righteous anger proportionately with humane understanding.

CHRISTINE DE PIZAN'S
ADVICE TO WOMEN

Charity Cannon Willard

Advice to women on how to behave in society has never been lacking, at least not since the days of St. Paul, and no doubt a considerable body of such advice already existed long before any was written down. At the same time, women's advice to other women had been singularly lacking, so the work of Christine de Pizan is especially remarkable. Without question she owes a significant portion of her literary reputation—today as well as in 1405—to her participation in a debate over Jean de Meun's continuation of the *Romance of the Rose,* the long, popular, anti-feminist allegory which Christine considered unfairly slanderous of women. Although it has now been demonstrated that she did not stir up the argument originally,[1] one must still wonder at her courage in publicly taking to task several royal secretaries who prided themselves on their intellectual accomplishments. She also dared to call into question the whole concept of "courtly love," as practiced by her contemporaries, some of whom had recently been engaged in founding a Court of Love supposedly devoted to writing poetry in honor of ladies.

Critics have not always been generous in their comments about Christine's role in the *Rose* affair, often disregarding or dismissing the validity of her viewpoint by labeling her, as did Gustave Lanson, a "tiresome bluestocking" or, as John Fleming has more recently written, an "hysterical woman."[2] Nonetheless one thing is certain: the debate and the letters she circulated about it led her to write two of her most important works, *Le Livre de la Cité des Dames (The Book of the City of Ladies)* and *Le Livre des Trois Vertus (The Book of the Three Virtues*—which we have called *The Medieval Woman's Mirror of Honor).* Both of these were devoted to the problems of women in society, and both probably were finished in the course of 1405.

Until now it has not been easy for contemporary readers to know just what Christine had to say about women beyond her letters written during the debate, for these two works on the subject have remained unpublished since the sixteenth century. Fortunately, modern translations are beginning to appear,[3] and my edition soon will make available to the interested reader the French text of this book, *Le Livre des Trois Vertus,* dedicated not only to a fifteenth-century princess but also to all women of Christine's own day and of the future.

Christine's outlook inevitably was affected by her Italian origin, for she was born in Venice around 1365, at a time when Petrarch was a resident in that city. Her father and grandfather were both counsellors of the Venetian Republic and graduates of the University of Bologna. Christine learned about the ways of Italian cities from her father, Tommaso da Pizzano, but most of her life was spent in Paris, where he had been invited soon after her birth to become an astrologer and physician at the court of King Charles V. Thus, Christine's childhood was spent in the shadow of the French court.

When Christine reached the age of fifteen, a match was arranged for her with a promising young notary, apparently a university graduate. Official documents refer to him as Master Etienne de Castel, probably in deference to his having obtained a Master of Laws degree. The year of their marriage, 1380, he was given an appointment as one of the royal secretaries, a member of the king's chancellery. Such a position would not only have provided security and a certain cachet, but would also have held out hope of a promising future. Successful public careers frequently began in the chancellery. But after ten years of happy married life and the birth of three children, Etienne de Castel died unexpectedly during an epidemic while he was away from Paris accompanying King Charles VI on a royal mission. Thus Christine was left alone, at the age of twenty-five, to contend with an unsympathetic and highly materialistic society for which she had little preparation.

If Christine had been born in the twentieth century, she probably would have chosen to be either a journalist or an educator. Her enthusiasm for reforming society and for educating its members, especially its youth, is one of the most interesting aspects of her writing. French society at that time offered abundant scope for such concerns, for the country had already embarked on the disastrous course which would lead, during Christine's own lifetime, to civil war and defeat by the English at Agincourt. Christine's ideas concerning the status of women and the education of young children, however, were well in advance of her day. [4]

Christine's own children, only two of whom grew to adulthood, were undoubtedly the first objects of her interest in education, for her earliest writings on that subject were directed to her son, Jean. For him she wrote a series of "moral teachings" and some proverbs which were eventually translated into English and published by William Caxton. [5]

Thanks to her talent and the interest of the Burgundian princes and princesses, among others who became her patrons, Christine made her way to success as a writer in a society where women writers were few. However, her struggles and frustrations in accomplishing this feat gave her an everlasting concern for the situation of women of all social classes. Women were traditionally sheltered and guided by men as long as they were daughters, wives, or mothers, but they were unprotected when obliged by circumstances to make their own way in the world. The problem of how to give women a sense of their own worth in society and to prepare them better to face the problems which might confront them provides the basic inspiration for both *The Book of the City of Ladies* and *A Medieval Woman's Mirror of Honor*.

Although the model for Christine's *City of Ladies* was Boccaccio's *De mulieribus claris*, her title for it was no doubt inspired by St. Augustine's *City of God*, which had been translated into French by Raoul de Presles during the reign of Charles V. At least three manuscripts of this translation were illustrated by the same artist who illustrated four of the earliest manuscripts of *The City of*

Ladies.[6] Christine also borrowed from St. Augustine an important part of her concept of the Virtues who were to play such a major role in both *The City of Ladies* and its sequel, *The Mirror of Honor.* Christine's *Livre du Corps de Policie (The Book of the Body Politic)* outlines the education of the Perfect Prince. There she says:

Now see Saint Augustine in the book of *The City of God,* the XXth chapter. . . . He says that according to the philosophers, virtue is the end of human good and evil, which is to say that human felicity consists in being virtuous . . . and the ancient philosophers represented Felicity in the following manner; she appeared as a very beautiful and refined queen on a royal throne, and the Virtues were seated on the ground around her, looking her in the face to hear her commandments and to serve and obey her.[7]

So it is that three Virtues, dressed as goddesses and wearing golden crowns on their heads, appear to Christine in a vision in *The City of Ladies* to guide her in the construction of an ideal city devised for the welfare of women, and to discuss with her women's special qualities and contributions to society. It is significant that these three supernatural creatures are quite distinct from the traditional theological virtues—Faith, Hope, and Charity—and that they bear only a slight resemblance to the well-known Cardinal Virtues—Prudence, Magnanimity, Continence, and Justice. The Virtues who make their appearance in *The City of Ladies* are distinctly secular in nature, and, in her next book, *The Mirror of Honor,* they organize lessons with the help of Worldly Prudence for princesses and other women.

As they introduce themselves to Christine, the Virtues describe the attributes they carry like scepters in their right hands. Dame Reason's mirror is intended to show the one who looks into it an image of his or her true self. Reason explains to Christine: "I would thus have you know truly that no one can look into this mirror, no matter what kind of creature, without achieving self-knowledge. My mirror has such great dignity that not without reason it is surrounded by rich and precious gems, so that you see, thanks to this mirror, the essences, qualities, proportions, and measures of all things that are known, nor can anything be done well without it."[8] Christine thus recommends "holding the mirror up to nature" more than two centuries before Molière. She already had introduced Dame Reason enthroned in the heavens in an earlier work, the *Chemin de Long Estude,* written in 1403.[9]

The second Virtue, Dame Rectitude, carries a ruler in her hand and explains that this is intended to measure all things and to separate good from evil. "It is the rod of peace," she says, "which reconciles the good things and where they find support and which beats and strikes down evil."[10] Rectitude seems to have been borrowed from Philip de Mézières. As Chancellor of the Kingdom of Cyprus, he had been in Venice during the period when Christine's father was living there, and like her father, had later been at the court of Charles V. Rectitude had appeared in Philip de Mézières' *Songe du Vieil Pelerin (The Dream of the Old Pilgrim),* dedicated to Charles VI in 1389. Rectitude appears there as the handmaiden of Queen Truth, dressed in white and holding in her hand a golden ruler.

Although Justice was commonly known as one of the Cardinal Virtues, usually represented carrying a balance or a sword, Christine's concept of her is different.[11] Justice had already appeared in Christine's *Epître d'Othéa à Hector,*[12] where she is represented receiving from God the measuring vessel she carries in *The City of Ladies.* In *Othéa,* Justice is a measure that God has established on earth to limit all things. In *The City of Ladies,* Dame Justice explains to Christine that she dwells in Hell as well as on Earth and in Heaven, for it is her duty to judge, separate, and provide retribution or reward according to each person's individual merits. She also is charged with preserving the equilibrium of all things, which would otherwise lack stability. Of the golden cup she holds, she says: "This vessel of fine gold which you see me hold in my right hand, made like a generous measure, God, my father, gave me, and it serves to measure out to each his rightful portion. It carries the signs of the fleur-de-lis of the Trinity, and in all portions it measures true, nor can any man complain about my measure. Yet the men of the Earth have other measures, which they claim depend upon and derive from mine, but they are mistaken. Often they measure in my shadow, and their measure is not always true but sometimes too much for some and too little for others."[13]

The framework of *The City of Ladies* was Christine's own invention and is a most interesting aspect of the book, for three levels of creation take place. The first is the symbolic construction of the City of Ladies, which would be devoted exclusively to the needs of women and where the most worthy of them would dwell, free from the demands and preoccupations of ordinary life. Second is the discussion between Christine and her allegorical visitors, and third are the examples of famous women marshalled as proof of women's special qualities and their contributions to society from the beginning of recorded history.

When Dame Reason proposes to Christine the building of the city, Christine objects that she is not capable of such an undertaking. Reason assures her that all the answers to her problems can be found in books and urges her to start building the foundations at once. By the end of the first part of the book, the walls have been finished, and Dame Rectitude is ready to start constructing the dwellings within the walls. By the end of Part II, the buildings are ready for occupancy and Dame Justice gives Christine directions for adding the high towers and the battlements which will enhance the city.

Christine's conversation with the Virtues as the work progresses ranges over a number of topics, but first of all she raises the question of the motives for all the slanderous remarks about women which are to be found in literature written by men. She insists that these are against nature, for men and women are in truth capable of great love for one another, as she has already pointed out in a poem entitled *L'Epître au Dieu d'Amour*.[14] Dame Reason's response is to point out how greatly Christine is mistaken in feeling so distressed about the reputation of women in the past. To illustrate this point, she begins to cite examples of women from mythology who made important contributions to civilization. These examples are largely taken from Boccaccio, to whom Christine makes no attempt to conceal her indebtedness. She also uses several examples from his *Decameron,* as yet practically unknown in France.[15] To these examples she adds others from French history, even mentioning some contemporary French women, thus presenting parallels between past and present.

Christine also wants to discuss with her visitors the limitations placed on women by society, asking why women are not allowed to serve as judges or to occupy positions of authority. Dame Reason replies by citing the case of Nicola, the Empress of Ethiopia, following this with the story of Queen Fredegonde of France, who governed her realm after the death of her husband, King Chilperic. She then recalls the cases of other French queens— Charles IV's Queen Jeanne, King John's Queen Blanche, and the Duchess of Anjou—all of whom served as administrators for their husbands.

Christine then inquires of Reason if there have been any women of demonstrated scientific ability. The Goddess admits that women suffer a severe handicap in this field because they are generally expected to stay at home to look after their households and families, but she insists that if it were the custom to send girls to school with their brothers, there is no reason to assume that their scientific prowess would not be the equal of men's. One has only to consider the obvious differences between educated men and peasant men without any schooling to see that women's possible accomplishments cannot be judged unless they are given equal opportunities for proving themselves.

Finally, Christine says to Dame Reason: "My Lady, I greatly admire what I have heard you say, that so much good has come into the world by virtue of the understanding of women. These men usually say that women's knowledge is worthless. In fact, when someone says something foolish, the widely voiced insult is that this is women's knowledge. In brief, the typical opinions and comments of men claim that women have been and are useful

33

in the world only for bearing children and sewing."[16] Christine then confesses that she has come to the conclusion that women's practical contribution to humanity is as important to the general welfare as Aristotle's philosophy. This remark undoubtedly provides an important clue to Christine's thinking about women, which is that they are quite capable of dealing successfully with the practical problems of living.

Christine continues her discussion now with Dame Rectitude, as she occupies herself with the building of houses within the city. It is in the course of this exchange that Christine inquires whether it is true that marriage is really so distasteful to men through the fault of their wives, to the point where some writers have even advised men to avoid it altogether. Dame Rectitude replies rather sharply that far more women suffer from the married state than men, and some are indeed worse off than if they were slaves of the Saracens. What is written in books on the subject has little to do with reality, for everyone knows that men are masters of their wives rather than the reverse, and they would never allow it to be otherwise. All this recalls statements made earlier by Christine in one of her letters inspired by *The Romance of the Rose*. Fortunately, there are also many happy and tranquil marriages, but any woman who enjoys such a union was indeed born under a lucky star; there are also good wives, who serve their husbands with devotion, sustaining them and comforting them in times of tribulation, and even keeping their secrets, a contradiction of one of the most frequent complaints by the men who have written about the trials of marriage. Such women as these will be among the first to be welcomed into the City of Ladies.

An especially interesting part of this discussion with Dame Rectitude occurs when the question of a suitable education for women is raised. Christine and her mentor immediately agree that women are enhanced by knowledge, so that it is indeed surprising that some men should oppose it.

In considering who will inhabit the city, now nearing completion, Christine inevitably thinks that French princesses should be among the first to be invited, so at the end of the second part of the book she issues a special invitation to them, beginning with Queen Isabeau about whose qualifications there might well have been some question if the book had not been finished before the summer of 1405.

Having issued these special invitations, Christine addresses herself to all virtuous women, both in France and elsewhere, uring them to take advantage of the newly built city, the product of her great effort on their behalf.

It has been suggested that Christine should have ended her book at this point, [17] for the stories of saints which make up the third part are sometimes distasteful to the modern mind. But in the Middle Ages, even a person as free from excessive piety as Christine was convinced that the contemplative life was superior to the active life, although not everyone was adapted to choosing it. It is inevitable that the Virgin Mary should be chosen to reign over the city and so Dame Justice escorts her to the gates, inviting all women gathered there to come forward to receive her. She is escorted by a great company of saints—who were, after all, as Christine points out, the first women in Christian history to be given equal recognition with men for their achievements.

Christine ends her book with some words directed to the inhabitants of the new city, cautioning them that they should make good use of it and that above all they should not be arrogant because of their newly discovered heritage. But she also speaks to them of the necessity of defending themselves against those who might attempt to assault their honor or their virtue, especially those who might attempt to ensnare them with the lure of illicit love under the guise of so-called courtly love. Thus she returns to the issues raised three years earlier by the debate over *The Romance of the Rose*.

Having demonstrated that women are worthy of respect and admiration, Christine inevitably was faced with the necessity of explaining to her contemporaries how they might develop the qualities which would make them worthy of dwelling in the city she had devised. Previously, little attention had been given to preparing women for more than religious and domestic duties. Such manuals as were available, the *Livre du Chevalier de la Tour Landry*[18] or the *Ménagier de Paris,*[19] had been written by men for the purpose of molding wives or daughters according to their own desires. Even in Italy, where there was somewhat more interest in instructing women in social graces, Francesco Barbarino's *Del Reggimento e dei Costumi delle Donne,*[20] written in the early fourteenth century, was primarily directed toward preparing girls for suitable marriages. Nothing had ever been written to help women deal with the problems which they faced as adults, whether married, widowed, or members of religious communities. Christine herself was painfully aware of the price she had had to pay for her own ignorance when she was widowed, and she had since had the opportunity to observe the sorts of problems other women had to face in a variety of circumstances. This became the basis for her second book, *Le Livre des Trois Vertus (The Book of the Three Virtues),* which was printed in 1497, more than sixty-five years after Christine's death, with the title *Le Trésor de la Cité des Dames (The Treasury of the City of Ladies).* We have elected to call it here *A Medieval Woman's Mirror of Honor.*

Although *The City of Ladies* and *The Mirror of Honor* undoubtedly were intended to complement each other, there is a distinct difference in tone between them. Whereas the three Virtues unite the two works, their role in the second book is much less important than in the first. They appear to Christine in the first pages to urge her to bestir herself to continue writing and to organize the school conducted by Worldly Prudence not only for princesses but also for women of all social classes. Only the first of three parts of the book is devoted to princesses, the second addressing itself to other noblewomen, and the third to all the rest of womankind. Since this great variety of women was expected to form her audience, Christine greatly simplifies her usual style, giving up most allegory and literary references. She limits her quotations and examples to texts these women might reasonably be expected to recognize—above all the Scriptures, plus common proverbs and quotations from a popular manual which was much used by medieval preachers, the *Manipulus Florum,* a collection of quotations dealing with virtues and vices.[21] Indeed, individual chapters of *The Mirror of Honor* sometimes recall sermons of the time, except that Christine is concerned with worldly rather than spiritual salvation.

It is especially significant that the ideal lives she prescribes for all—from the princess to the agricultural worker—are nothing if not active. A great burst of social vitality is reflected here. Christine has no patience with idleness.

At the same time, Christine shows herself well aware of the shortcomings of society, interspersing her recommendations with vignettes of people around her—the lazy, arrogant queen; the jealous and gossiping ladies-in-waiting at court; the extravagant and ostentatious wives of prosperous merchants; the servants who deceive an inexperienced mistress as they feather their own nests; the women who go on pilgrimages for dubious reasons—all of these are entertaining examples of social satire, sometimes recalling scenes from a notably satiric medieval book called The *Quinze Joies de Mariage.*[22]

Throughout *The Mirror of Honor* there are certain recurring themes which reflect Christine's particular concerns. First, of course, is widowhood. It is interesting to note how much of what she says differs little from advice given to widows by modern psychologists. There are also constant references to a woman's insecurity in a society where she lacked most civil rights and was obliged to remain in the good graces not only of her husband but also of his family and friends and others who could do her harm if they became her enemies. Many other elements contributed to the uncertainty of life, of course—not only the political instability brought on by recurring conflict between France and England, but also, from 1405 onward, the threat of civil war in

France.

Christine repeatedly attacks indolence, envy, and extravagance, not to mention the overwhelming desire to appear to be more than one really is, all shortcomings which contribute to giving women a bad name. This last foible suggests a certain upward mobility in fifteenth century French society which Christine, for one, was not prepared to condone, although it foreshadowed the subsequent history of the bourgeoisie.

She also attacks the hypocrisy and deceptions which were the unpleasant reality of courtly love. Although Christine earlier had admitted that it might once have been a noble ideal, times obviously had changed, inspiring her repeated warnings about the ensnarements of illicit love and the high price which almost inevitably has to be paid for it. (The situation had not changed a century later when problems of feminine honor figured in the conversations surrounding the tales in Marguerite of Navarre's *Heptameron,* where women are so often shown as the victims of just such snares as Christine describes. Marguerite of Navarre was certainly among Christine's readers.)

Christine's views on the subject of honor are best summed up in a letter written by Madame de la Tour (Book I, Chapter 27), a lady charged with the education of a susceptible young princess. The role of this elderly governess is particularly interesting, because she offers advice entirely opposed to the sort given to the Lover by the Old Woman in *The Romance of the Rose.* She also stands in contrast to the go-between Trotaconventos in *La Celestina* and to the nurse in *Romeo and Juliet.* It is quite evident that Christine believed that the elderly have a duty to give good advice to the young and not to encourage them in their follies. At the same time, she did not close her eyes to the results of frail morality, for she also includes a chapter on the plight of prostitutes in which she proposes a program of reform leading to ultimate salvation.

Christine's *Livre des Fais et Bonnes Meurs du Sage Roy Charles V,* commissioned by the Duke of Burgundy, had been intended to provide a suitable model of kingship for the heir to the French throne, Louis of Guyenne. [23] It is therefore not surprising to find that *The Mirror of Honor* was dedicated to Louis' young wife, Marguerite of Nevers, who was expected to become Queen of France in due course.

Marguerite, granddaughter of Christine's patron, the Duke of Burgundy, had been married to Louis of Guyenne in August 1404, about a year before Christine finished writing *The Mirror of Honor*. She was eleven years old at the time of her marriage. Born in 1393, she had almost immediately become a pawn in the sophisticated Burgundian diplomacy of marriages. [24] At the age of seven months, she had been promised to an older brother of Louis. From the time of their formal betrothal in January 1396, when the small princess was three, she had been known as "Madame la Dauphine," even though she had never left her own nursery.

But Marguerite's betrothed died in 1401. Her grandfather then made another treaty with the French crown in 1403, which was intended to ensure his continued dominance at the French court. This agreement was based on no fewer than three marriages between his grandchildren and the French royal children. The Duke of Burgundy did not live to witness any of these marriages he had so carefully planned; he died unexpectedly during the spring of 1404.

As soon as the formal marriage between Marguerite and Louis of Guyenne had taken place, the princess, according to the usual custom, was sent to live at the French court, although the chronicler Juvenal des Ursins tells us that the union was not consummated until June 1409. [25] In any case, the first part of *The Mirror of Honor* was quite evidently written to guide the steps of this young princess as she grew up at the French court. What is less certain is whether Christine wrote the book at the request of Marguerite's parents, John the Fearless and Marguerite of Bavaria, or whether she herself saw the opportunity to launch a new work which would give expression to some ideas which were especially important to her. The only clue is an ambiguous entry in the Burgundian accounts, dated February 20. 1406:

To Damoiselle Christine de Pizan, widow of the late Master Estienne de Castel, for a gift made by my Lord, 100 *ecus,* in recompense for two books which she presented to my Lord, one of which she was asked to do by my late Lord, the Duke of Burgundy, My Lord's father... shortly before he died, which she has since finished and which my Lord received in his place, and the other book which my Lord wished to have, which books and others of her letters *(épîtres)* and poems with which my Lord is well pleased....[26]

It is evident that the first book mentioned is the biography of Charles V which, according to her own account, Christine finished at the end of November 1404. It seems probable that the other book mentioned is *The Mirror of Honor.* The dedication to John's daughter Marguerite would certainly have commended it to his attention, whether he had specifically asked for it or not. In spite of the relentless Burgundian matrimonial policy, both John the Fearless and his father, the Duke, Philip the Bold, gave evidence of genuine devotion to their wives and children and a concern for their welfare. It is understandable that Marguerite's parents might have had some misgivings about sending her to the French court in Paris, dominated as it was by a power struggle surrounding the insane king, Charles VI, who was little more than a figurehead, and presided over by a frivolous and self-seeking queen, Isabeau of Bavaria.[27] Although the scandal which linked Isabeau's name to that of the king's brother, Louis of Orleans, had not yet become public knowledge at the time of Marguerite's marriage, one suspects that the portrait of the vain and lazy queen in the early pages of Christine's book is a veiled criticism of this notorious woman. However, the book contains no direct suggestion of the storm that was brewing during the summer of 1405, a storm brought on not only by the increasingly obvious nature of the relations between the queen and her brother-in-law, but also by the growing rivalry for political domination between the Duke of Orleans and his cousin, John the Fearless, the new Duke of Burgundy.

This latter problem came to a crisis in August 1405, when John the Fearless arrived in Paris for the avowed purpose of doing homage to the king for the County of Flanders, which he had recently inherited from his mother, Margaret of Flanders. Whatever the duke's true motive for this visit, he arrived at the head of a formidable army, and at the news of his approach, Louis of Orleans hastily left Paris accompanied by the queen. Furthermore, the two of them arranged for not only the Duke of Guyenne, but also the Duke's young wife, Marguerite, to be brought to them at a royal hunting lodge some miles south of Paris. When the new Duke of Burgundy learned of this kidnapping, he rode posthaste across Paris after his daughter and son-in-law, overtaking them near Corbeil. After a heated encounter with the children's escort, John the Fearless succeeded in having the royal litter turned around and sent back to Paris, where the young duke and duchess were placed behind the protecting walls of the Louvre.

The affair brought Paris to the brink of civil war, and the quarrel was settled only with the greatest difficulty. Nobody was really in favor of a show of force, so by mid-October the armies were successfully disbanded. It is significant that no hint of this crisis appears in *The Mirror of Honor*, although it is the subject of a public letter which Christine addressed to Isabeau at the beginning of October,[28] in which she made an appeal to the queen to act as peacemaker and to shoulder her responsibility for the welfare of the country. This letter refers to examples of virtuous queens of antiquity, who had already appeared in *The Book of the City of Ladies*, and recalls the concept of queenly duties which are developed in *The Mirror of Honor*, so it seems probable that it was written after both books were completed.

These events make it clear that, within a year of Marguerite's marriage, her life would not run smoothly. One of the most remarkable aspects of Christine's book is that it provides advice for so many of the contingencies the princess would be called upon to face, even if she was never to become queen of France.

The lives of Marguerite of Guyenne and her sisters reflect the model set forth by Christine to an intriguing extent. Marguerite, widowed at eighteen, was rescued with some difficulty from what had become enemy territory for her family and then lived for several years near her mother in Burgundy, establishing and maintaining a separate residence in the Château of Montbard, which had been part of her dowry. In 1423, however, she was married again, this time to promote the political interests of her brother, Philip the Good. He married her to the Duke of Brittany's younger brother, Arthur of Richmont, who since the French defeat at Agincourt had been a prisoner in England. True to Christine's precepts, Marguerite facilitated his liberation by refusing to marry him until he was free. At least he was someone she already knew, for he had been one of the Duke of Guyenne's companions at the French court. After the marriage she became his devoted wife, sometimes even in the face of danger. When, for a short time, Richmont fell from grace at Charles VII's court, the king, seizing the Château of Chinon where Marguerite was living at the time, offered her protection if she would renounce her husband. This she refused to do and, making her escape, she went to join her husband at his estate in Parthenay, near Poitiers, supervising it for him while he was leading armies to relieve France of English occupation. She eventually returned with him to Paris when the city was restored to French control in 1436, and she continued to live there, usually without him, until her death in 1446. Her will reflects a generous spirit and warm affection for the household which shared her years of relative solitude. Richmont's biographer paid her touching tribute when he wrote:

Richmont lost the companion of his youth, of his years of trial, the widow of a French dauphin, who had, by her own choice, raised him to high rank, furthered his ambition, hastened his good fortune, faithfully shared his disgrace and seconded his efforts. The role of this princess extended beyond the domestic sphere. By working to reconcile her brother-in-law with her brother, the Duke of Burgundy, by preferring to live in Paris rather than at the royal court, representing in a certain way the royal family there, she had served both the king and France, and so merits a place in the history of this memorable reign.[29]

Christine would certainly have considered that she had earned a place in the City of Ladies.

The numerous manuscripts of *The Mirror of Honor* which still exist (eighteen or nineteen in all), together with three printed editions in French and a Portuguese translation, attest to the fact that Christine's advice was read by many women for more than a hundred years after she wrote it.

Agnes of Burgundy, wife of the Duke of Bourbon, was a bibliophile, which probably accounts for one of two copies of Christine's book in the Bourbon library at Moulins. Christine's book was also known to another duchess of the same family, Louis XI's daughter Anne de France, who drew inspiration from it in writing her own book of advice for her daughter, Suzanne de Bourbon.[30] Anne also was responsible for the early education of two other princesses, both of whom had copies of *The Mirror of Honor,* Louise of Savoy and Margaret of Austria. Louise's copy is lost, but Margaret's copy (Brussels, Bibl. Roy. Ms. 9237) still has traces of candle wax discernible on the velum folios. Both these princesses, widowed, ruled as regents, Louise for her son Francis I and Margaret for her nephew, the Emperor Charles V.

The three French imprints of *The Mirror of Honor,* all of which bear the title *The Treasury of the City of Ladies* and all of which depart slightly from Christine's original text, were published under the patronage of the French Queen Anne of Brittany, a notable patroness of the arts who gathered about her a court of distinguished young ladies. The Portuguese translation was published in the early years of the sixteenth century, at the direction of Queen Lenore, wife of Portugal's King João II.

Possibly because many copies were worn out from use, only one manuscript which is known to have been contemporary with Christine survives. (There is no trace of the one which was presented to Marguerite of Guyenne.) This oldest manuscript, which

is the one we translate here as *A Medieval Woman's Mirror of Honor,*
Boston Public Library Ms. 1528, bears the signature of Jean de
Poitiers, father of the celebrated Diane. Obviously, Jean de
Poitiers, who acquired the title of Seigneur de Saint-Vallier mentioned in the manuscript only in 1510, was not the original owner
of this manuscript, but it could have been among books his father
inherited in 1490 from his cousin, one of the Boucicauts, along
with the famous Boucicaut Book of Hours now in the Jacquemart-
André Museum in Paris.[31] The Marshal Boucicaut, founder of
an Order of the White Lady on the Green Shield for the defense
of noble women, was a contemporary of Christine, and she celebrated the foundation of his order in one of her Ballades. It would
not be surprising that he and his wife, Antoinette de Turenne,
should have had a copy of this book.

Of particular interest is a group of manuscripts written on
paper, rather than velum, either unillustrated or with rather crude
illustrations. In spite of their doubtful quality as art objects, these
copies call attention to the appeal of Christine's books to non-
aristocratic readers, perhaps the literate wives and daughters of
merchants or public officials, who would soon form an important
audience for printed books. Some of these manuscripts show traces
of the vicissitudes of domestic life; for instance, one in the Arsenal
Library in Paris (Ms. 3356) has drawings scribbled on the end
papers by some long-forgotten child. Such manuscripts bear witness to the observation of the late Professor C.E. Pickford that,
as the fifteenth century progressed, the reading public was no
longer primarily aristocratic, but included members of a better-
educated middle class and, to an increasing extent, women.[32]

All this would have delighted Christine, who had hoped to
reach just such women and who, with a thoroughly unmedieval
concern for worldly renown, wrote at the end of *The Mirror of
Honor:*

And to this end I thought that I would multiply this work in various copies
throughout the world, whatever the cost might be, so that it can be presented

in various places to queens, princesses, and noble ladies . . . that through their efforts it may be circulated among other women, which thought and desire I have already put into effect. . . . Thus it will be seen and heard by many valiant ladies and women of authority both at the present time and in times to come.[33]

NOTES

1. *Le Débat sur le Roman de la Rose,* ed. Eric Hicks (Paris, 1977); E. Hicks and E. Ornato, "Jean de Monstreuil et le Débat sur le *Roman de la Rose,*" *Romania* 98 (1977), pp. 34–64; 186–219.
2. G. Lanson, *Histoire de la Littérature française* (Paris, 1952 ed.). pp. 166–167; J. V. Fleming, "Hoccleve's 'Letter to Cupid' and the 'Quarrel' over the *Roman de la Rose,*" *Medium Aevum* 40 (1971), pp. 21–40.
3. Christine de Pizan, *The Book of the City of Ladies,* trans. E. J. Richards (New York, 1982).
4. W. H. Woodward, *Vittorino da Feltre and Other Humanist Educators* (Cambridge University, 1877; reprinted New York, 1970), especially pp. 247–250.
5. M. Roy, *Oeuvres poétiques de Christine de Pisan,* Vol. III (Paris, 1896), pp. 27–57. *Morale Proverbes of Chrystine,* Facsimile of Caxton's 1478 edition of Anthony Woodville's translation (Amsterdam-New York, 1970).
6. *La Cité de Dieu:* Paris, B. N. Mss. fr. 23–24, 174, 2324; *La Cité des Dames,* Brussels, Bibl. Roy. Ms. 9393; Paris, B. N. Mss. fr. 607, 1178, 1179. See M. Meiss, *The Limbourgs and their Contemporaries* (New York, 1974), pp. 377–382.
7. *Le Livre du Corps de Policie,* ed. R. H. Lucas (Geneva-Paris, 1967), p. 4.
8. *The Book of the City of Ladies,* trans. E. J. Richards, p. 9.
9. *Le Livre du Chemin de Long Estude,* ed. R. Puschel (Berlin, 1887; reprinted Geneva, 1974), pp. 109–112.
10. *The Book of the City of Ladies,* trans. E. J. Richards, p. 13.
11. *Le Songe du Vieil Pélerin,* ed. G. W. Coopland (Cambridge University, 1969), Vol. I, p. 536.
12. *L'Art Religieux de la fin du Moyen Age en France; étude sur l'Iconographie du Moyen Age et sur ses Sources d'Inspiration* (Paris, 1908), pp. 306–340.
13. *The Book of the City of Ladies,* p. 14.
14. Roy, ed., Vol. II, pp. 1–27.
15. Carla Bozzolo, "Il *Decameron* come Fonte del *Livre de la Cité des*

Dames de Christine de Pisan," in *Miscellanea di Studi e Ricerche sul Quattrocento Francese* (Turin, 1967), pp. 3–24.

16. *The Book of the City of Ladies*, p. 77.

17. Enid McLeod, *The Order of the Rose* (London, 1976), p. 131.

18. *Le Livre du Chevalier de la Tour Landry*, ed. A. de Montaiglon (Paris, 1854).

19. *Le Ménagier de Paris*, eds. G.E. Brereton and J.M. Ferrier (Oxford, 1981).

20. Begun around 1290, not printed until 1815; reprinted 1842.

21. Richard H. and Mary A. Rouse, *Preachers, Florilegia and Sermons: Studies on the Manipulus Florum of Thomas of Ireland* (Toronto, 1979).

22. *Les Quinze Joyes de Mariage*, ed. J. Rychner (Geneva, 1967).

23. *Le Livre des Fais et Bonnes Meurs du Roy Charles V*, ed. S. Solente (Paris, 1936), Introduction, pp. xxvii–xxix.

24. C.A.J. Armstrong, "La Politique Matrimoniale des ducs de Bourgogne de la Maison de Valois," in *England, France and Burgundy in the Fifteenth Century* (London, 1983), pp. 237–342.

25. R. Vaughan, *John the Fearless* (London, 1966), p. 246.

26. Lille, *Archives du Nord*, B 1878, fol. 124.

27. J. Verdon, *Isabeau de Bavière* (Paris, 1981), especially pp. 79–105.

28. B.N. Ms. fr. 580. C.C. Willard, "An Autograph Manuscript of Christine de Pizan?" *Studi Francesi* 27 (1965), pp. 452–459.

29. E. Cosneau, *Le Connétable Richmont* (Paris, 1886), pp. 329–330.

30. *Les Enseignements d'Anne de France à sa fille Suzanne de Bourbon* published by A.M. Chazaud (Moulins, 1878).

31. M. Meiss, *French Painting in the Time of Jean de Berry: the Boucicaut Master* (London, 1968), p. 131.

32. "Fiction and the Reading Public in the Fifteenth Century," *Bulletin of the John Rylands Library* 45 (1963), p. 435.

33. Boston Public Library Ms. 1528, fol. 98.

A NOTE ON THE TEXT

The text of this volume was translated from the only complete manuscript that seems to date from Christine de Pizan's lifetime, Manuscript 1528 in the Boston Public Library.

For the reader's convenience and enjoyment, an extensive bibliography of translations and related books has been provided, as well as a glossary which offers details of general medieval ideas and matters specific to this book. Each word which appears in the glossary has been underlined when it first appears in the text.

Illustrations

1. Avoiding the tangled theological debate over the two first female figures of Judaeo-Christian tradition, tempted Eve and temptress Lilith, Christine de Pizan assumes woman's basic morality and goodness. To act virtuously, women need not fight against nature, but follow selectively and intelligently the dictates of their truest selves.

2. "Every heart which truly loves God should show this love through good works," says Christine. Such ardent, active generosity is exemplified by St. Elizabeth. The more exalted one's social place, the more humane graciousness is required.

3. The allegorical woman Temperance in Christine de Pizan's *Othéa* teaches four ladies the mechanism and the theory of the newly invented mechanical clock: to everything there is an appropriate time, place, and season.

4. The three Virtues—Reason, Rectitude, and Justice—who inspired Christine to write *Mirror of Honor* gather around her bed chiding her laziness and urging her to get up and write.

5. Pen in hand and dog at her feet, Christine de Pizan writes in her study one of her twenty internationally influential books.

6. Christine presents her female readers a choice of two lifestyles: the contemplative and the active. The contemplative woman studies and prays, absenting herself from the ways of this world. Christine's own experience and predilections are for the active life where one accrues merit through good works.

7. Hunting, not simply a sport but a princess's social duty, is among many seemingly ceremonial activities combining necessary politics and personal pleasure. Sitting sidesaddle, falcon at hand, the lady of the castle riding past field workers and bathing peasants asserts her political primacy while keeping a trained eye on her estate.

8. A feast with her ladies allows the princess to impress her companions with generosity, wealth, and good-heartedness. Entertaining has the political consequences of ensuring the subjects' loyalty and reaffirming the ruler's power.

9. The gentleman has already removed his sword but the gentlewoman still carries her keys on a chatelaine around her waist. The lovers sit on a curtained bed raised on a wooden platform under which are thrust slippers and a chamber pot.

10. The efficient castle kitchen has both male and female cooks who simultaneously prepare meat on a spit, soups and sauces on the stove, and bread in the oven below.

11. Necessaries such as linseed oil one could buy from itinerant vendors. This man carries the customary measures and funnels and is bound by market laws to deal honestly with consumers.

12. The intelligent lady of the castle keeps one eye on her embroidery, the other on her hired overseer, who must responsibly represent the lady in all dealings with the staff. Here the chief gardener receives instructions for the men working in the well-ordered herb garden.

13. Women such as baronesses who manage large estates must plan the planting, harvesting, and sale of crops as well as the proper raising, grazing, care, then slaughter or sale of livestock. Constant supervision of the staff ensures the efficient daily and seasonal care of the sheep, cows, pigs, and poultry. The peacocks were not only ornamental but culinary stock.

14. This bakery is identified by the pretzels hanging over the door. One woman bakes at a portable oven, while the other sells the bread. Female bakers were called *baxters,* the functional origin of the family name Baxter, just as male bakers' children carried the family name Baker.

15. Not all women in *Mirror of Honor* have meals served with entertainments and fanfares. Christine also addresses herself to the women of the crafts and trades who serve and enjoy comfortable, modest feasts with family, cat, and blazing fireplace.

16. Christine directs part of *Mirror of Honor* to women who work in the fields, raking, baling, and forking the grain with their men, and to the craftswomen who use or control the commodity mills.

17. Farmwomen milk the cows, lead them out to graze, and churn butter. Christine insists that well-to-do farmwomen and even women living at subsistence level who have a hard labor-filled life can learn much from her book.

18. The obstetrician and her assistant surround the expectant mother who sits on a birthing stool. Female obstetricians and gynecologists were formally trained, licensed, and their practices regulated by medical guilds and civil authorities, just as were the men practitioners. Physicians such as Dr. Trotula of Salerno (12th century) wrote gynecological texts dealing with normal and complicated birthing techniques plus pre- and post-natal care.

19. Whores of Venice were famous for their flamboyant costumes. In many cities, the so-called sumptuary laws controlled design, fabric, fur, and ornamentation of people's garments according to social rank. Prostitutes garb usually figures prominently in these regulations. Christine maintains that women of light morals can reform their ways if they subscribe to her precepts.

20. Entertaining their clients in bath tubs filled with scented water, the women wear only hats and jewels. The couples eat and drink aphrodisiacs to the sound of lute music, and then retire to bed in this pleasure palace.

Illustration Credits

We thank the gracious curators, librarians, museum and library trustees, and private collectors for their generosity in permitting these illustrations from their collections to be reproduced:

1. *Eve and Serpent. Der Spiegel der Menschen Behaltniss,* Speyer (Drach), woodcut, German, ca. 1481, The Metropolitan Museum of Art, Harris Brisbane Dick Fund, 1931, New York.
2. *St. Elizabeth of Hungary.* Artist unknown, woodcut, German (Southern), 1470s, The Metropolitan Museum of Art, Harris Brisbane Dick Fund, 1930, New York.
3. *Temperance Clock.* From Christine de Pizan's *Othéa,* Ms. Laud Misc. 570, mid-fifteenth century, Bodleian Library, Oxford.
4. *Christine and the Three Virtues. Le Livre des Trois Vertus,* Ms. 1528, Boston Public Library, Boston.
5. *Christine de Pizan in Her Study.* From Christine de Pizan's *Collected Works,* Harley ms. 4431, The British Library, London.
6. *Scholar in Her Study.* German print, fifteenth century, Galeria Medievalia, London.
7. *Woman Hunting.* From the *Très Riches Heures* of Jean, Duke de Berry, ca. 1415, Musée Condé, Chantilly.
8. *A Ladies' Feast.* Flemish, fifteenth century, Western MSS, Ms. Douce 374, f. 17, Bodleian Library, Oxford.
9. *Lovers.* Israel van Meckenem, German, fifteenth century, engraving, The Metropolitan Museum of Art, Rogers Fund, 1918, New York.
10. *Kitchen.* Froschaeur, woodcut in Diederich's *Deutsches Leben I,* #574, German, 1507, The Metropolitan Museum of Art, Rogers Fund, New York.
11. *Oil Vendor. Tacuinum Sanitatis,* Ms. 65, Italian, ca. 1475, Spencer Collection, The New York Public Library, New York.
12. *Herb Garden.* From *Petrus Crescentius,* Ms. 65, f. 86 v., Italian, fifteenth century, Spencer Collection, The New York Public Library, New York.
13. *Castle Barnyard.* From *Petrus Crescentius,* Ms. 232, f. 212, fifteenth century, The Pierpont Morgan Library, New York.
14. *Pretzel Baker.* Ulrich Richental. *Concilium zu Constanz,* f. 25 v., German, 1483, Spencer Collection, The New York Public Library, New York.
15. *Dinner Before the Hearth. Da Costa Hours,* Ms. 399, f. 2 v., Bruges, 1520, The Pierpont Morgan Library, New York.
16. *Haymaking. Da Costa Hours,* Ms. 399, f. 8 v., Bruges, 1520, The Pierpont Morgan Library, New York.
17. *Milking and Sheep Tending. Da Costa Hours,* Ms. 399, f. 5 v., Bruges, 1520, The Pierpont Morgan Library, New York.
18. *Birthing. Mutterleben,* late fifteenth century, German, Galeria Medievalia, London.
19. *Whores in Costume.* Woodcuts from *Liber Sartorum,* Heidelberg, early sixteenth century, Peter Drach, Dover Pictorial Archive, New York.
20. *A Bathing and Pleasure Palace.* Valerius Maximus, Master of the Housebook, late fifteenth century, Galeria Medievalia, London.

A Medieval Woman's Mirror of Honor
THE TREASURY OF THE CITY OF LADIES

1. The first chapter, which tells how the Virtues, by whose command Christine had composed and compiled *The Book of the City of Ladies,* appeared once more and commissioned her to write this present book.

After I built the City of Ladies with the aid and instruction of the three lady Virtues: Reason, Rectitude, and Justice, as I described in my book called *The City of Ladies,* I was worn out by that strenuous labor. My body was exhausted by such long and sustained effort, and I was resting, idly, when suddenly the three radiant creatures appeared to me once more, saying: "Studious daughter! Have you spurned and silenced the instrument of your intellect? Have you let your pen and ink dry out? Have you given up the labor of your hand which usually delights you? Are you willing to listen to the seductive song which Idleness sings to you? Surely you will hear it if you are willing to listen: 'You have done enough; you have earned your time for rest.' But remember what Seneca says: 'Although the wise one's intellect deserves repose after great effort, still a good mind should not neglect further good work.' Do not be distracted in the middle of your long journey! Shame on the knight who leaves the battle before victory! Only those who persist deserve the laurel crown. Now up, up! Lend a hand! Get ready! Stop crouching on this dust heap of fatigue! Obey our words, and your work will prosper.

"We are not fully satisfied with your labors as our handmaiden in the furthering of our grand scheme. Therefore, we deliberated and decided in the Council of Virtues to follow God's example: At the beginning of the world, God saw that His work was good, blessed it, and then went on to create man, woman, and the animals. So may our preceding work, *The City of Ladies,* which is fine and useful, not only be blessed and praised throughout the world—but now may it grow further. Just as the wise birdman prepared his cage before trying to catch birds, we have prepared the bower of ladies. Now, with your help, we will devise and fabricate benevolent snares tied with knots of love to cover the ground where honored ladies and all sorts of women will walk. Even the shy and unwilling will be caught in our nets. None will be able to resist or escape, and all will be taken within the beneficent boundaries of our glorious city. They will learn to sing the sweet song that those who live there already sing in splendor, perpetually chanting *Alleluia* with the blessed angels."

Hearing those harmonious voices, I, Christine, began to tremble with joy. Kneeling before the three, I vowed to carry out their desires. So, they commanded me: "Take up your pen and write. Blessed be those who will inhabit our city and swell the number of its virtuous citizens. May all of this College of Women learn Wisdom's lesson. Our first students must be those whose royal or noble blood raises them above others in this world. Inevitably, the women, as well as the men, whom God establishes in the high seats of power and domination must be better educated than others. Their reputations will lead to great worthiness in themselves and in others. They are the mirror and example of virtue for their subjects and companions. The first lesson, therefore, will be directed at them—the queens, princesses, and other great ladies. Then, step by step, we will begin to explicate our doctrine for women of the lower degrees, so that the discipline of our College may be useful to all."

2. Wherein it tells how the three Virtues exhort all princesses and great ladies to come to their college, where the first and basic teaching is to love and fear Our Lord.

Greetings from the three sisters, God's daughters, named Reason, Rectitude, and Justice: To all princesses, empresses, queens, duchesses, other great ladies reigning over Christian lands, and to all women. Love and charity motivate our desire for the well-being and the increasing honor and the prosperity of the University of Women, and we hope for the decline and destruction of anything which might hinder it. Here follows our doctrine. Come, all of you, to this College of Wisdom. Women of high estate, please do not be ashamed to humble yourselves by taking lowly seats to hear our lesson; for, according to God's word, the humble shall be exalted.

What in this world is more congenial or more delightful to those seeking worldly riches than gold and precious stones? Consider this: Ornaments cannot beautify as well as virtues. Virtues enhance the body of one desiring to live well because they are nobler than worldly riches. Why are they nobler? Because they endure forever and are treasures of the soul, which is everlasting. Other treasures pass like smoke. Therefore, those with a taste for virtues desire them more than any worldly thing can be desired. Shouldn't those whose grace and good fortune seat them in the highest places be served the best? Virtues are the food of our table. Happily we will distribute them.

First and foremost, our doctrine's foundation is the love and fear of Our Lord. This is the beginning of wisdom and the source of all other excellences.

Hear then, princesses and other ladies honored on Earth, how you must love and fear Our Lord. Why love? Love Him for His infinite goodness and the very great benefits you receive from Him. Fear Him for his divine and holy justice, which leaves no evil unpunished. If you keep both this love and this fear before your eyes, certainly you will walk the path leading straight to the place of virtue.

Every heart which truly loves should show this love through good works. The Scriptures themselves say: "My Father's sheep love me and I protect them." Creatures who love Him follow His footsteps of perfection, and He protects them from all peril. Thus, the princess who loves Him will demonstrate it by dutiful labor in her exalted occupation. She will not stray from the light of His way, and that light will protect her from temptations and shadows of sin and vice, radiantly conquering and expelling them.

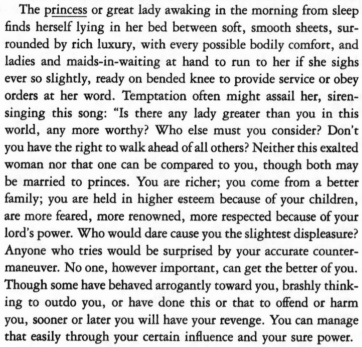

3. Wherein the sort of temptations which can assail a great princess are described.

The princess or great lady awaking in the morning from sleep finds herself lying in her bed between soft, smooth sheets, surrounded by rich luxury, with every possible bodily comfort, and ladies and maids-in-waiting at hand to run to her if she sighs ever so slightly, ready on bended knee to provide service or obey orders at her word. Temptation often might assail her, siren-singing this song: "Is there any lady greater than you in this world, any more worthy? Who else must you consider? Don't you have the right to walk ahead of all others? Neither this exalted woman nor that one can be compared to you, though both may be married to princes. You are richer; you come from a better family; you are held in higher esteem because of your children, are more feared, more renowned, more respected because of your lord's power. Who would dare cause you the slightest displeasure? Anyone who tries would be surprised by your accurate counter-maneuver. No one, however important, can get the better of you. Though some have behaved arrogantly toward you, brashly thinking to outdo you, or have done this or that to offend or harm you, sooner or later you will have your revenge. You can manage that easily through your certain influence and your sure power.

"How can you do all this? However great the person, no one achieves prestige or accomplishes anything without great financial resources. Therefore, amass treasure to carry out your intentions. Money is women's best friend and the surest means to any possible end. Who would dare disobey you when you freely distribute gifts? Even if you give only a little, people still will serve you willingly in the hope of receiving more later. After all, you would have the reputation for great wealth. Only the dead fail to reach out with both hands. Dispense for gain, no matter who may be harmed or displeased by it. You know you can do this very well if you put your mind to it. Who cares what others may say? Talkers cannot harm you, so why let them bother you? Heed only things which please you. You have only one life to live and it passes quickly. What can trouble you? Food and drink never will be in short supply; delight in all such delicacies. Dwell on nothing but the pleasures and amusements you can enjoy in this world. Nobody has a good life beyond what she provides for herself. Think only enticing thoughts to amuse yourself. For whom will you be pretty? You must have just such a robe, such ornaments, such jewels, such gorgeously wrought, newly fashionable apparel . . . ."

4. Which tells how the good princess who loves and fears Our Lord can resist temptation through divine inspiration.

Words such as those are the meats Temptation serves to any creature living in ease and luxury. What does the good princess do when she finds herself so tempted? Love and fear of Our Lord will sing her a different lesson: "Foolish idler? What are you thinking of? Have you forgotten what you know about yourself? Don't you remember that you are only a wretched, frail creature, subject to illness, maladies, passions, and pains inherent in all mortal bodies? What advantage do you have over another human being? A ball of clay covered with rich cloth is worth little more than a ball of clay under poor rags. Inclined to sin and every possible vice, you, wretched creature, deceive yourself into forgetting that your feeble vessel, yearning after honor and ease, will decline and die. Soon it will be food for worms, decaying in the dust as readily as any indigent woman's body. The released soul will carry away only the good or evil works that the feeble body has done on earth. What use, then, will be the honors, wealth, or status you have been so proud of in this world? Will they save you from the pains you will suffer if you have lived this life badly? Certainly not. Rather, all you have done wrong will be held against you.

"You would have better spent your life as a very poor woman

than to have been raised so high with so far to fall toward damnation. Amidst the flames you will be tortured, forever burning without being consumed. Don't you know that God says in the Gospel: 'Blessed are the poor, for theirs is the Kingdom of Heaven'? As a loaded camel cannot pass through the eye of a needle, neither can the rich expect to enter the Kingdom of Heaven.

"You are so blind! Wretched creature! You do not even see the great peril your pride causes. Vain honors blind your reason so that you consider yourself not only a princess or great lady but a veritable goddess in this world. How do you endure your own pride? Surely you know from the Scriptures that God cannot abide pride. Because of it He caused Lucifer, the Princess of Darkness, to fall from Heaven to Hell. He will do the same to you. Watch out!

"O Pride, root of all evil, I know that all other vices come from you! You drive my anger to seek vengeance. I thought I ought to be feared and esteemed. I thought I should take precedence over all, never tolerate what displeased me, take revenge for any trivial slight. But, Pride, perilous wind, inflated courage, boil filled with poison! The flesh you corrupt is in greater danger than if swollen with plague.

"Perverse creature! You seek vengeance because you think yourself great. You expect nobody to contradict you or to cross your wishes, no matter what. Blind ignorance, bred of arrogance, prevents your seeing that everyone, great or small, who ill-uses these mortal days deserves to suffer later. Perversity will merit you little esteem from anyone. People will rebel against you, countermanding your expectations and demands. Not even noticing your own mistakes, you always feel free to suppress the desires and opinions of others. You dislike anyone who resists or contradicts you. You despise, plot, and connive against them, secretly or openly. Yet you neglect to take into account the great harm and danger to your body and soul, let alone the distress you cause others. And if you do not chastise people who anger you because

74

for some reason you are not able to, then you bear them an eternal grudge.

"Faithless Pride casts you into the Sea of Perdition. It agitates you over trifles. You want revenge. You covet extravagances for which you gather money without conscience. Wretched wealth! It is almost impossible to amass it without causing others harm or suffering. You extort from others your particular profit. Rest assured, however, you will never enjoy possessions acquired dishonestly. Though you have assembled them for your pleasure, God will send you so much adversity, illness, or burden that this ill-gained treasure will be dissipated and put to uses far less pleasant than you expected. What then will you do with this treasure? Will you take it with you when you die? Certainly not, although you will take the burden of everything ill-got and ill-used.

"Consider again how accursed Pride pricks you into believing that you surpass others in grandeur and worthiness. Your heart is sick with chills and fever lest others equal your lofty estate. You always want to be greater than what you know you are in your heart. So you are spiteful, angry, and puffed up with animosity. Another of Pride's infernal brands inspires you to say to yourself that you don't have to work, or, indeed, do anything at all: You may live at your ease, lying abed late into the morning, then resting after dinner. Inspecting your jewel boxes and your wardrobes should be your sole occupation. Does it seem that God's gift of time to everyone to use for good purpose allows you to be more idle than the rest? Wicked creature, surely you have learned from <u>Saint Bernard</u>'s sermons on the *Song of Songs* that idleness is the mother of all frivolities and the smotherer of virtues. Idlensss makes even the strong and constant stumble into sin. It extinguishes goodness, nourishes pride, and paves the way to Hell.

"What else can happen to you? That Pride-nourishing ease and ease-encouraging Pride makes you a glutton for food and drink. Ordinary dishes and usual meats are no longer good enough; you are sated with all that. To please you and to earn their wages, cooks must invent flavors, sauces, and new concoctions to make food more delectable to your palate; so, too, with wines.

"Thus you fill the bag, which is nothing more than meat for worms and vessel of every impurity. What will become of it when it is full? What then will it want? Just as the log nourishes the fire, so superfluous sensuous foods and drinks stimulate lechery. Sensual abundance inflames Pride, which makes the heart desire things most pleasing to the body. The body thus indulged resembles a horse so well fattened by its master than when the master expects to ride it, it is too plump and cosseted to respond. Nonetheless, led out and ridden, the horse rears and falls, breaking its neck. Just so the body, made too fat by indulgence, kills both its own virtue and its own soul. Pride, of course, delights in such rich nourishment, making you covet not only superabundant food but also clothes, jewels, and ornaments, until you scarcely think of anything else—neither what they cost nor where they come from—as long as you have them when you want them.

"This vice, and the endless other disreputable habits into which it leads you, makes you so disdainful and so difficult to please that almost no jewel, no costume, nor any ornament really satisfies you. You always find some detail to complain about. Furthermore, no person pleases you. You are so overbearing and presumptuous, you think not even God can cross you.

"Miserable, weak, blind woman! Your overweaning pride seduces you to forget God's punishments. Though for a long time He may watch you plunged in your vices without giving you what you deserve, remember: The longer God's vengeance tarries, the more perilous it is when it comes, just as the more a bow is stretched the more piercing the arrow when it strikes. Have you forgotten how God punished the pride of Nebuchadnezzar, King of Babylon, who was such a prideful prince that he feared nobody in the whole world? Likewise Antiochus, King of Persia, and Emperor Xerxes, and such others were so powerful that they feared nothing in Heaven or Earth. But the vengeance of God humbled them according to their merits, reducing them to such tribulations that no men in the world were more wretched or more unfortunate than they. Remember what is written in the tenth chapter of the *Book of Ecclesiasticus:* 'God has destroyed the seats of mighty dukes and has put the merciful in their places.' He dried up the roots of the arrogant and planted the selfless in their places. This means that he confounded the overbearing and raised up the humble. So it will happen to you if you deserve thus to be humbled.

"You foolish, simple, ridiculous, little woman! You have no force, power, or authority other than what is given to you by someone else, namely the Lord. Nevertheless, seeing yourself surrounded by luxury and honors you think you can trample on the world and dominate it according to your will."

5. Where the helpful advice and knowledge which come to a good princess through the love and fear of Our Lord are set forth.

So counseled by God, the good princess who loves and fears Our Lord will realize that however virtuous she may be, she must consider herself the least worthy. She will say to herself: "Now, with God's grace, know the great and shocking trouble you have fallen into because of damnable Pride. Now what will you do? Will you continue deserving and wanting to be damned? Which will profit you more: to live a short time at your ease in this world—(Though, of course, you really are not living in luxury, for the more the world delights you, the more desires torment your heart. You can't fulfill them nor suit everything to yourself. Never satisfied, your heart perpetually will be anguished.)—or to resist trivial delights, live in the fear and love of Our Lord, and be saved for Eternity?

"What is damnation like? Holy Scripture says that it is to live forever deprived of the vision of God, always in frightful shadows, in the company of terrible devils—enemies of humankind—and, with the other damned souls, raising their voices in horrible cries and lamentations, cursing God, their parents, and themselves, in unspeakable torment amidst burning fires. As Job said, it is to live in fearsome stench, perpetual horrors, and, worst of all, despair of ever leaving that despair.

"Folly will lose for you the grace God promises you may have if only you will make a little effort to deserve it. He has promised you that, by virtue of His Holy Passion, if you will serve Him and keep His holy commandments, you will go to Paradise.

"What is Paradise? Saint Gregory in his *Homilies* speaks of that Holy City of Paradise: 'Where is the mind that can know, where is the tongue that can tell how great are the joys of Paradise? Paradise is to be ever in the company of angels with the blessed saints in the glory of Our Creator, to see the Blessed Trinity, to know God's glorious face, to behold and to feel His unbelievable radiance, to be free from all desire, to have infinite knowledge in eternal quiet, to fear no death, and to be ever assured of that company, never separated from that glorious joy.'

"Now do you see the difference between the two ways? Which one will you take? Will you foolishly remain in the swamp to drown and perish, neglecting the holy, lovely, and sure way which leads to salvation? Certainly not! You must not abandon the good to choose the evil.

"O Holy Trinity, One God in sovereign unity, perfect power, wisdom, and infinite goodness: Advise and succor me. Help me escape from the shades of ignorance that have fearfully blinded me. O Virgin—worthy, pure, and sacred—comfort of the hopeless and hope of the faithful; please grasp my hand, by your Holy Mercy, to pull me from the swamp of sin and iniquity. Most holy and blessed College and Court of Paradise, angels, archangels, cherubim, seraphim, thrones, and dominations, holy apostles of God, martyrs, confessors, and all the communion of blessed saints, virgins, and chaste martyrs: Pray for me and help me now."

6. Which describes the two holy ways, the contemplative and the active.

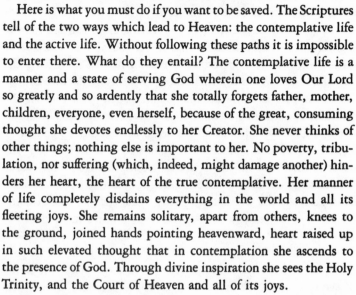

Here is what you must do if you want to be saved. The Scriptures tell of the two ways which lead to Heaven: the contemplative life and the active life. Without following these paths it is impossible to enter there. What do they entail? The contemplative life is a manner and a state of serving God wherein one loves Our Lord so greatly and so ardently that she totally forgets father, mother, children, everyone, even herself, because of the great, consuming thought she devotes endlessly to her Creator. She never thinks of other things; nothing else is important to her. No poverty, tribulation, nor suffering (which, indeed, might damage another) hinders her heart, the heart of the true contemplative. Her manner of life completely disdains everything in the world and all its fleeting joys. She remains solitary, apart from others, knees to the ground, joined hands pointing heavenward, heart raised up in such elevated thought that in contemplation she ascends to the presence of God. Through divine inspiration she sees the Holy Trinity, and the Court of Heaven and all of its joys.

The perfect contemplative often is so ravished that she seems other than herself, and the consolation, sweetness, and pleasure she experiences can scarcely be told, nor can any earthly joy be compared with them. She feels and tastes the glories and joys of Paradise. She sees God in spirit through her contemplation. Her burning love gives perfect sufficiency in this world because she feels no other desire. God delights his servant, offering the sweets of His Holy Paradise. Pure, holy, heavenly thoughts give perfect hope of joining that joyous company. No other exultation compares; those who have tried the contemplative way know this. To my regret, I cannot speak of that exultation any more than a blind man can describe colors. But this is the way, above all others, manifestly agreeable to God. Certain holy contemplatives are said to have risen physically, soaring above the earth in their contemplation, by God's miracle, as if the body were following the thought as it rose toward Heaven. I am not worthy to speak of this holy, elevated life, nor to describe it as adequately as it deserves. But the Holy Scriptures are filled with words on it for anyone who wishes to learn more.

The active life is the other way of serving God. The one following this way is so charitable that if she could, she would serve all for the love of God. So she serves in hospitals, visiting the sick and the poor, aiding with her own wealth and her own efforts, generously, for the love of God. She has such great pity for the creatures she sees in sin, misery, or tribulation that she weeps as if the trouble were her own. She seeks her neighbor's good as if it were her own; and since she always is striving to do good, she never is idle. Her ardent desire to accomplish charitable works is unceasing; she devotes all her energies to them. Such a woman bears all trials and tribulations patiently for the love of Our Lord. This active life, as you can see, serves the world more than the other.

Although both ways are excellent, Our Lord Jesus Christ gave his opinion as to the more perfect of the two. Mary, the figure of the contemplative life, seated herself at His feet, as one who had no heart for anything else and was totally consumed by holy love. Martha, her sister, the example of the active life, was the hostess of Our Lord, busying herself to serve Him and the apostles; she complained to Him because her sister did not help her. Our Lord excused Mary, saying: "Martha, you are very diligent, and your work is of great excellence and necessary for the aid and succor of others. Nevertheless, the contemplative life represents the abandonment of the whole world and all its demands only to meditate on Him. That is of greater dignity and more perfect."

For this reason holy men long ago established religious orders, for that life is the nearest estate to God. Those wishing to love in contemplation can separate themselves from the world for the service of God without other cares. Along with pleasing themselves, such contemplatives greatly please God when they are faithful to their duty.

7. Here is set forth the way the good princess, counseled by God, will decide to follow.

You must then decide which of these two ways you will follow. So the good princess inspired by God speaks to herself. Discretion truly is called the mother of Virtue. Why the mother? Because she conducts and leads, and the one who fails to follow her finds that enterprises without her come to nothing and are worthless. Therefore, I must work discreetly. Why discretion? Before I undertake anything, I consider first of all the strength or weakness of my own body and my fragility. Then I weigh the demands I must balance in this human state to which God has committed me. Considering these things honestly, I know that however excellent my will, I have a very weak body for suffering great abstinence or intense pain, and a feebleness of spirit from that fragility and inconstancy. Knowing myself thus, I do not deceive myself into imagining that I am of such great virtue to act when God says, "You will leave father and mother for my sake." I could not. I could not leave husband, children, my worldly state, and all earthly preoccupations with the intention of serving God completely in the contemplative life, as the most perfect human beings have done. I must not try to do what I know would be inadequate for the demands.

What then should I do? Should I follow the active life? Happy are those who can fulfill its demands successfully. Good Lord, why didn't You create me poor, so that I could at least serve You more perfectly for love of You? I cannot leave everything to devote myself only to good work. Good Lord, advise me and inspire me! Tell me what I must do for salvation. Though I know well enough that I should not love or desire anything but You alone, and though I know all other joy is meaningless, still I don't find the strength in myself to relinquish the world completely. So I am troubled. For You say that it is impossible for the rich to be saved.

Holy Information then comes to the rescue of the good princess and says: "Here is what you will do. God does not insist that you leave everything to follow Him except for those who wish to devote themselves to a perfect life. Rather, each can save herself according to her own state. When God says that it is impossible for the rich to be saved, he means the rich without virtue; those who do not distribute their wealth in alms; those whose only pleasure is in their possessions. Truly God hates them, so they never will enter the Kingdom of Heaven. When He says that the poor are blessed, He means the humble in spirit. That could include the wealthy and well-endowed who do not prize wealth, but rather disperse it in good works and in the service of God, and who are not unduly proud because of honors or money. Even those with abundance of worldly goods who yet are humble can possess the Kingdom of Heaven.

"Surely you can see this for yourself. Haven't there been kings and princes who now are saints in Paradise? Saint Louis and others like him did not abandon the world but rather reigned and governed their lands in a manner pleasing to God. These people lived justly and were not unduly impressed by vain glory or by their own achievements, realizing that their honors were for their positions as God's vicars on earth and not directed to them as individuals. Similarly, many queens and princesses now are saints in Paradise, such as the queen of King Clovis of France; Saint Badour; Saint Elizabeth, the Queen of Hungary; and others. God doubtlessly is willing to be served by people of any estate. Any who wish it can be saved; for it isn't the position which brings damnation but not knowing how to use it wisely."

Therefore, since I conclude that I am not strong enough to follow either of these paths, at least I will try the middle way, as Saint Paul advises, and select from each path as much of the best as I am able.

8. Which shows how the good princess wishes to attract virtue to her.

Guided by divine inspiration, the good princess will think of all these things. Here is how she will act. She will choose well-informed, ethical, and wise advisers to help her elect what is good and avoid what is evil. Although every mortal creature, by nature, is inclined to sin, she will strive to avoid specific mortal sins. As in medicine, she will be the good doctor who cures ills by their opposites. She will follow <u>Chrysostom</u>'s *Commentary on the Gospel of Saint Matthew* which says: "Whoever wishes importance in Heaven must observe humility on earth." The most significant in the eyes of God is not the most honored on earth, but whoever is most just on earth will be exalted in Heaven. Since the good princess knows that honors generally inflate pride yet befit her husband's status and her own authority, she will direct her heart toward humility, protecting it from damage by arrogance and puffery by pride. She will thank God and attribute all honor to Him, never ceasing to recognize that she is poor, mortal, frail, and sinful, and that her worldly status is only an office for which she will be accountable to God shortly. In the eyes of eternity, her life's span is very short.

Though the dignity of her position requires this noble princess to receive homage from others, she will not take undue pleasure when it is rendered to her. She will avoid it whenever possible. Her manner, her bearing, and her speech will be gentle and kindly, her face friendly, her eyes lowered. Returning greetings to all who greet her, she will be so humane and courteous that her words will be pleasing to God and to all the world. This virtue of humility will make the noble lady patient. Although the world brings ample adversity to great lords and ladies as well as to the lowly, she never will be resentful no matter what happens. She will accept all adversity for the love of Our Lord, thanking Him humbly. If people wrong or injure her, as they might by accident or intention, she will not punish or pursue them. If they are rightfully and justly punished, she will pity them, remembering that God commands one to love one's enemies. Saint Paul says that charity is not self-seeking. Therefore she will pray to God to give them patience in suffering and to be merciful to them.

This noble lady's great constancy, courage, and force of character will not heed the darts of the envious. If she learns of frivolous slander against her, as happens every day to the best of people no matter how great they are, she will not be troubled nor take offence but will pardon readily. Nor because of her greatness will she suspect ill will if anyone slights her, recalling what Our Lord suffered for us and nevertheless prayed for His tormenters. Instead, this humble lady will question whether she could have offended in any manner, remembering virtuous Seneca's teaching to princes, princesses, and people in power: "It is great merit in the sight of God, praiseworthy in the world, and a sign of nobility to let pass lightly the slight which might easily be avenged." That is also a good example to lesser people.

Saint Gregory speaks similarly in the twenty-second book of the _Moralia:_ "Nobody is perfect who does not have patience with the damage his neighbors may inflict upon him." He who cannot bear the trespasses of others shows by impatience that he is far from virtuous himself. The same saint's praise of patience says that just as the rose smells sweet and looks beautiful among sharp thorns, a patient creature shines victoriously among those who attempt to wrong her. The princess trying to amass virtue upon virtue should remember that Saint Paul says: "Whoever has all the other virtues, prays unceasingly, goes on pilgrimages, fasts at length, and does all good, but has no charity, profits in nothing."

Therefore, the princess contemplating all this will be so merciful toward everyone that she will suffer for them as for herself. Not content merely to note people in trouble, she will put her hand to the task of helping. As a sage said: "Charity is extended not only through aiding others with money from one's purse but also through comforting words, fitting advice, and all other good one can do." Through charity, this great lady will be the advocate of peace between the prince, her husband (or her son, if she is a widow), and her people, those to whom she has a duty to offer her assistance. If the prince, because of poor advice or for any other reason, should be tempted to harm his subjects, they will know their lady to be full of kindness, pity, and charity. They will come to her, humbly petitioning her to intercede for them before the prince. Poor and unable to request it themselves, they merit the lady's clemency.

9. Wherein it is explained how the good and wise princess will attempt to make peace between the prince and his barons if there is any difficulty between them.

If any neighboring or foreign prince wars for any grievance against her lord, or if her lord wages war against another, the good lady will weigh the odds carefully. She will balance the great ills, infinite cruelties, losses, deaths, and destruction to property and people against the war's outcome, which is usually unpredictable. She will seriously consider whether she can preserve the honor of her lord and yet prevent the war. Working wisely and calling on God's aid, she will strive to maintain peace. So also, if any prince of the realm or the country, or any baron, knight, or powerful subject should hold a grudge against her lord, or if he is involved in any such quarrel and she foresees that for her lord to take a prisoner or make a battle would lead to trouble in the land, she will strive toward peace. In France the discontent of an insignificant baron (named Bouchart) against the King of France, the great prince, has recently resulted in great trouble and damage to the kingdom. The *Chronicles of France* recount the tale of many such misadventures. Again, not long ago, in the case of Lord Robert of Artois, a disagreement with the king harmed the French realm and gave comfort to the English.

Mindful of such terrible possibilities, the good lady will strive to avoid destruction of her people, making peace and urging her lord (the prince) and his council to consider the potential harm inherent in any martial adventure. Furthermore, she must remind him that every good prince should avoid shedding blood, especially that of his subjects. Since making a new war is a grave matter, only long thought and mature deliberation will devise the better way toward the desired result. Thus, always saving both her own honor and her lord's, the good lady will not rest until she has spoken, or has had someone else speak to those who have committed the misdeed in question, alternately soothing and reproving them. While their error is great and the prince's displeasure reasonable, and though he ought to punish them, she would always prefer peace. Therefore, if they would be willing to correct their ways or make suitable amends, she gladly would try to restore them to her lord's good graces.

With such words as these, the good princess will be peacemaker. In such manner, Good Queen Blanche, mother of Saint Louis, always strove to reconcile the king with his barons, and, among others, the Count of Champagne. The proper role of a good, wise queen or princess is to maintain peace and concord and to avoid wars and their resulting disasters. Women particularly should concern themselves with peace because men by nature are more foolhardy and headstrong, and their overwhelming desire to avenge themselves prevents them from foreseeing the resulting dangers and terrors of war. But woman by nature is more gentle and circumspect. Therefore, if she has sufficient will and wisdom she can provide the best possible means to pacify man. Solomon speaks of peace in the twenty-fifth chapter of the *Book of Proverbs*. Gentleness and humility assuage the prince. The gentle tongue (which means the soft word) bends and breaks harshness. So water extinguishes fire's heat by its moisture and chill.

Queens and princesses have greatly benefitted this world by bringing about peace between enemies, between princes and their barons, or between rebellious subjects and their lords. The Scriptures are full of examples. The world has no greater benevolence than a good and wise princess. Fortunate is that land which has one. I have listed as examples many of these wondrous women in *The Book of the City of Ladies.*

What results from the presence of such a princess? All her subjects who recognize her wisdom and kindness come to her for refuge, not only as their mistress but almost as the goddess on earth in whom they have infinite hope and confidence. Keeping the land in peace and tranquility, she and her works radiate charity.

10. Which speaks of the paths of devout charity which are to be followed by a good princess.

The good princess will do even more than tread the pathway of charity. She will personify <u>Saint Basil</u>'s words to the rich: "Your temporal possessions come from God." You have more of them than others more deserving. Was God not just in dividing them unequally? Not at all. By sharing with the poor you can merit God's gifts to you; and because of their suffering, the poor will be crowned with a diadem of Patience. Do not let the bread of the hungry mildew in your larder! Do not let moths eat the poor man's cloak. Do not store the shoes of the barefoot. Do not hoard the money of the needy. Things you possess in too great abundance belong to the poor and not to you. You are the thief who steals from God if you are able to help your neighbor and refuse to do it.

Therefore, the well-guided princess must hire fine administrators to help her in her good works. No matter how deserving of compassion are princes who act on bad advice or who are betrayed by dishonest ministers, I believe that the truly good-intentioned select competent <u>counsellors</u> who would not dare to give them bad advice. Ordinarily, a master chooses servants according to his own disposition, and they counsel their master to good or evil according to what they think he wills. Likewise, a good lady will retain servants in her own likeness. She will commission them to inquire throughout the town or elsewhere to find the destitute people, gentlefolk who have fallen on hard times, neglected widows, unfortunate wives, poor girls of an age to be married, women in childbed, students, priests, and monks living in poverty. She will send them help by her almoner, whom she will know to be devout, charitable, and generous even before she appoints him. She will not imitate the custom of certain lords, noblemen, and prelates, who make the most dishonest servant master.

The noble lady will send her almoner secretly to these poor, good people so that even they themselves will not know whence the help is coming; that was what <u>Saint Nicholas</u> counseled. Nor will the good lady, accompanied by her ladies, be ashamed occasionally to visit <u>hospitals</u> and the poor in their homes. Speaking to the poverty-stricken and the ill, touching them and gently comforting them, she will be distributing the greatest charity of all. For the poor feel especially comforted and prefer the kind word, the visit, and the attention of the great and powerful personage over anything else. They think the world despises them. If someone of importance deigns to visit and speak with them, they thereby recover a certain self-respect, which everyone naturally desires.

So doing, the princess or great lady acquires greater merit than a lesser person who performs the same good deed. Three reasons justify that disparity. First, the more exalted the donor, the deeper comfort the poor person receives. Second, the greater the person, the more she must humble herself, and thus the more profound the virtue. Third, and most important, she sets a good example for those who see a good work performed with such spirit of humility. Nothing so well instructs subjects as observation of their lord or lady. Therefore, it is as great a benefit when the highborn or others in authority are graciously well-bred as it is a great misfortune when the opposite is true. No lady is so important that it is shameful or unsuitable for her to go devoutly and humbly to <u>pardons</u> or to visit churches or holy places. A lady ashamed to do good is ashamed to work for her own salvation.

Perhaps you will ask me how a great lady can give alms if she has no money, for I have already said that it is dangerous to amass worldly treasure. But, of course, there is no inevitable harm in the princess gathering treasure through revenues or income rightfully her own and gotten without extortion. The question is what she does with these treasures. Certainly God does not oblige her to give all to the poor if she does not want to. She can rightfully use it for her own necessities, to preserve her worldly station, to pay her servants, to give suitable gifts, and to pay her debts. Debts must be paid even before alms are distributed, for there is no merit in giving as alms what truly is due another. The good lady, however, should avoid the temptation of extravagances. Denying herself numerous robes and superfluous jewels and using her money instead for alms is true generosity. Admirable is she who so acts!

She might be compared to the wise man elected governor of a city who, being prudent and clever, realized that former holders of that office later had been deposed, banished, and exiled. Deprived of everything, they were left to die of hunger in a poor country. He thus provided for such a contingency, so that if ever he were exiled he would not starve. He arranged that his pay and the wealth earned in office that was left over after providing for necessities was stored safely. In the end it happened to him as to the others, but his wise provision preserved him from want. Likewise, what one saves out of abundance to give to the poor and to other works of merit is the treasure laid aside in holy provision to serve after death as protection against the exile of hell. This is the incessant message of the Scriptures: "Lay up treasures in Heaven! Lay up treasures in Heaven!" One can take along nothing but such treasures. As the Bible truly demonstrates, not only princesses but all women who are good housekeepers understand this manner of thrift.

In short, then, charity (joined to other noble virtues in her heart) will provide the benevolent princess with such good will that she will celebrate other people's worthiness as greater than her own and rejoice in their welfare as if it were her own. Their good reputation also will delight her. Accordingly, she will encourage the good to persevere in their virtue and the wicked to desist.

11. Which begins to expound the moral teachings which Worldly Prudence will give the princess.

Worldly Prudence's teachings and advice do not depart greatly from God's, but rather arise from them and depend on them. Therefore, we shall speak of the wise governance of life according to Prudence, who will teach the princess or noble lady to cherish honor and good reputation above all things in this earthly world. Prudence also will say that God is not in the least displeased with a creature living morally in the world, and she who lives the moral life will love the good renown called honor. Saint Augustine's *Book of Corrections* tells us that two things necessary for living well are conscience and good repute. Similarly, the wise author of the *Book of Ecclesiasticus* exhorts: "Cherish good repute for it will endure longer than any other treasure."

Agreeing that, above all earthly things, nothing so suits the noble as honor, the good princess will ask what qualities belong to true honor. Certainly not worldly riches, at least not according to the world's normal habits. Riches are of meager value in perfecting honor. What things, then, are suitable? Good morals. What in the world is the use of good morals? They perfect the noble creature, achieving the good repute wherein lies perfect honor. No matter what wealth a prince or princess possesses, if she does not lead a life of reputation and praise through doing good, she lacks honor regardless of the blandishments of her entourage to suggest that she has it. True honor must be above reproach. How greatly should the noble lady love honor? Certainly more than her life, for she would pay more dearly for the loss of it. The reason for this is clear. Whoever dies well is saved, but the one who is dishonored suffers reproach, living or dead, so long as she is remembered.

Good reputation is the greatest treasure a princess or noble lady can acquire. No other is so great or should be sought more eagerly. Ordinary treasure is useful only in the locale in which she finds herself, but the treasure which is the reputation of her honor serves her in lands near and far. Like the odor of sanctity, good repute is a sweet fragrance from the body wafting across the world so that everyone is aware of it. The fragrance of good repute thus goes forth from a worthy person so that everyone else may sense her good example.

After this admonishment by Prudence, the princess might well ask what she must do to put these ideas into practice. Her life will pivot around two particular points. One is the morals she will observe and abide by, and the other is the style of life which will direct her. Two moral considerations are especially necessary for women who desire honor, for without them it is unattainable: namely, Sobriety and Chastity.

Sobriety, the first, does not concern merely eating and drinking, but indeed all else serving to restrain and moderate excess. Sobriety will prevent a lady from being difficult to serve, for she will not be unreasonable in her demands. Despite her high estate she will be well satisfied with whatever is served of wines and foods. Not dwelling on such matters, she will partake of only the necessities life requires. Sobriety also will keep her from excessive sleep, because Prudence tells her that too much repose encourages sin and vice. Furthermore, Sobriety will deflect her from avarice. A small amount of wealth will be a great sufficiency for her. Above all, Prudence will restrain her from coveting extravagant clothes, jewels, headdresses, and an unreasonable mode of life. Unfailingly, Prudence will tell her that although all princesses and wealthy ladies customarily ought to be richly adorned with robes, headgear, and ornaments corresponding to their station in life, discretion must rule decoration. If you, good princess, are not content with your station nor the traditional styles and would prefer to acquire something finer or desire to introduce new styles, you are mistaken. For all frivolous things redound to your dishonor and insult the virtue of Sobriety. Therefore, do not do it. It benefits no one unless somehow it is in accord with the desires of one's lord. Even so, the good princess should not imitate anything extravagant without good advice, counsel, and just cause.

Sobriety also should be evident in all the lady's senses, as well as in her actions and costume. Her glance will be slow, deliberate, and without vagueness. Sobriety will protect her from too great curiosity about sweet scents, to which many ladies give great attention, spending large quantities of money on perfume. Likewise, it will tell her that she should not seek out or indulge the body in such delights, when she would do better to give the money to the poor. The same Sobriety will duly correct her tongue, for her speech must be free from extravagances so unbecoming to great ladies, and, indeed, to all worthy women. Heartily despising the vice of falsehood, she will prefer truth, which will be so habitual in her mouth that always what she says will be believed and respected. She will be known as a person who never lies. The virtue of truth is more necessary in the mouths of princes and princesses than in others because everyone must trust them. Sobriety also will prevent her from speaking words she has not carefully considered in advance, especially in those places where they will be weighed or reported.

Prudence and Sobriety teach a lady well-ordered speech and wise eloquence. She never will be coy, but will speak well-considered words, soft and rather low-pitched, uttered with a pleasant face and without excessive motion of the hands or body, nor facial grimaces. She will avoid excessive or uncalled-for laughter. Refraining from speaking ill of others, she will not blame, but rather will encourage goodness. Gladly she will keep in check vague, dishonest words, nor will she permit others to speak them to her. Her humor also will be discreet.

In the midst of her own entourage, the princess will speak a virtuous language of good example, so that those who listen to her directly, as well as those who hear later reports, will perceive that her words come from her goodness, wisdom, and honesty. Never speaking ungraciously to her companions or servants, nor quarreling or speaking viciously, instead she will instruct her household retainers and friends gently, correcting their shortcomings softly, politely, threatening to expel them if they do not reform, punishing them in a quiet voice without being needlessly unkind. Crude brutality from the mouth of a lady or, indeed, any woman turns more against herself than against the one to whom it is addressed. Moreover, her commands must be reasonable for the time and place, as well as suitable for the person receiving them, each according to his own proper duty.

The lady willingly will read books inculcating good habits, as well as studying on occasion devotional books. She will disdain volumes describing dishonest habits or vice. Never allowing them in her household, she will not permit them in the presence of any daughter, relative, or lady-in-waiting. Examples of good or of evil doubtlessly attract the attention of those who see or hear them. Hence the noble lady who takes pleasure in remembering or in speaking good words likewise will be pleased to listen to them; above all, she will delight in the words of God. Whoever belongs to God willingly hears His word. As it is set forth in Scripture: "Those who love me hear my word with a full heart and observe it." Consequently, she will invite good, notable clerics to deliver sermons on feast days, sharing these with her daughters, ladies, and her whole family, desiring the refinement of her own knowledge of our faith's articles, commandments, and ideas on Salvation.

Regarding worldly affairs, she will listen gladly to worthy people, brave knights, and gentlemen who speak of their deeds and accomplishments, as well as to great churchmen cherished for their knowledge, and to all noble men and women worthy of hearing for their fine sensibilities and exemplary lives. Appreciating them with honor, she also will lavish upon them suitable gifts. Similarly, the wise noblewoman will gather about her those who lead admirable, elevated lives of devotion. Seeking them out and receiving them humbly, she will talk to them in private, listening to them devotedly, and requesting remembrance in their prayers.

Thus the virtue of Sobriety will govern the noble princess. From this will follow naturally the regime of the second of the two virtues: the practice of Chastity. It will direct her to such purity that her word, deed, appearance, dress, countenance, bearing, status, and high regard will be unreproachable.

12. Wherein is described the lifestyle of the wise princess according to the admonitions of Prudence.

Prudence will suggest that the wise princess order her life according to such a regime as this. Rising early every morning, her first words will be addressed to God. She will pray: "Lord, keep me free this day from mortal sin, from sudden death, and from all misfortunes. So be it with my family and friends. Grant pardon to the dead. Grant peace and tranquility to our subjects. Amen." She would end with a Pater Noster and any additional prayers her devotion might suggest.

She will prefer not to surround herself with an elaborate morning service. Such was the habit of Good Queen Joan, formerly wife of King Charles V of France. During her lifetime she arose every morning before daybreak and lighted her own candle to recite her Hours, thus not permitting her serving women to rise up and lose necessary sleep. When ready, the wise princess will go to chapel to hear morning Mass either as often as her devotion dictates or her time allows. The lady with great responsibilities in government has little time free from ruling. Lords often give over their rule to their ladies when they know them to be wise and good and when they themselves are obliged to be absent. Such women have enormous responsibility and authority to govern their lands and serve as council chief. These ladies should be excused even by God if they do not spend so much time in lengthy prayers as those with greater leisure. Certainly they merit no less for attending to the public good and welfare of all in their power than if they spent more time in prayer.

Of course, a lady might elect total dedication to the contemplative life, completely renouncing the active life. However, while that contemplative life can exist without the active, the active cannot endure without some portion of the contemplative. Therefore, the active lady leaving her chapel will personally, with humility and devotion, give alms with her own hands, showing by her actions that she does not despise the poor. Any requests for mercy or aid she will listen to kindly, replying graciously, and immediately attending to those which can be fulfilled. By so doing, she will enhance not only the gift but her own reputation. If time will not allow her to hear all the requests, she will refer the rest to virtuous men accompanying her who have been charged with listening to them and who by nature and character are charitable, efficient, and honorable.

After this, the lady who governs will go to her council on those days when it meets. There she will carry herself with such presence, such bearing, and such a countenance that, seated on her high throne of office, she will indeed appear to be the ruler of them all. Everyone will revere her as a wise mistress of great authority. She will listen diligently to all propositions and to the opinions of everyone present. Carefully remembering the principal points of each problem and the suggested conclusions, she scrupulously will note which members speak the best, with most due consideration, and which offer the finest possible advice. Then she will weigh the wisest, most lively, most honorable opinions. Naturally, she will consider the causes and reasons inspiring the speakers' diversity of opinions, instructing herself on the cause of each effect. When her own time comes for speaking or replying, her reasoning will be so wise that nothing could be further from simplicity or ignorance. Moreover, she will be informed in advance of what will be proposed in the council. Such preparation for important matters by wise advice will permit her to speak and act to her own advantage.

Moreover, the lady will have appointed a certain number of wise gentlemen as advisers, those she knows to be good, intelligent, upright, and free from greed. Greedy retainers shame everyone. The entourages of certain princes and princesses sadly demonstrate that counsellors who are known to be greedy give false advice to the ones they counsel. Those having this defect will not give loyal, dependable advice either for profit of the soul or for honor of the body. Therefore, a prudent lady will test in advance her counsellors' honor and suitability. With them, she then will take counsel daily at a particular hour concerning the duties which she and they must execute.

After this morning session she will go to table, which on certain feast days, or more frequently, will be set in the great hall. There she will be seated among her ladies, handmaidens, and other significant people, each placed according to proper protocol of rank. She will be served the foods befitting her status as ruler, and throughout the meal will maintain the fine old custom of having some worthy man standing by her table to recite poems about ancient deeds of virtuous ancestors, or to tell exemplary tales. Beneficent order will rule the hall. After grace has been offered and the tables removed, she will hold court. Lords, knights, squires, ladies, or strangers who have come to see her, each will she receive correctly, in her customary gracious manner, as one well trained for such duty. She will offer each due honor so that everyone will be content. Speaking politely and showing a cheerful face, she will address the elderly more seriously and the young more gaily. So agreeably will she welcome those coming simply to talk or to hear an entertainment that all will say she is charming and a true lady for all seasons.

After spices have been served at the feast's end, the lady will go to her private apartment. There, if she wishes, she will rest for a while. If it is a working day (as opposed to a Sabbath) and she has no more pressing occupation, she will avoid idleness by taking up some handiwork and will gather her handmaidens and ladies to do the same. Then she will allow all to indulge in various honest amusements of their own choice. Laughing with others, she will amuse herself, talking with them informally so that all will praise her great friendliness and kindness and love her with great devotion.

Remaining thus until the hour of <u>Vespers</u>, she will hear the service in her chapel if it is a feast day and if no other business detains her. In any case, she certainly will say prayers with her chaplain. After that, particularly if it is summertime, she will enjoy herself in the garden until suppertime. She will meander here and there for recreation, but if some of her subjects need her, she will welcome them to come in and will listen to their petitions. After supper, toward bedtime, her thoughts will return in prayer to God. So will conclude the order of ordinary days for the prudent princess engaged in good and holy activity.

Yet other pleasures delight ladies, such as hunting, boating on the river, dancing (if they are young), and certain games. I do not prescribe or teach these, preferring to leave them to the discretion and wish of the ladies themselves and their husbands. Such sports and entertainments can be allowed without hesitation to even the most virtuous ladies when time and place are suitable, disporting themselves with moderation, always avoiding excess.

13. Here begins the discussion of Prudence's six principal teachings which should be observed by every princess who loves and desires honor. The first of these concerns her attitude toward her lord and master.

Now that we have spoken both generally and specifically about the princess's devotion to God, good habits, and recommended style of life, we are pleased to present for her benefit seven teachings which, according to Prudence, are fitting and necessary for all desiring to live wisely and honorably. Princesses, and all ladies of great, ordinary, and low degree ought to note well and practice these seven points. Good theory is worthless when not followed by good practice.

The first of the seven rules is: A lady loving honor, or any woman in the estate of marriage, must love her husband and live with him in peace. Otherwise she already has encountered the torments of Hell, where storms rage perpetually. Although doubtlessly women of all sorts may love their husbands dearly, either they do not know all of these rules or, because of their youth, do not know how to demonstrate their love. This lesson will teach them how.

The noble princess wishing to love according to the rules of honor will conduct herself toward her lord, whether he is young or old, in all ways expected for good faith and true love. She will be humble toward him in deed, word, and attitude. She will obey him without complaint and will keep her peace as punctiliously as did Good Queen Esther in the Bible's first chapter of her book, where her lord so loved and honored her that she had no wish he would not grant. The lady will show her love by lavishing care and attention on all matters pertaining to his welfare, that of his soul as well as of his body. In order to attend to his soul she will win the confidence of his confessor, to whom she can turn if she sees in her lord any indication of sin whose practice could lead to his perdition. She might hesitate to mention such frailty to her husband for fear of displeasing him; instead, she will have his confessor admonish him, begging him to serve Our Lord faithfully. And, when giving alms and doing good works, she always will say: "Pray God for my lord and me."

Parallel to her concern for her lord's soul is the lady's concentration on his bodily needs. She must assure that his health is maintained and his life preserved from threat. Therefore she will wish to talk frequently with his physicians, inquiring about the state of his health, sometimes being present at their consultations, and wisely heeding their opinions. Similarly, she will want to be sure her husband's servants serve him well. If need be, she will not hesitate to take personal charge, no matter who has been appointed to this duty. Because it is not customary for royal ladies to be in such close contact with their husbands as other women are with theirs, the lady frequently will inquire for information about him from chamberlains and others of his suite. She will see him as often as possible, always expressing joy at their meeting. In his presence she will show a joyful face and say things which she knows will please him.

Of course, some of you may reply that we are telling only part of the story, insisting that women must always love their husbands and show it, not saying whether men always deserve to be so well treated. Certainly some husbands conduct themselves abominably, showing little love for their wives or none at all. We reply to this objection that our doctrine in this present treatise is not addressed to men, however much they might need to be instructed. Since we are speaking to women alone, we intend to provide them with the remedies useful in avoiding dishonor.

Thus we advise them to follow the path of virtue no matter who may choose the contrary and whether it profits them good or ill. Presuppose for the moment that the husband is marvelously perverse in his morals, rude, whatever his background, is ungracious to his wife, and is involved with another woman, or even several. Nevertheless, the wise woman's good judgment and prudence are manifest when she knows how to bear all this, dissembling, without appearing to be aware of his perfidies or showing that she observes anything unusual. Even if every suspicion is true, there is nothing she can do about it. She may well reflect to herself: "If I speak to him harshly, I will gain nothing. If he mistreats me, I am headed into a storm. Perhaps he might send me away. Then people would mock me all the more, thus adding shame and disrepute to the whole despicable affair. Even worse might overtake me. Alas, I am obliged to live and die with him, whatever he may be."

All things considered, the wise lady will try to attract her husband to her by charm and gentleness. If she realizes it is for the best, she will speak to him about his peccadilloes in private, gently and kindly. One time she will caution him, playing upon devotion; another time she will emphasize the mercy he should have toward her; another time she will speak laughingly, as if she were teasing. She also will have good people such as his confessor speak to him. However, this noble lady will excuse him if she overhears others speaking about him, and she will not permit them to speak ill of him nor to come bearing vicious tales. She will defend him, knowing that listening to what they say will bring her only sorrow. Nothing will be gained by it. After she has made every effort to remain in peace with him, and when she has tried all of these methods for a reasonable time and still he does not wish to change his ways, then without further mentioning the subject, her only sure refuge is God.

No man is so perverse that in the end his conscience and reason will not say to him: "You have wronged and sinned against your good, honest wife." Consequently, he may reform and love her as much or even more than if he had never strayed from the path of virtue. She will have gained her ends by patient endurance. And if her lord leaves on a long, perilous journey or goes off to war, the good lady faithfully will pray to God and also have others pray for him, conscientiously making religious processions and oblations in his honor. Furthermore, she will increase the amount of money she donates in alms, conducting herself humbly and simply in her manner of life, her behavior, and her dress during his absence. On his return she will receive him joyfully and with honor.

Moreover, she will hospitably receive all his companions, gladly discovering which of his men were bravest and most valiant and how they all conducted themselves in battle. Enthusiastically, she will hear them tell of all this and will receive them with great honor, giving them fine gifts. She also will inform herself about how her lord's servants attended to their duties and served his needs, and will reward the best and most devoted.

Observing such amenities brings great credit to the lady. Even though she does these things willingly, she should always want their forms to be seen (if not their spirit) and known in the world rather than concealed from view. The reason: She loves honor and good repute. No greater honor can be paid a prudent lady than to say of her that she is true and loyal to her lord, that certainly she appears to love him, and that consequently she is faithful to him. Everyone assumes that a wife who loves her husband never will be false to him. No better proof of loyalty is there than the love she shows for him and the external signs by which sentiment ordinarily is judged. People's intentions cannot be judged except by their acts, which when good, give evidence of good thought and personal virtue; the opposite is likewise true. So much for the first teaching which befits all noble women whoever they may be.

14. Which sets forth Prudence's second teaching: The way in which the princess will conduct herself toward her lord's relatives.

Prudence's second precept indicates for the princess, and any other woman, that if she esteems honor and, presumably, loves her husband, she also will love and honor her husband's relatives. She will demonstrate enthusiastic cordiality whenever she meets them. In front of others, she will show them even more consideration than her own parents. By taking pains to please them and adhere to their reasonable requests, she will draw them to her both amiably and cheerfully. She will intercede on their behalf with her lord if there is need. If disagreements arise among them, she will make every effort to pacify them. Speaking well even of those who don't deserve it, she will avoid quarreling and prevent animosity, ill will, or discord from erupting. Those relatives who are particularly difficult and trying, she will attempt to regard in the best possible light and be as kind to them as is feasible, never forgetting the honor due herself. This way she will love not only her lord's relatives but also those of whom she knows he is fond.

Even people who are not admirable she will receive hospitably. Why? She cannot make them good, nor can she hinder or deflect her lord's preference for them. The only result of showing ill will would be altercations. She would acquire enemies who would say that truthfully the wife does not like her husband's friends. However, if she is sure that he trusts her judgment, and she knows for certain that particular people are vicious and evil and might harm her husband through his association with their persons, deeds, or behavior, she will tell him so, explaining the matter in private, quietly and gently. Or she will convince someone else to speak to him. Her lord will be grateful for such behavior. And she will have the good will of his relatives. That can be useful to her and protect her from other burdens and more serious perils. Moreover, enjoying the favor of her husband's relatives will make her feel more secure. Many troubles have come to women through antagonistic relatives. Concord with her in-laws proves a woman's love and loyalty to her lord.

15. Which sets forth Prudence's third teaching: How a wise princess will carefully arrange the upbringing of her children.

Prudence's third teaching is dedicated to the princess with children, who must diligently arrange for their care and upbringing. Ordinarily it is the father's duty to find good tutors and provide suitable governors, especially for the sons. Nevertheless, the lady, who might be less preoccupied with other duties and by her nature as a mother more inclined to concern herself with children, will consider carefully all aspects of their welfare.

Proper development of their habits, especially their moral and intellectual instruction, is even more critical than the care of their bodies. Therefore, the good princess will plan exactly how to properly nurture good habits, will select the men and women to take charge, and will supervise how they fulfill their duties. She will leave nothing to the report of others. Personally visiting her children in their rooms, seeing them put to bed at night and awakened in the morning, she will direct their care. Such attention will satisfy not only the princess's maternal interest but also her honor. The greatest protection and ornament she can have is her children. Often someone wishing to harm the mother will refrain from doing so <u>for fear of the children.</u>

Thus, she should cherish her children as evidence that she is both wise and good. The intelligent lady who loves her children dearly will assure their being well taught. The masters must teach at suitable hours. First, let the children learn to serve God. Then they should be taught their letters. They should also be instructed in Latin and have some knowledge of the sciences, which are most desirable and suitable subjects for the progeny of princes and the nobility. As her children grow in age and understanding, the wise lady also will wish them to be taught about such worldly matters as the quality of government later to be expected from them and all such other things that princes must know. Needless to say, she must ensure their instruction in following virtue and avoiding vice.

Character and competence of her children's masters also are the lady's concern, as are the characters of those in their company. She will fire unsuitable masters and then replace them. Having her children brought to her frequently, she will observe their manners, behavior, and speech, correcting them herself if they misbehave. She will make them respect her, wanting them to show her great honor. Her talks with them will inform her of their knowledge, and she herself will instruct them wisely.

Benevolent, intelligent women will be hired to guide her daughters. Before entrusting them with her children's care, however, she will assure herself of such women's good judgment, habits, and the quality of their private lives. Any woman or girl given supervision of the lady's daughters must have an excellent reputation, being devout in the eyes of God and sensible and honorable in the eyes of the world. Wise and prudent, she will serve as example of the virtue, the bearing, and the behavior that a daughter of a prince and princess must both learn and practice. This governess must be old enough to be more mature in her behavior than the child she will supervise, so that the child and others at court will respect and fear her.

No woman or maiden of doubtful reputation must be allowed in the daughter's entourage, nor anyone ill-bred, frivolous, foolish, or badly behaved. The child must have no bad examples to follow. When the princess's daughter has reached suitable age, she will be taught to read and thereafter to learn her Hours and her prayers. Then she will be given devotional books and others describing virtuous behavior. She will not be allowed to read of vain things, folly, or loose living. No such books will be permitted in her presence, for a child's learning and what is taught to her in her early youth remains with her throughout her life.

Consequently, the wise mother will devote great attention to the upbringing and instruction of her daughters. As they grow older, she will be especially careful, keeping them close by her side much of the time and always making sure they respect her. Her own virtuous bearing will be example to her daughters for comparable conduct.

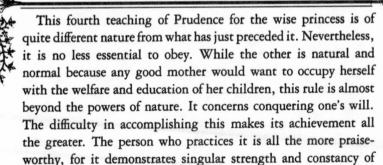

16. Which speaks of Prudence's fourth teaching: How the princess will maintain a discreet manner even toward those whom she well knows do not like her and are envious of her.

This fourth teaching of Prudence for the wise princess is of quite different nature from what has just preceded it. Nevertheless, it is no less essential to obey. While the other is natural and normal because any good mother would want to occupy herself with the welfare and education of her children, this rule is almost beyond the powers of nature. It concerns conquering one's will. The difficulty in accomplishing this makes its achievement all the greater. The person who practices it is all the more praise-worthy, for it demonstrates singular strength and constancy of courage.

All wise princesses who prize honor and repute should know how to use this strength. Otherwise, Prudence cannot properly reveal herself, announce her presence, or achieve perfection. Let us explain. According to the ways of the world and the turnings of the <u>Wheel of Fortune</u>, no person, however great and however just, and no prince, lord, or lady ever alive—or any other man or woman who ever was—has been loved by everyone. Even if a person were completely perfect, still he inevitably would suffer from others' heartfelt, hateful envy.

Pleasing to everyone, such a paragon is loved by no one. Even the death of Jesus Christ, who alone was perfect, was the result of envy. Various other valiant people similarly have perished. The greater and more virtuous the person, the greater the war Envy wages against him. Nobody and no one who ever was, except God, could ever avenge himself upon such <u>jealous hatred</u>.

Therefore, it seems evident that the wise princess, and all wishing to conduct themselves prudently, must be forewarned and provided with a remedy. If Fortune assaults, as she has done in the past and continues to do against good people, and if the princess knows that particular powerful people do not wish her well or would harm her if they could (such as removing her from the love and grace of her lord, who possibly might believe their malicious blandishments and flatteries), or that these connivers gladly would slander her through false reports of barons, vassals, or commoners, then she should appear not to notice nor to consider these people her enemies. Rather, by showing them unsuspecting and cheerful countenance, she will lead them to believe that she esteems them and never could judge them otherwise, for she apparently trusts them more than others. This appearance must be so well controlled and so discreetly and cleverly acted that no one will perceive it is all pretense. If on one occasion her sweet, dissimulating demeanor is overdone, and on another it is accompanied by a sharp look so that someone notices the laugh is not from the heart but false, everything will be ruined.

Prudence therefore demands moderation. Courage, too, must be well fortified. The lady will pretend that she wants these people to advise and direct her. So she will invite them to her private councils, where she will appear to tell them things in great confidence. Of course, this will be the opposite of what she truly thinks. But all must be done so ingeniously that they are not put off by it. She must be mistress of her tongue, for if she should say any equivocal word behind their backs which could be repeated to them, it would indeed be very dangerous. No lord or lady is so great that all his servants are to be trusted. Hence, the princess always must be careful before whom she speaks. Though a heart swollen full with regret and displeasure suffers with difficulty a mouth constantly closed and silent, that heart must be trained to its essential skill.

The dissembling lady would ruin herself if found out. Not only would it bring discredit, but it would diminish her stature if her enemies realized that, aware of their dislike for her, she would still put up such pretense. They would imagine her doing it from fear. Thus they would be all the more overbearing and bold to harm her. They would respect her so much the less. So she must protect herself from such revelation. If anyone tells her anything wherein she imagines that her reply might be repeated, she will chastise the gossips by saying she is sure those in question seek only her good and honor, for they are fine and loyal to her as well as being her friends.

Suppose these enemies do or say something obviously hurtful. If it is impossible to suggest that they did it for some reason other than her harm, she still must pretend to be so ingenuous or ignorant that she does not notice it. Surely such a thing could have nothing to do with her. Surely she could harbor no thought of suspicion against such people. Nevertheless, despite this great pretense, she will keep as sharp an eye on them as she can and henceforth be on guard against them.

Thus, the wise lady will use this prudent device of discreet dissimulation, which should not be considered vicious but rather a great virtue whem employed for the common good, to maintain peace, or to avoid detriment or greater harm. Not only will she escape trouble but she will also achieve great benefit if she pretends not to notice conspiracy against her. Of course, it is sometimes necessary for her to disagree and debate with her enemies and to strive to avenge herself upon them. By so doing, however, she would create a huge uproar in the realm, putting her friends into conflict and peril and risking that her husband might believe her enemies rather than herself and their well-disposed barons and subjects. The bitter quarrel would result in serious trouble. Furthermore, she might not even be avenged, but rather be given greater cause for sorrow.

But the way of tolerance and dissimulation appeases the ire and ill will of her enemies and perhaps might even convert them into friends. At least they would never have the heart to injure her as much as if she had shown herself to be their enemy. The height of disloyalty is to harm a reputed friend. Suppose they persist. Their wicked betrayal would be the more apparent to the world, leading to their censure and dishonor. Others would be less likely to rally to their cause. Everyone would blame them. Undeniably, a lady has more to gain in such case by disciplined dissemblance. Not only princesses and great ladies but all women ought to remember this idea: If flatterers' reports to husbands cause problems in marriage, then dissemble! Many women cannot dissemble or they do not do it well; God knows this, as do others.

17. Which sets forth Prudence's fifth teaching: How the wise princess will try to be in the good graces and the kind thoughts of all her subjects.

The wise princess governing her affairs with Prudence's guidance cultivates honor. This fifth teaching requires her to be in the good standing and good graces of the clergy, the religious orders, the prelates, the counsellors, the monks, the doctors, the bourgeoisie, and even the people. Though some will be surprised that we insist on these groups rather than on the barons and nobles, we assume the princess already has their friendship, as it is usual for her to frequent such nobility. Two reasons, however, make these other groups desirable. First, the good and devout will pray to God on her behalf. Second, they will praise her in sermons and other public discourses, so that their voices can be a necessary shield and defense against the murmurs and false reports of her jealous defamers. Perhaps their words might silence the gossips; consequently, she would be in better repute with her husband as well as with the common folk. Hearing their lady well spoken of, the more powerful among them might sustain her if she should ever need their help.

Therefore, she will learn which clerics, masters, and people in religious orders are the most capable and highly regarded, and which are the most respected for what they say. On occasion she will send for them, sometimes one, sometimes another, and converse with them amiably. Not only will she seek their advice but she will follow it. Inviting them to dine at her court, she will ask them to join the company of her confessor and other members of her chapel, themselves distinguished people, and will honor these guests, expecting her entourage also to render honor to them. Homage, after all, is fitting; those ennobled by knowledge should be venerated.

Not only will she entertain them but, according to her financial potential, she will make gifts to their communities and to their monasteries. Although alms normally should be given secretly so that the donor will not be encouraged in the mortal sin of vanity, nevertheless if the lady does not have undue pride in her heart, such gifts are best given openly rather than in secret. Overt giving sets a good example for others. Whoever so inspires others to give performs not only a good deed but doubles her own merit. Free of vanity, the lady would wish her important gifts and alms to be known and noticed publicly. Major benefactions include the reconstruction of churches, convents, or other religious necessities; and donations for memorials, paintings for the churches, and prayers to God on her behalf. Such gifts recorded publicly will assure that others appreciate them and that, led by her example, they will make similar gifts. If this open way of giving and this acquaintance with particular people capable of enhancing one's reputation seem to suggest hypocrisy, or if these are so labeled, they ought better to be called "justifiable hypocrisy." Their intent is cultivation of virtue and avoidance of its contrary. Clearly we are not suggesting that evil and sin be committed in the shadow of expedient giving, nor that great pride result from it.

So we repeat: Justifiable hypocrisy is necessary for princes and princesses who must rule over others and thus be accorded more respect than others. Moreover, expedient hypocrisy is not unworthy for others desiring honor, as long as they practice it for worthy ends. As Valerius Maximus reminds us, long-ago princes requiring their subjects' reverence and respect pretended that they were related to the gods.

The lady of authority will want the good allegiance of her lord's counsellors, prelates, knights, and others. So, from time to time she will have them come before her, receive them honorably, speak to them eloquently, and make an effort to like them as much as possible. Such courtesies are valuable in many ways. Those people will praise her judgment and her ability to manage her affairs and will perceive them to be fine and estimable. Moreover, if envious people machinate against her, the counsellors will not permit the matter to pass a vote in the council nor exploit anything to her prejudice. Nor would they adversely influence the prince against her if he misjudged or was misinformed. Conversely, any measure she would wish passed through the council they would shepherd through as friends favorable to her desires.

Equally important, the wise lady will cultivate good will among lawyers involved in ordinary legal causes of the people—the Advocates of Parliament, as we call them in Paris. Throughout the country there are similar defenders of causes. The lady in power will receive on a certain day the officials and other significant, outstanding members of this group. Speaking cordially, she will urge them to observe and understand her honorable estate. Not that she should speak boastfully, but she ought to let them see for themselves her noble bearing and wisdom. Such action is valuable to increase their admiration and her fame. All sorts of people from various countries come to seek the counsel of such lawyers. Consequently, they speak with many people to whom they could thus bear witness to her praiseworthiness and respectability, to both strangers and friends. So her renown will increase. Similarly, she will maintain good relations with <u>bailiffs</u>, <u>provosts</u>, and all those concerned with the administration of justice.

Occasionally she ought to call to her presence the most important citizens of her lord's cities and towns, as well as certain important merchants and even some of the most respected artisans. Receiving them well, she must pragmatically cultivate their good will so that if ever she is in difficulty they will support her. If she should find herself in need of money, for example, she could request the merchants' help, which would be forthcoming willingly and benevolently. If she should need to borrow money, she must observe all contractual terms and pledges, not failing to pay back the loan on the appointed day. In this way her word invariably will be honored, unfailingly and faithfully.

While, of course, we already have explained in the fifth chapter of Prudence's seven teachings that the princess must maintain good relations with all her subjects, some readers might think it useless for me to repeat this now, finding it unsuitable for a princess to lavish attention on her lowlier subjects. They might think it is appropriate only for her to give orders without hesitation, and for her subjects to obey them in order to win her favor and not she theirs. But, without offense to those who believe the contrary, we maintain that the more overtly considerate course is splendid not only for princes and princesses but for everyone. (We pass over all but two of the many reasons for this, for it is a subject we could elaborate on extensively.) First, despite the prince being the lord and master of his subjects, still the subjects create the lord, not vice versa. If people want to be troublesome, they will much more easily find somone else to take them on as subjects than a lord will find subjects to accept him as their ruler. Moreover, the lord alone could not repress so large a group of people if they were to rebel against him. Even if at any given moment he had the military power to destroy them, he would also destroy himself. He is obliged to maintain their deferential admiration. Their respect for him will arise from his concern for them, rather than from force. Otherwise his power will be in question. A common proverb reinforces this point: "No one is lord in his country who is hated by his people."

Nothing is more sensible for a prince or princess wishing to be called a true ruler than to hold the people in genuine affection. There is no city or fortress so well defended, so strong and powerful, as one protected by the love and good will of loyal subjects. Therefore, the second reason for the prince and princess to cultivate homage from the people is to assure their subjects' deferential devotion. Subjects respecting them never will be so bold as to approach them either in contemptuous familiarity, or when an audience is unsuitable. Though courtesy demands the first welcome always to come from the prince or princess, the subjects themselves should joyfully celebrate their coming and feel duly honored. Love and loyalty of the subjects is increased two-fold by the kindness they perceive in their rulers. A wise man has said that nothing so impresses the hearts of subjects nor attracts them to their ruler so much as knowing him to be benevolent and gentle. Similarly, it is written of a good emperor that he would like to be regarded by his subjects as they themselves would like him to be regarded. Aware of this, the good princess will follow that example.

Therefore, when from time to time the wives of the princess's subjects come to call on her, she will receive them courteously and speak to them so amiably that they will be well disposed to praise her graciousness and benevolent manner. When she holds full court she will send for them, and also invite them to celebrations, to _gesines,_ and to the weddings of her children, asking them to be in the company of her attendants. Because of such estimable acts, she will attract the love of everyone, men and women alike.

18. Which prescribes the sixth teaching of Prudence: How the wise princess will organize the women of her court.

Prudence's sixth teaching compares the wise princess to the good shepherd. She will assure that her sheep are kept in good health, and if any one should become afflicted with mange, she will separate it from the flock for fear the others might become infected. Therefore, she will watch over the conduct of her ladies-in-waiting, whom she will have selected carefully for their dependability and honesty. She would not wish to surround herself with any of lesser quality. Because knights, squires, and other men who are attracted to women generally will make advances to them and attempt to lure their attention whenever possible, the circumspect princess will do well to establish a rule of not allowing anyone to frequent her court who boldly converses with her women in private and tries to excite their interest. If any man should try this, or if the lady sees a man acting questionably, she straightaway will give him such a severe condemning look that he will not dare to try such a thing again. According to the master, so the household goes.

A completely honorable lady will want her companions to meet the same standards as she, on pain of exclusion from her company. Amusing themselves in honest entertainments, they will not in any way give men the opportunity to mock them or disparage them, as men are all too ready to disgrace women even at the moment they themselves may be laughing and disporting themselves with them. Her ladies should conduct themselves with decorum among knights, squires, and other men. They should speak simply and quietly, without coquetry and effrontery, as they amuse themselves in dancing and diversions. Certainly they should not be foolish, bold, or loud in their speech, countenance, or laughter.

Nor should women walk about with their heads held high, like antlered deer. Such appearance and manner would be most unbecoming and cause ridicule at court, where, more than any other place, should appear good breeding, courteous bearing, and chaste elegance. Indeed, where greatest honor dwells, there should live the most exemplary behavior.

Ladies of the court are totally misguided if here or in any country they believe that they are privileged to be more brazen and forward than other women. Because we hope our doctrine will be carried to many kingdoms and prove useful anywhere such social shortcomings exist, we say to all courtiers in general and in any country whatsoever, that all ladies- and maidens-in-waiting, be they young or old, ought to be wiser, better educated, and better behaved in every way than other women. Courtiers should serve as examples of honor and excellence to others. Doing otherwise would be of no credit either to their mistress or to themselves.

To assure that all aspects of her court are equally estimable, the wise princess will make certain that her ladies' gowns and headdresses, although suitably rich and handsome, are also modestly stylish, neatly maintained, and proper for the occasion—no arrogant fashion, suggestive low-cut necklines, or similar outrages. Hence, the wise princess must watch over her attendants in all matters, just as the benevolent, prudent abbess does in her convent. Thus disrepute will not circulate abroad, in town, or elsewhere.

The princess will be so feared and famous far and wide for her intelligent management of her court that no one will dare disobey her orders or unsuitably arch an eyebrow. A lady is more awesome, more venerated, and more revered when she is known to be wise, circumspect, and just. Even if such a lady is by nature amiable and complacent, if she rules well nobody would be so foolish as to be obstinate or troublesome, for her mere glance and reproving look should be sufficient warning to correct misbehavior and oblige people to deference.

19. Which sets forth the seventh teaching: How the wise princess will oversee her revenues, and how her finances will be managed, and which speaks of the state of her court.

Prudence's seventh instruction for the wise princess is to supervise carefully her revenues and expenses, a habit that should be cultivated not only by the nobility, but by anyone else desiring to live wisely. No princess should hesitate to find out for herself the amount of her <u>revenues</u> and pensions or to insist at certain times upon reviewing the records of her agents and paymasters. The princess should know how her stewards supervise her servants and how they regulate her daily household expenses, distributing food and wine and overseeing other court affairs. No woman should consider herself either too exalted or too modest to know that each steward, before she engages him, is prudent, respectable, and trustworthy. If she learns the contrary after having hired him, she should dismiss such a person at once. In this way she will keep careful watch on the nature and extent of her household expenses. She will want to know what is bought for her from merchants and from the people, ordering that they be paid appropriately to avoid incurring their ill-will or hatred. She will want to avoid debt, preferring to live more economically with less. Forbidding the taking of anything from people against their will, she will buy at fair price, and pay promptly. She will not allow poor people of the village to endure great trouble and expense in going to her counting house or to her agents one hundred times or more with the same bill before they are paid.

She will forbid her treasurers or those who distribute her finances to follow that common practice of making false promises of payment to vendors, carrying people along term to term. Conversely, she will insist that each person owing her money or produce be given terms possible for him to carry through in prompt payment.

The wise lady will distribute her revenues in the following manner: She will separate her receipts into five parts. The first portion will be devoted to alms and gifts to the poor. Second is the sum necessary for expenses of her household, if she must pay all salaries from her own revenues and income, presupposing her lord does not fully provide for them without her contribution. The third part will pay her officers and the ladies of her court. Fourth are gifts to strangers or to those subjects giving evidence of particular merit. And the fifth part she will put into her treasury, drawing from it as she wishes to purchase jewels, gowns, or personal apparel. Each of the five portions will represent the amount she can afford in accordance with her income. By following this plan in orderly fashion she will maintain her financial affairs without confusion, and without enduring shortages of necessary funds which otherwise might require her to juggle accounts or make unsuitable loan arrangements at great cost and financial loss.

So, by following these seven teachings of Prudence herein recommended, along with other virtues—none of which is particularly difficult to live by, but all of which enhance the quality of her life, being quite agreeable to anyone attracted and accustomed to them—the wise lady will acquire praise, glory, fine reputation, and considerable honor in this world. In the end, she will gain the Paradise promised to all mortals who live virtuously.

20. Which explains how the gifts and largesse of the wise princess should be distributed.

We spoke at considerable length of other virtues befitting a princess, suggesting the worldly generosity she must display by giving gifts beyond her ordinary expenses and by bestowing favors for special occasions. Since gift-giving is important for a princess, here we will consider that subject again at greater length.

Because the princess desires to avoid reproach in all of her dealings, she must avoid the vice of stinginess, a form of unwarranted avarice. It is as reprehensible as undue extravagance, which also is a vice. Rather, she will govern her gifts with discretion and prudence, for if any single thing in the world enhances the reputation of great lords and ladies, it is generosity. John of Salisbury in his *Polycraticus* (Book 3, chapter 14) argues that the virtue of generosity is essential to those governing public affairs. His example is Titus, the noble emperor who gained such reputation for generosity that he was called "The Clement, the Help of All." Titus so admired this virtue that it is said that on any day that he had not made a gift to anyone he could not be happy. Because of this generosity he won all people's grateful approbation.

Similarly, the wise lady will demonstrate her generosity. For example, if she has the capacity to give and she learns of a foreign gentleman or some other who by long imprisonment or because of ransom has lost his wealth or otherwise is in great need, she gladly will help from her own resources—graciously and generously. Since generosity consists not merely in gifts, as a wise man has said, but also in comforting words which give hope of better fortune, perhaps benevolent conversation may do more good than the money she gives. As I have mentioned before, a troubled person is extremely pleased when a prince or princess gives him personal encouragement.

Furthermore, if this lady sees some gentleman, knight, or squire of good courage who is eager to promote his honor but not able to outfit himself with armor as custom requires, and if she thinks it a good idea to help because he is so deserving, then she will assist him. Representing all noble virtues herself, through her gifts she will encourage nobility and high standards in others. Her prudent largesse will be distributed as occasion merits it.

When she receives gifts from great lords, she will reward the messengers so promptly and so generously that not only will they praise her for it but, especially if they are foreigners, they will also report to their lords in their own countries. Gifts from great ladies she will reciprocate even more generously with some of her own jewels or something from her most beautiful possessions. However, if a poor or simple person should do her service or give her some curious trifle because of affectionate regard, she will consider the person's situation in life as well as the service, value, beauty, or curiosity of the gift, and suitably return the gesture with praiseworthy largesse. Her evident pleasure in that gift will be half the repayment.

Recently we observed something which disturbed us greatly at the sophisticated court of a particular prince and princess. A person reputed to be wise was summoned there for all to hear and appraise his talents. Everything appreciated and satisfactory, this person's several services were agreeable, praiseworthy, and deserving of reward. Simultaneously, the court was frequented by one reputed to be a fool, who entertained the lords and ladies with jokes, flattering remarks, gossip, and idle chatter to make them laugh. When the time came to reward them, the fool was given a gift valued at forty crowns and the other a gift of only twelve crowns. Seeing this, we three—Reason, Rectitude, and Justice—blushed at this evidence of unsuitable judgment and lack of discrimination at a well respected court. Not only did it err in the value of the gifts but in appreciation of the two people and their contributions. The wise princess will not emulate such behavior toward fools, gossips, or other such worthless people. She will not even cultivate them. Rather she will lavish gifts upon the virtuous and those who will appreciate them and use them well.

21. Which discusses what excuses are suitable for the good princess who for some reason cannot put into practice the precepts set forth in this book.

Before continuing our discussion on the generosity of a wise princess, lest we forget them we should raise two particular questions you might ask concerning this subject. We explained the benefits for the princess of becoming acquainted with all classes among her subjects. We also discussed the generosity she must personify. Concerning the first, you might ask this question: "You say a wise princess must gain the good will of her subjects and therefore should become acquainted with them. But can this precept serve everyone?" No doubt some women who are wise and prudent nevertheless have husbands with abominable habits who restrict them so severely that they scarcely dare to speak to their servants or to the staff of their own houses. They cannot become acquainted with anyone. So this teaching will be quite useless to them.

A like caveat concerns the next point: "There are many princes and other men who keep their wives so short of money they don't have a sou. Surely these cannot practice the virtue of generosity, no matter how benevolent their spirits are." Thus we answer these two questions at the same time and in one long sentence. We are not speaking of those who find themselves in such extremities, for Prudence has nothing to advise princesses and other ladies kept in such servitude, beyond this recommendation, which is not without value: "They must be patient and do such good as they can manage, being obedient in order to keep the peace." We speak, rather, to those who have the authority, judgment, and possibility of doing good.

Also, of course, we do not include the very young still under the supervision of other women who direct and teach them. However, the young ones who study and remember our doctrine will govern themselves so prudently that when they are at an age of greater discretion, their husbands and lords will observe in them such competence and training as to give them great authority to act and to govern themselves. Later and in the proper place we will discuss the preparation of the young for such work. No matter what a man's status, he would be foolish indeed if, having a good, wise spouse, he did not give her authority to manage their affairs whenever the need arose. However, some stubbornly ungracious, unappreciative men are incapable of recognizing the existence of women's talents and common sense and so cling to the notion that they cannot leave responsibility to women or trust their judgment. Of course, the opposite often is seen to be true.

All things considered, then, those ladies who cannot practice their own discretion in becoming acquainted with their subjects or distributing gifts simply must be excused. However, just as it is impossible to keep a great light from being seen in every corner, their husbands cannot keep virtuous, wise women from good relations with their subjects. For such women will be loved by all and known for the beneficence of their actions even through the mere, discreet, radiant glimpses others will have of them, making them praised and extolled everywhere. For the moment, this must suffice.

22. Which speaks of the government of a wise princess who is widowed.

Thus far we have spoken about teachings for the married princess. Yet in order for this doctrine to be useful for women of all estates, we now must address the princesses and great ladies who are widowed, young or old, and discuss those differences in their plights resulting from age.

The good princess becoming a widow will grieve and cry for her spouse, as good faith dictates. After the burial service she will follow custom's requirements and withdraw for a time in dim light, in piteous and <u>mournful costume</u> and headdress. Ever mindful of her lord's soul, she will pray and will have prayers said devoutly in masses. She will organize services, alms offerings, and oblations, and will recommend his memory to all devout people, requesting their prayers. Such remembrances and good deeds will not be limited to a brief period but will continue as long as she lives.

Nevertheless, Prudence will advise this lady of great wisdom, as will her father-in-law and others who would frequently counsel her: in spite of her great loss, her mourning, her sorrow over her lord's death, and the admirable, loyal love she bore him, still she must be patient in accepting all it pleases Our Lord to do. All of us are born to walk that same way whenever He so decides. So, it is sinful and displeasing to God for mourners to grieve overmuch and for too long a time. Therefore, she must adopt that manner of life which will avoid damage both to her soul and to her health. Furthermore, she must turn from deep grief to her noble children, who still have need for her.

Thus advised by reason and good counsel to help her better pass through this period of great tribulation, the lady will devote herself to guarding her own interests. First of all, she will wish to have precise knowledge of her lord's last will and testament. As soon as possible she will relieve the anxiety of her beloved's blessed soul by assuring that his wishes are carried out. Next, if the children's father has not provided for them during his lifetime, she will divide the lands and other holdings of wealth among them with due regard to the advice of the barons, to the satisfaction of as many as possible. She will plan valiantly to raise the children together, tranquilly, without quarrels, so the younger ones will serve and honor the eldest one, their new lord.

Then she will take stock of her own assets, both her furniture and her dowry. If she has no children and someone wants to wrong her by claiming what should be hers—as often happens to widows of both the exalted and the humble—she will seek and follow dependable advice to protect and to defend her rights boldly, through justice and reason. Without becoming agitated to the point of immoderate language, she will strongly voice her claims or have them stated publicly with notable courtesy. However, she will assert her due rights.

As long as she lives, she will try to remain on affectionate terms with her lord's parents. By honoring them she will be greatly revered and praised.

If the princess is widowed while her oldest son is still young and a minor, and if war and civil troubles arise among the barons concerning the government, then necessarily she will employ all her prudence and her wisdom to reconcile the antagonistic factions and maintain peace among them. No war waged against her by foreigners could be as dangerous as such civil war. Therefore, the wise lady will be such a good mediator by her prudent conduct and her knowledge that she will succeed in appeasing all factions. Her constant thought must be to avoid the troubles resulting from quarrels consequent upon the youth of her child. Therefore, she will try all practical expediencies. The troublemakers she must handle with gentleness and courtesy. Good and loyal counsel will guide her every act.

Certain lands might rebel. Enemies might attack the country, as often happens after the death of a prince who has very young children. Hence war may be necessary. Then the prudent lady wishing to protect her children's rights must conduct herself with very great wisdom indeed. She will require the affection of her barons, counting on their dependability, loyalty, and good advice to her son. The knights, squires, and noblemen must be willing to fight bravely, if it is necessary to wage war for their young lord. Furthermore, the people must be ready to help unsparingly with their money to support the war. In order to keep the barons as loyal subjects and to prevent others from subverting them, the lady frequently will speak to them graciously. She will say eloquently that she does not want to burden them, knowing they are often offended by the great expense of wars, but, may it please God, it will not last long. She will not forget their support, and will always remind her son of their goodness and loyalty. Thus the wise princess will speak suitable words to inspire them to contribute their wealth willingly and to keep them from the rebellions that so frequently occur among people too greatly oppressed and treated inconsiderately by their lords. The benefit such a princess hereby would give to her realm is immeasurable.

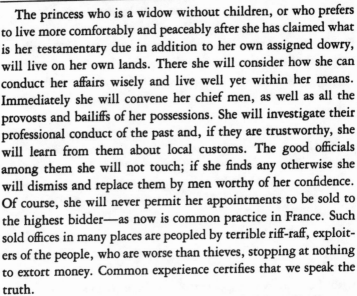

23. Concerning the same, but especially young widowed princesses.

The princess who is a widow without children, or who prefers to live more comfortably and peaceably after she has claimed what is her testamentary due in addition to her own assigned dowry, will live on her own lands. There she will consider how she can conduct her affairs wisely and live well yet within her means. Immediately she will convene her chief men, as well as all the provosts and bailiffs of her possessions. She will investigate their professional conduct of the past and, if they are trustworthy, she will learn from them about local customs. The good officials among them she will not touch; if she finds any otherwise she will dismiss and replace them by men worthy of her confidence. Of course, she will never permit her appointments to be sold to the highest bidder—as now is common practice in France. Such sold offices in many places are peopled by terrible riff-raff, exploiters of the people, who are worse than thieves, stopping at nothing to extort money. Common experience certifies that we speak the truth.

Well informed about her appointees, the lady will allow no offices to be bought, sold, nor traded but, as always should be the case, will see that they are given by choice to the most worthy and wise. She will make special regulations and give her appointees recommendations to assure that justice is maintained. If it is not, she will depose and punish them. Moreover, she expressly will forbid her officers and members of her household to allow anyone to take anything without paying for it. For she would not wish to burden her soul with the possessions of the poor. Therefore, she will insist upon being informed of any major extortions, such as often are made by the representatives of lords and ladies. Extortions not known will not be excused by God. So they must be recognized and strictly forbidden. The lady should aim to keep the people in peace, protect and defend them from all possible harm, and, in short, keep them benevolently disposed to serve her.

She will wish her men, and their wives, to visit her frequently. She will greet all graciously. Ladies and young women from the country, as well as the city women, will assemble in her private residence where she will receive them pleasantly, honoring each one according to her just merit, and will send for them to join her company when noblemen or foreigners are to be present. Even the common women of the village who hold her in great affection sometimes will bring a noble lady small presents—fruit and other little things. She will have these women brought before her, wishing to see them, receiving their gifts enthusiastically and making much out of trifles, saying there is nothing so good or so beautiful, and thanking them warmly. Talking to these good women, she will discuss their food and their households. When the women return home they will be flattered and talk a great deal about the way their lady received them. Considering themselves greatly honored, they will gossip about it with their neighbors.

Never ashamed to call on women in childbed, both the rich and the poor, the noble lady will visit them and will give alms to the poor. She will honor the rich, sponsoring the christening of their children. She will appear so charitable, so admirable in all things, and so humane toward her subjects that they will speak only good of her, praying for her and holding her in deferential affection.

The very noble queens and princesses of France observed in their widowhood such good and suitable manners. I have mentioned them before: Queen Jeanne; Queen Blanche; the Duchess of Orleans, former daughter of Charles IV; and others, who all governed themselves so well and wisely that they are examples to their successors.

This concludes Prudence's teachings for the wise princess who is of an age to know good from evil. Since we have embarked on the subject, we will speak a bit about the very young princess who is widowed, and then about young wives.

So long as the very young widowed princess does not remarry, she should return to her parents' supervision. Obeying their will and governing herself entirely by their advice, she will not undertake anything new without their knowledge and counsel. She ought to wear a simple gown and headdress, according to the style of the country where she is living, conduct herself modestly, present a gentle, unassuming appearance, and avoid overly boisterous amusements, all dancing, tight-fitting gowns, and all disapproved or forbidden frivolities. Even though by nature she may be lively, and may be encouraged by her youth to play, laugh, and sing, it is important, if she wishes to protect her good name, that she amuse herself in private and not in the presence of men. Especially among ladies and gentlemen, foreign knights, and others of importance, she must conduct herself discreetly, with tranquil face, speaking little, wearing an air of innocence. People will be pleased to see a young woman bear herself so well, with so composed a countenance.

Speaking with men in private is not suitable for her, whoever they may be, knights, squires, or otherwise. She must not be found in their company too frequently, nor should they be around her, especially in her bedroom. Such things easily could turn to her disadvantage and cause slanderous talk in a bad season, even with little cause. Her chaperone here must be vigilant. But to avoid boredom and idleness, she should look for amusements on feast days, play _martre_ with her attendants, and enjoy other simple, quiet games. On weekdays she can do handwork or embroidery.

Marriage is a subject she must never speak of privately to anyone without the knowledge of her friends. Nor should she listen to idle recommendations. This could redound to her dishonor and result in deception. She must depend entirely upon her friends, carefully avoiding any action without them. By marrying at will, without their consent, she would incur both danger and blame. If, for example, she chose unwisely and the marriage failed, she would never be pitied and would forfeit her friends' good will. Therefore, she must realize that they recognize her best interests better than does she herself.

24. Wherein it speaks of the supervision which should be provided for the newly-married young princess.

Earlier, I explained how the wise princess will arrange for her daughter's instruction during infancy and childhood. Now we can proceed to consider arrangements suitable for a young princess who wants to live properly after she has married, away from her parents' protection. A young, newly-married princess ought to have her own household of men and women organized in the manner appropriate to the importance of the lord or prince she has married. Those selected for her service will be gentlemen who are not too young, nor too talkative, nor too handsome; rather, they should be wise, discreet, and virtuous. If they are married, so much the better, especially those who will serve her at table and be around her and her serving-women most frequently. And if it can be arranged, it is useful for their wives also to live at court.

Her <u>major-domos</u> particularly should be mature, experienced men. To teach and train the young princess the better for the salvation of her soul and her conscience, a good priest ought to be appointed for her, one knowledgeable in theology, prudent in habits, and inherently dependable in judgment—in short, an admirable man of impeccable character. Her serving-women properly should include both older and younger women. Before they are appointed it is essential that they prove themselves suitable in judgment, background, and style of life. More attention must be given to their character than would be necessary for women selected for the household of an older princess. For, despite the fact that <u>women attendants</u> should be virtuous in any court, nevertheless, inappropriate courtiers chosen for a young princess would place her in greater peril than they would an older woman. Two reasons for this are significant. First, the standard of behavior observed by a household commonly leads to a judgment concerning the character and condition of the lord or lady. If the attendant women are not all particularly well-behaved, some might possibly suppose that neither is their mistress. That certainly could damage her honor.

Second, a young mistress, even a mere infant, could learn or see something among her women which would provide quite an unsuitable example for her. Hence, one particular woman must be entrusted with the upbringing of the young lady, even if there reside at court many more distinguished ladies, among them her own relatives, who would be pleased to honor her and bear her company. This one governess must be sufficiently old, prudent, good, and devout. She must have principal responsibility for the princess's care. If this lady performs her duty well, she will have no minor undertaking, no trivial, perfunctory job. She must keep two major considerations ever in mind. First, she must instruct her mistress in prudent behavior and courteous conduct, and always so supervise her that no talk or gossip will prove detrimental to her honor. Second, she must cherish her young charge, always keeping her affection and maintaining her good graces. These two, that is, giving correction and instruction to the young while at the same time retaining their love and devotion, often are difficult to achieve simultaneously.

Therefore, the governess must act with great discretion. Just as it is far more difficult to extinguish a fire when it already has spread and is burning down the house than it is to keep it from starting in the first place; and just as the wise housekeeper, always on guard to avoid peril which might threaten her, often must search through the house, especially in the evening, lest some careless servant has left a candle or torch or any other dangerous thing unattended which might cause damage; just so, this wise instructor will be prepared for whatever must be done to <u>bend the twig</u> in the desired direction while it is young. She will direct her mistress into such a desirable shape that henceforth the young lady will retain it. But she will direct that force gradually, rather than all at once, lest the twig break.

Starting their association in the manner appropriate to attaining her desired ends, the governess will begin immediately to direct her charge with a pleasant and courteous manner, giving her mistress inconsequential gifts of the sort which please young people. Thereby she will gain her young mistress's confidence and affection. Presupposing that the governess is not too old, she will sometimes indulge in games and diversions when she and the young princess are alone. Or she might tell fables or stories of the type customarily told to young children or young girls. This will attract her mistress to her so that the child will take it better when it is necessary to reprove or correct her. For if the governess were to appear serious every day, without humor or playfulness, youth's inclination to gaiety and pleasure could not abide it. The young princess would be so afraid of the governess she would take offence at her admonitions and thus behave badly.

When the governess has won the confidence of her mistress and has her well in hand, then, depending upon the child's age or the level of judgment she observes in her, she will begin telling her stories when they are talking together in their rooms, relating histories of ladies and maidens who have governed themselves intelligently, thus having turned out well and gained much honor from good conduct. Contrariwise, she will tell how misfortune pursued those who behaved foolishly. She will say that she has seen all these things happen in her own time. Moreover, she will repeat all sorts of contemporary anecdotes bearing upon these matters. But she must not appear to be giving examples, only recounting adventures. By telling these stories well, she will touch her mistress' heart, as well as that of others who may be hearing her who have gathered around her to listen. Sometimes she will tell them stories of the saints, their lives, and their passions. So that her tales won't become boring, she will interrupt them to tell some little jokes. Also she will encourage the others to tell stories and jests, so that each may have a turn at speaking. Such methods the wise lady will use to lure the young princess's affection.

As for specific correction and instruction, she will counsel with wise, benevolent words. First advice of all is to arise early. Then she will teach the young princess some good, short prayers which she will urge her to say upon getting up, hailing at the beginning of day Our Lord and the Virgin. She will tell the princess that she has always heard that the one who sincerely makes it habit to address the first words of the day to Our Lord upon arising in the morning will not suffer misfortune during that day. She will be telling her the truth; many good people believe this. Then she will have her mistress dress and array herself suitably, without devoting overmuch time to clothing, as some ladies do. That is a ridiculous waste of time and, furthermore, an unseemly custom. Then directing her to attend mass, she will have her say her Hours devoutly and attentively.

She will urge the young princess to maintain excellence in speaking, propriety in facial expression, suitability in ornaments and clothing for a highborn princess, and perfection in conduct, allowing nothing about her to be criticized. The instructor will accomplish all this in as few words as possible, offering wise commentary and counsel. So doing, she will train the young princess so well that everyone will say that they never saw a lady at such a young age with such charming manner nor better brought up. These same people will say of her: "How praiseworthy is the young heart, so mature and wise through benevolent habits."

Of course, we must assume that the young princess is already so well trained as to wish herself instructed, and to remember what she has learned. For she might well be so obstreperous that the governess must be excused if unable to do anything for her improvement. In such a case, the wise instructor will reprove her young mistress for the mistakes that young people tend to make. With such a wild one it is less effective for her to be kind, gentle, and have her mistress's control in hand, than it is to threaten that if she does not behave differently, or if she continues to do and say forbidden things, she, the governess, will no longer continue to serve her, and will return home. Further, such bad behavior is completely unsuitable for such a lady as her mistress. If the princess really is good, gentle, and fond of her governess, she will fear losing her and will reform with little further reproof. If, however, she is contrary, contemptuous, spiteful, and emotionally cold, the lady must speak severely to her in private. Whether the young one likes it or not, the governess necessarily will report her to her parents or to her lord if she does not conduct herself better.

Nevertheless, the lady responsible for teaching good behavior to her young mistress wisely will understand that young people sometimes must play and laugh. So, she will arrange for this at particular times and in the company of the younger ones among the ladies, particularly when no strangers are present, and according to her mistress's temperament. One cannot, and indeed should not, deny young people pleasures unless they are harmful or unsuitable. Concerning these morals and good behaviors necessary for the princess we will speak no further here, but will discuss them presently in the letter which the governess may send to her mistress.

25. Which teaches the manners which the wise lady who has charge of a young princess should observe to keep her mistress in good repute and in her lord's affections.

Because a young woman nourished in delicacy and courtly ease may incline toward excessive gaiety of spirit, which may deflect from virtue a youth who really has no malice, it is necessary to restrain her with a long arm to prevent her harm. The remedies the wise lady in charge of the young princess might attempt are these.

If she notes great love between her lord the prince and her mistress, the sort young people recently married usually experience, she will do all she can to nourish that love, encouraging the lovers to say sweet, affectionate words to each other and to delight in one another's company. She will carry between them gracious messages and pleasing gifts, as well as beneficent, affectionate greetings to instill in them peace and love. Likewise, she will attempt to avoid and to turn aside all disturbing or unfavorable circumstances. When the lord is absent and the young princess is preparing for bed, the older woman will talk to her about him, recalling pleasing words that she heard him say about his love for his lady, and how good he is, how handsome, how gracious. She will wish God to give him a good night, and in every way commend his virtues to her lady.

Because it is customary for lords, knights, squires, foreigners, and many others often to be in the presence of the princess, whether or not her lord and parents are escorting her, the young married lady will receive and speak with a certain number of these courtiers, entertaining them suitably with feasts and dances, and conversing and providing pastimes in keeping with the occasion. It sometimes happens that certain courtiers may be struck with love for the lady, or at least pretend to be. Then the wise governess, always near her mistress, will note carefully the appearance and behavior of the guests to see if she can detect any with such ideas. If something suspicious comes to her attention, she will not mention it to anyone, keeping it entirely to herself.

When everyone has departed, the party ended, and her young mistress withdrawn to her own apartments, then, if she has the young woman's confidence, she will speak to her in such wise as this. "We have danced magnificently. Such and such people particularly were gracious." (Or, they were not.) And she will add words such as these: "I do not know how it is but I did not see anyone who seemed to me as pleasant nor as handsome nor as gracious as my lord, your husband. I noticed particularly, for it seemed to me that, among all other courtiers, he spoke and behaved most impressively." Or, if the lord is old and plain, she might say: "In truth, I paid no attention to any of the company except to my lord. It seemed to me that among all others he was the most impressive, lordly of princes. How good it is to hear him speak, for he talks so wisely." If the prince was not there at all, she still can recall him in some manner, praising him. Saying nothing of any suspicions she may have had, she will take care to notice if the one or ones who attracted her attention try to frequent the presence of her mistress, or if they seek out acquaintances with her relatives or others near to the princess, or if their servants ingratiate themselves with her serving-maids. However, if after the feast or assembly she notes that nobody is doing any of these things, she can forget the whole matter.

On the other hand, if she observes any of these or other similar signs, then she will not rest until she has remedied the situation. That is her duty. She will have to work very cautiously, for revealing her suspicions to anyone would be a grave mistake.

What can she best do? When she has assured herself that her suspicions are justified and someone indeed is attempting to get into her own good graces for love of her mistress, before he has time to accomplish anything bold she will be exceedingly gracious to him, so that he will have every occasion to become acquainted with her. Readily he will do it, thinking that she is the closest to the lady and thus potentially the most helpful to him. Perhaps the affair will advance to the point where he boldly will tell the governess what is in his mind, with all the offers and rewards he will propose to her, as men customarily do in such cases.

Then the wise woman, ever ready with her reply, will speak to him, without the knowledge of her lady and free from the hearing of as many other people as possible. She will address him boldly, though in a low voice, if he is the sort of person for whom this is suitable. "My lord, I have suspected from your behavior that you had in mind just what you now reveal to me. Because I wanted those words to come first from you, I have cultivated you so that I might hear them from your lips, rather than from someone else's who might repeat them, concealing the matter so poorly it would be noticed by others. I am pleased now to have the opportunity to answer you directly. The question is decided in my heart and never will be changed any day of my life. This I swear both to God and to you. So without lengthy preaching to you or wasting any words, I say briefly, once and for all, that as long as I am a living woman and in her company, this young lady given into my care by the trust of her lord and her friends, however unworthy I may be, will do no wrong or anything else which might bring reproach or gossip to her, a lady born of such noble blood. For with God's help I will protect her from it. She is, however, easy to protect. I know that all her love belongs to her lord. That is as it should be. She is so entirely good and well brought up that she would not become involved in or even think about any such other love.

"I know her well enough to say that if you or anyone else had spoken to her, or if she had noticed anything odd, she would be quite displeased with anyone who might believe that she could think of any such thing. So, my lord, I beg of you, insofar as I have the power to do so, that you go away. Give no further thought to the matter. I swear to you as a Christian that you will be wasting your effort. In order that you may have no further hope, I swear on my soul that even were she attracted to you— which I know she could not be—I would erect such barriers that she could not do anything about it. So believe me, truly. Do not attempt any comings or goings or other such pretenses. Upon my soul, I could not permit it and would be obliged to tell someone who would not be pleased about it and who indeed would keep her out of your hands. I have only one death to die. I prefer to have it overtake me now rather than allow harm or dishonor to my mistress. So it is better that nothing further be said. Let the affair rest where it is."

Making such a reply, the lady must not—for promise, gift, offer, or threat—change her mind, then or at any time later. Nothing should influence her otherwise. Moreover, when she takes leave of him, she must take care not to show an altered or inflamed face or hard eyes. Rather, she should have a composed face and an assured manner, as if they had spoken of other matters. Thus no one will suspect anything. She also must be careful not to say any word of this to her mistress, nor to anyone else, however intimate.

But of course she will not by any means leave it at that. She will see to it that none of the serving-women, court servants, or anyone else speaks with her mistress privately in such manner as would seem to have anything whatever to do with the affair. She will notice it soon enough by the way they laugh or speak. Even what she does not hear directly, she will notice nevertheless. She must not remain silent. Rather she will threaten the guilty person with the possibility of being dismissed if she should involve herself in her mistress's affairs, for this is clearly none of her business. She will keep such close watch that nobody will have the opportunity to speak to her mistress alone.

If it should happen that the man disobeys her words and somehow manages to come and go in some obscure way, found through an acquaintance, which allows him to be present from time to time in spite of the governess, then as she has promised, great trouble must come of it. She will not permit this affair and will guard her mistress closely without the young woman's notice. If, by her mistress's manner and covert words, the governess knows that the man has spoken to her of his intentions, still she should not fear anything overmuch. She knows well that many ladies are sought after and loved without paying any attention to it. Certainly they do not necessarily fall in love.

But she will try to notice discreetly if the young lady takes any pleasure in it. If she speaks of that man more willingly than of another, or shows pleasure when he comes, or changes countenance or color, then in private, when only the two of them are present, the governess will try by subtle, sweet words to draw from her mistress her intentions with regard to the man, and learn if he has made any serious impression upon her. The song her mistress sings will determine her response. If her mistress says that truly she is aware of the proposal and he has spoken to her, causing her annoyance and regret, the lady of wisdom will perceive by the movement of the words whether the young woman is troubled and seeking her advice, or whether she is pretending not to be rebellious at all in order to make the governess believe that she would never think of such a thing, when she is indeed interested. If the young lady is speaking sincerely, and the governess assures herself that her young charge has no serious thought of the affair, then she will be relieved and pleased, urging her mistress to remain good in her resolve. Repeating to her examples of the trouble which can result from flirtation, which truly has come to some as the result of such folly, she will document the likely great dishonor and reproach to come of it, as well as the deceptions of which men are capable.

Counselling the princess to answer carefully and wisely whenever he speaks to her, the governess will recommend that she tell him briefly that he is wasting his time, insisting always that never will she change her intentions, whatever he may do; that it displeases her to hear such language; that she wants none of his advances. With that, she will stay away from him as much as possible. She must be sure that her glance, words, laughter, or expressions do not give him any encouragement which might further attract him to her or give him any hope.

The governess also will instruct her mistress how she ought to discourage him courteously by having him told when he comes that she is resting or busy doing something else; may it not displease him, she simply cannot see him at that time. She will have him told the same thing as often as he comes, until he finally perceives he is wasting his time in thinking about it any longer. In addition, the wise lady will advise her mistress that she should be careful not to speak of the matter to any other man or woman, for trouble certainly would result. It is far more sensible to keep quiet about it, for it never is to a woman's credit or advantage to boast of such interests. She will so counsel her mistress because if the princess speaks of the affair to someone who would not offer good advice or who might even comfort or encourage her in her folly, or who would conceal it badly, then some smoke might come from it, forcing someone to suspect fire. So, wisely counselling her, the good lady will persist until she has stamped out the flame.

Thus ending the whole affair, she will have acted circumspectly, whoever may hate her or bear her ill will. However, she would pay no attention to such hatred, but simply would do her duty. The one resenting her at the beginning will praise her at the end, prizing her a thousand-fold more upon seeing her great prudence and admirable constancy. A good deed always conquers its own results. The young princess in her time may become an extremely wise and honest lady, possessing all the admirable virtues, thus having been protected from flirtatious folly.

26. Which tells of the young noble lady who might wish to stray into illicit love, and the teaching which Prudence gives to her governess.

All people are not alike; some men and women are so perverse that no matter what good advice and teaching they are given, they will persist in following their foolish or wicked inclinations. Trying to teach them otherwise is a waste of time and will result only in provoking their hatred. Therefore, I will speak here of how the instructor ought to conduct herself if she has in her charge some young princess or noble lady unwilling to profit by wise, good counsel who thus strays into illicit love.

A certain young princess or noble lady might be so deficient in knowledge or constancy that she is unable or unwilling to resist the blandishments of the man making every effort to attract her to his love by various semblances and manners. Men know so well how to do this. The lady who has charge of the princess perceives by various signs and indications that her heart is most susceptible, whatever she may give her governess to understand by her words. Or she might not even deny it or say the contrary. The older woman will be grieved from the bottom of her heart. But in spite of her mistress's possible resentment or that of anyone else, she will do her duty to admonish her for her own good. Not dissembling or concealing her views, she will not fail to speak to the young woman in private, now kindly, now severely, if she sees her persist. She will remind her of the great evil, peril, and misfortune which could result. She will continue to pursue the matter on the chance that realization of the truth or the very force of her words will influence her mistress and dissuade her before folly has gone too far.

But she may find this to be all to no avail. She may see her mistress talking privately to one of her other attendants, whom she may well suppose knows about her plans and intentions, observing that they are at pains to consult with outside messengers and that they make various signs to one another, avoiding her at all costs. Now she is aware that her mistress, with proud and lofty manner, no longer wishes her around. Rather she indicates she no longer is a child to be in her charge and under her direction, taking badly whatever she says to her, answering haughtily, half-menacingly, seeming quarrelsome and ill-tempered. By all these signs the lady will see she is held in contempt and disliked. The younger lady most certainly would prefer to be free to follow her own devices. Then she may hear the princess saying to one of her attendants who is in better favor: "What the devil are we going to do with that old hag? She just complains. May the fires of Hell burn her! We'll never get rid of her." The other may reply: "So help me God, Madam, we will have to scatter peas on the steps so that she will fall and break her neck." And other such words as these.

What, then, will the wise lady do, now that she sees the case is hopeless? She knows she has done her duty, following her conscience in having shown the young woman the folly of her ways. She even had her father-in-law tell her of the evils which could result from such indiscretion. Yet her mistress is so carried away that there is no remedy for it. She has discovered a way to do as she pleases, whether anyone likes it or not.

It is not possible to protect one who does not want to protect herself. Murmurs are beginning. People are starting to notice. Some among her ladies-in-waiting are talking because of the envy they feel toward the one or ones enjoying the special confidence of their mistress, thus being preferred over others. Tales circulate which lead to no good. Therefore, though her heart may be heavy indeed, the prudent governess will consider her best choice, considering the misfortune and peril the affair would cause her if she were to remain at court longer. For, granted that she is not in agreement with her charge's behavior and never in her life would allow the matter to come to the attention of the young lady's husband or parents, nevertheless she would bear responsibility for it. They could well say: "Why didn't you tell us? We would have remedied the situation. We depended on you." Of course, she would not have told such a thing for anything in the world because of the resulting dangers and troubles. Anyone of conscience and sense hesitates to report philandering to the husband or friends, or to anyone else.

Furthermore, the governess remaining at court would not be without another explosive danger: the personal harm which might come to her from her mistress herself or from the one who had captured her heart, if in any way they feared her or thought she might hinder them. Now the good lady, being well advised in all matters, must use every bit of her great knowledge. She will maintain her silence about all this, not speaking further to her mistress of good or evil, nor giving the impression by her face or bearing that she is in any way displeased in her heart. But as soon as she can, by any good way she had prepared for herself in advance when she saw her mistress's intentions change, she will forthwith take leave of the court. With her lord's good will, if possible, or if not she wisely will take care that he does not realize why she wants to leave. If she knows that he would prefer above all to keep her, she will fabricate a reason: illness or age or some weakness or difficulty within her own body.

If he wishes to inquire too deeply into her departure's cause, she will say even before she has asked permission to leave that because some illness afflicts her she is unfit to be around such a lady as her mistress until she has been cured. Thus she will quickly excuse herself. Her mistress herself, seeing she will no longer talk to her, almost might be displeased by her departure. Perhaps she will recognize that she has better opportunity to do what she pleases as long as she has such a governess remaining with her, for people would be less likely to speak evil were she accompanied by such a person. Though the young mistress may try to flatter her and hold out promises to her so that she will stay, the good lady quickly will excuse herself from this, saying that, in truth, she is seriously ill, but when she is cured she may well return.

However much her heart aches at her departure, neither for this reason nor for the affection she has for her mistress will she stay for any blandishments whatsoever, if she is wise. She would sorely regret it later. If, on the contrary, when her time comes to leave, the young lady is joyous at her departure, then the ancient lady will speak to her in private, kneeling before her, thanking her humbly for the favors and honors she has accorded her. She will beg her pardon if she has not served her as befits her station in the world. If she has said or done anything to displease her, this has only come from great love and intense concern for her. Though it pains her to leave her, she is old and feeble and can no longer serve her. Perhaps old age has made her so cross and ungracious that she no longer can support, as she should, the amusements of the young. For this reason she prefers to leave, and may it be with her mistress's good will. So she begs that she may retain complete good grace, for she can assure her mistress that never in her whole life will she have serving her a woman who loves both her and her honor more dearly and more loyally, and who will continue to do so as long as she lives. This always will be her wish. The good governess will address her mistress with such words as these upon departure.

Perhaps the princess graciously will answer her fine words, feeling relief and joy at her leaving. Perhaps, because the governess has been with her for so long, possibly even from infancy, she will appeal to her heart and purposely pain her. Perhaps she will tell her that she has not held anything against her except that she has turned against her charge, which she never would have thought possible. Or she will offer other such excuses. To all these, the older lady will not want to argue with her mistress because she knows it is to no avail. She will reply that truly it may be the result of her own folly, because of her over-great concern, that has led her to have suspicions. She will beg her mistress to forgive everything, and will say that her mistress may be certain that however long she lives, whatever suspicions she may have had, or however it may have been in fact, she never will open her mouth to anyone. Nor has she ever done anything to her mistress except for her own good. So she will depart.

From the book of *The Duke of True Lovers* comes the letter <u>Sebile de la Tour</u> is said to have written to her duchess which will be included in the following chapter. Anyone who already has read it may skip it but it is good and profitable for all high-born ladies and any others to whom it might apply.

27. Hereafter follows the letter that the wise lady may send to her mistress.

Following the incidents in the previous chapter, the young woman might behave so badly after her former governess leaves that talk compromises her reputation. Slander spreads. The good, wise woman who used to have charge of her but now is living at home hears about it. She is so saddened to know the honor of her mistress has been so diminished, after she has made such an effort to bring her up and to instruct her properly, that she will not be able to bear it any longer. Not knowing what to do, finally, after having thought about it at length and moved by great affection regardless of the outcome, she will write. What is written in letters sometimes is better remembered and makes a deeper impression on the heart than what is merely spoken. Therefore, she will express once more, by <u>letter,</u> the warning she has already given several times, to see if any possible good can come of it. By the hand of a dependable priest who in confidence has written down her words, she will send such a letter as this:

"My revered, beloved lady.

"I commend myself to your good grace, well and humbly. Honored lady, do not take it amiss if I am moved to write to you for your good. Great love constrains me to do so. Noble and estimable lady, you have been in my charge from your infancy until very recently. Of course, I am not at all worthy of that great honor. However, having loved and protected you for so long, I now may not remain silent about something which would damage you if I were not to point it out to you. For this reason, beloved lady, I write to warn you for your own benefit. I beg you once more that you not bear me any malice. Realize that my great affection and my desire for your honor's continuity and your renown's excellence move me to caution you. My lady, I have heard rumors concerning your conduct which grieve me to the bottom of my heart. I fear the loss of your good name.

"Any princess or high-born lady exalted in honor and estate above all others must surpass others in goodness, wisdom, manners, disposition, and behavior, so that she may be an example after which other ladies, and women in general, can pattern their conduct. So, she must be devout toward God and have a tranquil, gentle, and calm bearing. In her diversions she must be restrained, not given to excess; in her laughter, low-keyed, never foolish; in her stature, stately, with a modest look and great dignity; in her manner, kindly, with a courteous word for everyone; in her dress and attire, rich but not too affected; in her greetings, gracious to strangers, restrained in her speech, never flighty, never too familiar, never too slow to answer. Never should she appear harsh, ill-tempered, or capricious. Never should she be too difficult to serve, always being humane and kind to her waiting-women and servants, not too haughty, bountiful within reason when giving gifts, knowing how to recognize those most deserving in merit and prudence, and benevolently generous to her best servants. These she will draw close around her, recompensing them according to their worth, not trusting or putting faith in flatterers, but rather identifying them and dismissing them. Furthermore, she will not lightly believe gossip she hears.

"Because the lady never permits herself the habit of whispering to strangers or intimate friends in any secret place, nor even to any of her retainers or serving-women, no one may assume that they know more of her private affairs than another. In the presence of others the lady never says in jest, to anyone whatsoever, anything which cannot be understood by all, so that no one listening could imagine that there is any foolish secret between them. She should not keep overly much to herself in her apartment, nor be too much in the view of others. But at particular times she should discreetly retire alone, while reserving other times to appear with her companions.

"These very habits befitting a noble princess you formerly practiced beautifully. Now I hear you are completely changed, amusing yourself more, more lively and flippant than ever you were. When outward signs change, commonly so the heart is assumed to have changed. Now you wish to be alone, withdrawn from others except one or two of your women and a few others of your suite with whom you share private conversations and laughter, even in the presence of others, speaking in covered words as if you had a secret understanding. Only the company of these, rather than any others, is pleasing to you. None of the others serves you to your liking. Such acts encourage envy in your other servants. Your appearances allow them to think your heart is attracted to someone other than your own lord.

"My very dear, esteemed, lady! For God's sake, remember who you are! Consider your high position. Do not consent for the sake of any foolish pleasure to forget your soul and your honor. Do not put trust in vain fancies, as many young women do, allowing themselves to believe that there is no harm in loving with a tender passion provided that it is not accompanied by any sinful act. For I am sure that you would die rather than contemplate any such sinful thing. Do not deceive yourself into thinking that one lives more happily if one makes some man valiant and famous forevermore. My darling lady, the truth is the reverse. For Heaven's sake, do not deceive yourself nor allow yourself to be deceived by others.

"Take warning from such noble ladies as you yourself have seen in your lifetime. Being merely suspected of such a love, the truth never really known, they lost not only their honor but their lives. Upon my soul, I am sure that they neither sinned nor did great wrong. Yet you have seen their children reproached and belittled. Such a love would be dishonorable for any woman, rich or poor. It is especially unfortunate in a princess and high-born lady—the more so, the more important she is. The reason is quite simple and just. The fame of a great princess travels widely through the world. Any stain on her good name is more widely known in foreign countries than for a simpler woman. Equally important, a princess's children are destined to be rulers over the land and princes over the people. There must be no doubt as to whether or not they are legitimate heirs. Terrible trouble arises from such uncertainty. Even if there has been no real wrongdoing, no one who wishes to believe otherwise will believe the woman innocent. They will have heard rumors that she is in love. Thus for her few tender glances, perhaps given thoughtlessly or because of inexperience, evil tongues will wag. Things which never were done, nor even thought of, will be said to have happened. Talk will go from mouth to mouth, never diminished, only growing.

"Hence it is more important for a noble lady than for another woman to attend strictly to her behavior, looks, and words. In the presence of a noble lady everyone pays attention to her in order to hear what she will say and to notice what she will do. The lady cannot open an eye, say a word, laugh, or jest without all separate, simple things being put together, discussed, remembered by multiple people, and peddled in many places. So, my very noble lady, do not ever think that it does not look very suspicious for a high-born lady, or indeed any woman, to appear gayer than usual, more fun-loving, and more eager than ever to hear talk about love. Suddenly, then, she changes, becoming discontented, ungracious, and quarrelsome. Nobody can serve her to her satisfaction. She pays no attention to her dress or appearance. Certainly people seeing such opposing behaviors will say that she has been in love but now is no longer.

"My dear lady, truly this is not behavior suitable to any lady. Always she must be careful that, whatever her intentions, she will conduct herself in such a way and maintain such an appearance that such judgments cannot be made of her. Although where love indeed exists it is difficult to maintain such decorum, the best way to assure oneself of following the proper course is to avoid and to shun temptation. My dear mistress, you can see that every noble lady, likewise every other woman, should more eagerly acquire a good name than any other treasure. This reflects honor on herself and endures eternally for both herself and her children.

"Noble lady, I can understand the reasons which inspire any young woman to be tempted by such a love. Youth, ease, and idleness can well make her say to herself, 'You are young! Enjoy yourself! You certainly can love without doing any wrong, for no harm will come because there is no sin. You will inspire a man to be valiant. You will live more happily because of it. You will have gained a true servant and a loyal friend.' Many such other excuses also are possible. Excellent lady, for God's sake be warned! Such foolish ideas only deceive. In such love affairs there are a hundred thousand times more griefs, injuries, and perilous risks, especially for the lady, than there are any chances of happiness. Such love brings in its train many sorts of troubles. Fear of losing honor if the affair is discovered makes the price of such pleasure exceedingly high. As for saying no harm because of no sin, alas, my lady, nobody dares ever be so sure of herself in such a love, however good her intentions to preserve moderation.

"Certainly, if discovered, the situation would be impossible. While there is no fire without smoke, often there is smoke without fire. As for saying, 'I will make a man valiant,' it is great folly to destroy oneself for another's gain, even presupposing he could

143

indeed be made valiant. She who destroys herself to improve another only dishonors herself. As for saying, 'I will have gained a true friend and servant,' good heavens! How could such a friend serve a lady? If she had real need of him, he would not dare help her for fear of dishonoring her. What then would be the value of such a servant, who could not act in her behalf? Some men say they serve their ladies when they do great deeds of arms. But I say they serve only themselves. For the honor and fame are theirs rather than their lady's.

"My lady, you and others might wish to excuse yourselves by saying, 'I have a difficult husband who is neither loyal nor loving. For this reason I can without blame seek my pleasure elsewhere to avoid melancholy and pass time agreeably.' However (no offense to your goodness or anyone else's who might say it), such excuses are without merit. She who sets fire to her own house to burn down the neighbor's indeed is ridiculous. The lady with such a husband who puts up with him patiently without giving in to temptation greatly increases the value of her soul and stores up much honor. As for finding pleasure, a great lady can entertain herself with sufficient, good, and acceptable pleasure, making time pass without falling into melancholy by other means than giving in to illicit love. For the lady with children, what greater pleasure can she want than to see them often, assuring herself they are being well brought up and beautifully trained for the courtesies and skills of their station in life? She will rejoice that her daughters are instructed and so refined in manner that even in childhood they develop the habit of living well, according to the example set by their good companions. If the mother is not decorous and wise, what example, then, is she for her daughters and for those who have no children?

"After prayers, an honorable lady ought to take up some piece of handwork embroidering either fine linen or silken fabrics with exquisite designs, or making other beautiful, useful things. Such worthy occupations prevent idle thoughts. Certainly I do not say that a great lady should not amuse herself nor laugh and play in suitable time and place even with the presence of great lords and gentlemen. Nor do I suggest that she should not honor strangers suitably. These entertainments, however, must have such dignity and decorum that not a single glance, laugh, or word is not properly restrained and governed by reason. A lady always should be on her guard lest anyone take exception to what she says, does, or appears to be. Heavens! If every noble lady and indeed every woman knew how becoming good bearing is, she would make a great effort to acquire it over every other ornament. No jewel enhances her so greatly.

"Finally, my dear lady, I must speak of the perils and difficulties which accompany illicit love. They are endless. First and greatest is that it angers God. Then, if the husband or his family should learn of it, the woman is ruined. At very least she bears reproach that she can never escape from.

"You might presuppose that none of the unpleasantness will occur because the lovers are loyal, secretive, and truthful. Usually men are not. Rather, the men generally are faithless, promising and saying what in actuality they would never think or do, in order to deceive women. Moreover, the ardor of such love does not endure long. Even with the most loyal, that is certain. Dear lady, what will you do when the time comes for this love to end? She who has been so blinded by foolish delight begins to repent bitterly, remembering follies and various dangers she has risked. How she would wish, whatever the cost, that it had never happened, that she had never allowed such a reproach! You cannot imagine what great regret, repugnance, and repentance remain in her heart.

"Moreover, you cannot imagine the folly of putting one's person and one's honor at the mercy of wagging tongues, or in the power of such servants. Indeed, although men call themselves servants, generally the service is such that however much they have sworn to keep their secret, so will they violate their word. In the end, all that is left to the lady is the regret of such a love and the gossip of others about it. The fear remains in the woman's heart that he in whom she has put her trust will talk of the affair, boasting of it to anyone else who happens to know about it. Thus she is changed from living in freedom to enduring bondage. You can well see the conclusion of such <u>service of love</u>.

"Don't you understand, my dearest lady, that such servants consider it much to their advantage to speak and even boast that they are or have been loved by a noble mistress or a well-known lady? Why should they remain silent about it? God knows, they even lie about it, speaking about what has not occurred or exaggerating what has. All women should understand this well! Also remember that the servants in your household who know your secret and whom you are obliged to trust certainly will not keep silent about all this, even though you have made them swear to do so. Most of them are such as to be vexed if it were not known they were more greatly in your confidence and more familiar with you than others. If they do not tell your secret openly, they will point their fingers and hint with various covert signs which they know will be noticed. Good heavens! What servitude for a lady who does not dare to blame or reprove her serving-men or -women even when she knows they are behaving very badly! She realizes she is in their power. They have risen up against her with such arrogance that she does not dare to say a word. So she must suffer them to say and do things that she would not allow to anyone else. And what do you think people who see and notice all this say? They think what indeed is the case. You may be sure they will whisper about it.

"If the lady becomes angry and sends some servants away, God knows that everything will be revealed and discussed widely. These same servants may have been the very means of bringing this love into being, having encouraged it with zeal and diligence in order to gain gifts, or offices, or other emoluments for themselves.

"Very honored lady! What more can I say to you about this? You might as well dig a bottomless pit as try to recount all the perils which exist in that amorous life. Never doubt it. It is so. Because of this, my very dearest lady, do not cast yourself into such jeopardy. If you had any thought of it, for God's sake, withdraw yourself from it before greater harm comes of it. Better early than late; but better late than never. You already can see what slander will spread if you persist in your new habits. Already they have been noticed and thereby discussed in various places.

"Therefore, I do not know what to write further. In so far as I am able, I humbly beg of you that you bear me no animosity but rather believe in the benevolent intention which constrains me to say this. Indeed, I should prefer your anger for my doing my duty in admonishing you from a sense of loyalty than ever your affection for my counseling you to your undoing or my remaining silent.

"Very honored princess and most dear lady, I pray that God may give you long life and a happy one.

"Written at La Tour, yours faithfully etc., etc."

HERE ENDS THE FIRST PART OF THE PRESENT VOLUME.

BOOK II. Which is addressed to ladies and
          demoiselles and first of all to those who
          live at the court of the princess or
          lady.

1. This first chapter tells how the three Virtues,
   Reason, Rectitude, and Justice, summarize
   briefly what has been said thus far.

Now we have instructed queens, princesses, and ladies of high
degree in the doctrine which is useful to them: teachings which
touch the soul's welfare and virtuous morals becoming to nobility.
Our lesson in this second part of the discourse is addressed to
ladies, demoiselles, and other women, those who live at the court
of a princess to serve her and to maintain her estate and likewise
those who live on their own lands and in their own castles or
manor houses, or in enclosed or open cities. We insist that this
doctrine applies to ladies, demoiselles, and indeed all women.
On certain matters affecting the soul, the virtues, and good habits,
we will not repeat all we have said before. It would be needless
effort and easily might bore our readers. So let what has earlier
been said benefit everyone where it fits. May each one take from
it what she thinks she may need for the good and profit of her
soul and her behavior.

Equally for ordinary women and great mistresses, it is important
always to have the love and fear of Our Lord before their eyes in
all their undertakings and ever in their memories. This will
remind them of the blessings they receive from Him: the soul
created in His image will possess the Kingdom of Heaven forever,
if only they expend a little effort and care. God gives many gifts:
the ability to know Him and to know what is good and evil;
bodily strength to put the good into effect; health; and many
other good graces. Women should be grateful for the love they

owe Him. As the first Commandment says: "You will love God above all things." Women must never forget this love, nor the fear of the Lord, nor the grievous punishment from His justice, which imperils any creature who does not follow the straight path. This love and fear will protect them from vice and lead them to virtues, vanquish pride and enthrone humility, destroy anger and stimulate patience, eliminate avarice and substitute charity, root out envy and plant instead true love for neighbors. This love and fear will discourage idleness and encourage care and diligence to do good, and will make women despise gluttony and love sobriety, banish luxury and invite chastity. So it will endow these ladies with all virtues helpful to the soul while driving out vices which could harm it. Likewise, Worldly Prudence must order the manner of life of all ladies and demoiselles in a suitable fashion, each according to her estate. May they love honor, good reputation, and excellent praise as much as the princesses. Thus we will begin.

2. Wherein it speaks of four points, two which are to be observed, the other two to be avoided.

The first point: how ladies and demoiselles at court should love their mistress.

Ladies, demoiselles, and women of the court in the service of princesses and great ladies: Once more, we three sisters—God's daughters, Reason, Rectitude, and Justice—will reiterate that which we already have said for the good of your souls. To the previously recommended good advice we add four points: the first two are to be followed, the second two to be avoided. Not merely useful, the first two are most necessary for the good of your souls and your personal honor.

The first point is that you must love your mistress as wholeheartedly as yourself. The second is that in your manner, words, and actions you must not be too approachable or too familiar with certain men. We will explain the reason for this in a moment.

As for the other appropriate behavior which you should observe, we already mentioned that the wise princess will treat and robe you well: in simple, handsome clothes without pretention, yet sumptuous enough and fittingly well designed. We will not discuss details of your composed countenance, quiet words, behavior, games, and honest laughter, because we already spoke of those in Chapter 18 of the first part of this treatise, where whoever wishes may read it.

The lady or demoiselle at court, and indeed any servant, must love her mistress faithfully and whole-heartedly, whether the mistress be good or bad, difficult or gentle. Otherwise she damages herself. I say the same for all servants, no matter who pays or hires them. You might answer: "But truly, my master or mistress is a wicked person. Am I still obliged to love him or her?" We reply: "Yes, without fail." If you think your master or mistress wicked or that you are not offered sufficient advantage, you should leave rather than stay and perform your duties badly, not giving the devotion and faith you should. Suppose your master does his duties badly. You still should not fail to do your own. Quit, rather than damage yourself while serving. I will explain how the lady or demoiselle should love her mistress. She must keep faith and loyalty in every way.

What manner of faith and loyalty?

First of all, she must love the good of her mistress's soul, encouraging her to do good and not giving her occasion to do the contrary. She must strive for a reassuring tranquility. Of course, she must not bear tales, nor speak untruthfully about others, nor talk against the value of honesty and honor, nor utter surly words or answers which might trouble her mistress. Besides this, she will tend to her own business and whatever else she is supposed to do and, however she is able, prevent outrageous behavior in others. Above all, she will strive to protect her own honor in both word and deed, even more behind her lady's back than in her presence. Thus she will promote her lady's good name. She will take care, however, that for the good of her own soul she will not flatter her mistress in order to maintain her good graces. Servants are inclined to do so with masters and mistresses, especially lords and ladies, though God despises such hypocrisy and the Scriptures firmly warn against it.

Let us explain more clearly what flattery is, so no one will be deceived by it. If you serve well and loyally, to the best of your abilities, you carefully protect the well-being, honor, and advantage of any master or mistress. You give care and effort to serving and pleasing in all licit and honest affairs. This is your duty, not merely a ploy to gain favor or reward. You always should respond to your master's or mistress's fortunes: If they suffer misfortune, you should be distressed, but you must be greatly pleased by their well-being and prosperity. You should feel sad and discontented to see your mistress displeased and joyous at her good luck, not only in her presence but behind her back. You should make proper excuses for her if you hear evil spoken of her and testify to her honor and good renown. These things done with good heart are not flattery, but rather show the true love and pure loyalty a good servant appropriately demonstrates to master or mistress.

On the other hand, flattery takes many false forms. If you know that your master has some vicious tendency which undermines the good of his soul, his honor, and his morality, and nevertheless you encourage him by giving him advice to confirm and sustain his despicable ways, by flattery you support his action in word or deed. If you hear him malign someone else or maintain wicked, false, or dishonest opinions, and you say: "My lord (or my lady) speaks the truth," this is flattery. If, contrary to the dictates of your conscience, you tell him that something truly evil would be pleasant, good, or wise, you would not only be a flatterer but would sin mortally; thus damning yourself. Likewise, you would contribute to his damnation. Certain servants, particularly of young people, will try to curry favor with and gain profit from their masters and mistresses by encouraging their various vices and sinful habits. Such people are not loyal servants at all.

They are false and reprehensible. However, those who keep them in service themselves are so blinded, they pay no heed. A holy doctor of the Church has said it well: "The flatterer by his word drives a nail into his master's or his mistress's eye. The flatterer blinds with blandishments."

But to return to your duty. You might ask: "If I serve a princess and find that my mistress wants to give her heart to some man in a foolish love, am I obliged by loyalty to support her behavior?" Certain women would think it most important to protect their mistress's honor and conceal her action. They would say: "Though I have had no responsibility in arranging this affair, my mistress wants it; she has confided in me, and if I refuse to help her, she will confide in someone else who would perhaps not conceal the matter as well as I."

The proper reply to your question is very simple. You would do wrong and there is no excuse for wrongdoing. You cannot support your mistress in sin without sinning yourself and participating in the wrong. Besides, suppose you say you are doing it to protect her honor. If you examine your conscience carefully, you will find other reasons prompting you. Perhaps you want to parlay her good will to your own advantage. Whatever motive inspires you, you are doing wrong. Like a blind woman leading another blind woman, you both will fall into a ditch.

If you want to use good judgment and preserve good conscience, here is what you should do. If your mistress trusts you enough to tell you her secrets, you should reply: "Madam, I thank you for confiding in me. Never fear for a moment that I will reveal your private thoughts. But it pains me greatly that you are considering an affair or even that you are so tempted. The only things that can result are the perdition of your soul and dangerous dishonor to your body. There is nothing I would not do to dissuade you from this idea and intention. And please pardon me, but my soul and my conscience would be seriously burdened by what you ask of me. Therefore, I will not do your bidding. Even if you may hate me and cast me out from your good service, I would prefer that you hate me for doing your good rather than that you love me for consenting to evil. Rather than involving myself in your affair, I would prefer to die. I know well that I am yours to obey you, but in this case I would be committing a mortal sin. That I am not obliged to do for any living person."

The good servant thus should reply to her mistress in such a case. But if this servant is wise and loyal, she will not go telling the tale for her own advantage, as some do to show their virtue. They say: "She asked me to do such and such, but I most certainly refused, for I would rather see *her* burn. . . ." Silence is far superior. Thereby, on the subject of her mistress, the good, discreet lady or demoiselle should govern her tongue.

Lest we forget an important aspect of this subject of faithfulness: If any real mishap overtakes the mistress, the good servant will protect her from all perils and defend her as if she were her own child. One lady was saved from being discovered in a compromising situation by her maid-in-waiting, who, when she realized the danger, immediately set fire to the grange so that everyone, thus distracted, would run in that direction and her mistress could escape from her awkward predicament.

Another had a mistress so desperate that she wanted to kill herself because she was pregnant without being married. The maid comforted her and dissuaded her from this unwise idea. Then she told everyone she herself was pregnant, so that when the child was born she could say it was hers. In this way, she saved her mistress from death and protected her from dishonor. In cases like these, once the deed is done and the decision made, if your deception will keep another from despair or from further sin, it is not wrong but rather great charity as long as one does not show approval of the sin. Pity the sinner. God does not wish her death, but rather that she should repent and live a good life. Again, however, the servant should refuse to obey her mistress not only in the case of love affairs but also in any case involving sin or vice. No one is obliged to obey another and thereby to disobey God.

3. Which discusses the second point, also good for women to remember, which is that they should avoid certain sorts of acquaintances.

Our second teaching is that a woman of the court, whatever her situation, should take care not to form acquaintances with too great a variety of men. Here are our reasons. Many people think that court ladies are supposed to be more friendly than other women. This idea is misplaced for at least two principal reasons. First, more than any other women, court ladies must guard honor. (The other reason we will explain in a moment.) Why should they protect honor more than others? Their honor or dishonor is reflected upon their mistress. As they behave well or badly, the mistress will be praised or blamed. We explained in the first part of this book that there is no lady to whom so much honor is due as to a princess. And the household, after all, mirrors its mistress. So it would greatly be to her disadvantage if there were shortcomings in her attendants. I conclude, therefore, that they must protect themselves from criticism even more assiduously than others.

To return to our point. Any woman, whoever she may be, who delights in knowing a variety of men will encourage gossip. Even supposing she did not intend any mischief but merely enjoyed laughter and entertainment, she could scarcely proceed without stimulating doubtful talk, which envious strangers who are only waiting for the opportunity and even some of her agreeable friends will join in. Women, do not be so trusting or act so blindly! If several men frequent your company, eventually one or more of them is bound to make propositions to you if he can. They will vie for your favors. When several are positioned where each would like to find himself alone, the men invariably speak ill of the woman and make fun of her behind her back. Whatever face they put on before the lady, however charming they may appear, they are dissembling. By word of mouth, in taverns and elsewhere, they spread mockery and lewd comments, with everyone adding a little something of his own. In such a way, without cause but merely because of her naivete, or actual sinfulness, the woman is blamed by the very ones she seeks to please.

Let whoever does not believe this find out for herself. May it please Our Lord for ladies and maidens of the court (and indeed all women elsewhere) to realize the peril of cultivating such talkative acquaintances. So realizing, they would withdraw their friendly advances and disregard fine words of men who laugh in their presence, who promise them body and service. Women then scarcely will be tempted to take these men seriously. Perhaps you will ask why it is not better to protect one's honor by turning a pleasant face to everyone, so that no one seems more important than anyone else. This, then, would preclude the comment: "She only frequents such and such a place; she approves of that one but does not even recognize the others." We reply that, in fact, one does not have to endure either of these two evils.

As we already said, if one is seen to associate with only one or two or four, suspicions would be cast upon those questionable associations. Neither this nor friendliness to everyone is desirable. But then you would say: "How are women, especially those at court, to dare to see anyone or amuse themselves in any company where there are men present without arousing evil thoughts? Are they to be so circumscribed?" We reply that the limitation is good, if displeasing, when it prevents more serious difficulty. Though the bridle may annoy and displease a horse, it sometimes prevents it from falling into a ditch.

Where suitable to time and place, by all means wear a friendly countenance. We do not intend to restrain anyone from that. For instance, in a court in France or elsewhere, the prince or princess may receive strangers, either princes, valiant knights, or squires. Of course they must be entertained and made welcome among the ladies and demoiselles, for it would be dishonorable not to do so. Our warning pertains to association with those men who, for no particular reason at all, exuberantly frequent places and boldly play and enjoy themselves in the state chambers when ladies and gentlewomen are present. Our restrictions should annoy no one who loves honor, be she young and vivacious or not, any more than it should displease one who prizes health to hear the doctor say: "You must use this particular remedy for your particular illness." So much for the first reason (for not forming too many acquaintances with men).

The second concerns any honorable woman just as much as it does those at court. The more a thing is held worthy, noble, and valuable, the more it is cherished, and the less it is taken for granted. So every honorable woman who is good and wise should be considered a fine treasure—an exceptional, rare object, worthy of veneration and reverence. Insofar as she is so and wishes so to remain, she should neither sell at high price nor generously donate this great treasure, namely acquaintance with herself. The more distant and difficult of access she is for all men—not because of pride but through the sort of dignity so becoming to a woman— the more she will be respected and prized by them. The more she employs the sort of distant dignity so becoming to a woman, the greater respect men will show her. Nothing is more enthusiastically sought after and desired than what is seen only with difficulty, particularly if it is good and beautiful. Therefore, not being too approachable suits a woman well. Excessive generosity with speech or other favors ill becomes her.

4. Which sets forth the third point (the first of the two which are to be avoided), which is to say the envy reigning at court and how it affects women who are living there.

Now we come to those two circumstances to be avoided particularly by women at court, and generally by all honest women; although they are widespread, at court these problems are especially virulent. These two wicked, most damnable devices are envy and slander, they attract an infinity of others. They are contemptible and despised by God. First I will speak of one and then the other. Because we are concerned for your welfare, we want to show you the way to cultivate a good and just conscience.

First of all, to know better the quality and nature of false envy, we must consider whence it comes and why it arises. Envy derives straight from the pride engendered in creatures who forget their poor fragility and their evolution from nothing. Overbearing from false arrogance, the pride in their hearts makes them forget their misery and their vices and consider themselves worthy of great honors and possessions. Because every creature so frequently deceives herself, each tends to want to outshine her neighbor and to rise above her not only in virtue but in worldly estate, esteem, or possessions. When such a person sees another ahead of her, she believes she has been outdone. Or fearing that, she is envious.

At the court of princes and princesses, honors and worldly status are distributed more generally than elsewhere. Envy therefore, here is most common because everyone covets the greatest share of those goods and rewards. But to return to the subject at hand: You women of the court, whatever your estate, whether you live there by right or in service of a princess, take good counsel! Fortify your courage with wise, useful advice so that you never find within yourself the mortal worm of false envy, which destroys the soul harboring it, gnaws at the heart, and anguishes the will.

5. Which speaks further on the same subject, explaining to women of the court how they may harbor the vice of envy.

What can the virtuous lady, the good noblewomen, or another person living at court do to avoid this dreadful envy? She can struggle against the causes of envy in the human heart.

At the court of princes, however well-born she may be she may happen to see or perhaps think she sees her mistress favor someone over herself. Or she truly sees her mistress do another lady more favors, calling her more often to her counsel, wishing her to be more intimate with her, or keeping her near more frequently. Then this woman will grieve, her heart pricked and punctured by envy. "Why should my lady favor this one or that one more than myself, or prefer her or take her more into her confidence? Am I not of equal lineage, or more noble than she, even if she is better dressed? I am wiser, more gentle born, and better suited to be where she is. She came up from nothing. She is ignorant. She isn't worthy. She is so forward, so obviously obsequious, however could my lady have advanced her, or given her such rewards or such status? How can my lady even look at her in the way she does? Already that one has advanced further in her short time at court than I who have been here since childhood. Why is this? But I will stop it if I can. I will get ahead of her in the end. I know how. I know such and such things about her. What I don't know I will invent. At very least I will add some spice to what I know. I will act fast before I let her get further ahead of me. Surely she wants to advance herself very deviously and she already lords it over everyone. She wants to outdo others, pushing them behind her. However, I will put stumbling blocks in her way, whatever comes of it, no matter what I have to do. I simply will not put up with this any longer. She wants to put herself in my place. Alas, my lady allows it, supports her, and permits her to go ahead of me (and others). I will not let her do it!"

These are the admonitions of envy. The wise lady or noble-women of the court immediately will cast them aside, mustering her good sense and her just conscience. Collecting herself, she will think quite otherwise: "Ridiculous idler! Whatever are you imagining? For God's sake, what do all these foolish things matter to you? If you do your best, if you are always loyal (even if you are not so well rewarded in this world as someone else), God—the only just, true judge—knows all hearts. From Him nothing can be kept secret. He knows all this well and will reward you without fail. In Him alone you should put your hope. As the Scriptures say, 'Whoever puts his desire and trust in princes or in other men is cursed.' Besides, if another has more of Fortune's gifts in this world—which is only a brief journey, like a pilgrimage—why should you complain or grieve about it?

"Do you want to prevent princes or important people from doing what they desire? If your mistress gives more of what is hers to someone else, what harm does she do to you? Certainly, none. Our Lord has given good example of this in the Biblical parable of the workers in the vineyard. Some started work at sunrise, others at noon, others in the evening. When payment time came, the owner of the vineyard gave as much to the ones who came in the evening as to those who came at daybreak. When the all-day workers murmured in discontent, the owner answered: 'My friends, what wrong do I do you? I am paying for the day's work, as I agreed. If it pleases me to give these others as much or more than you, that is not your affair. You have no reason to complain.' In the same way, you have no cause to grumble if your mistress gives what is her own wherever she pleases. It takes nothing from you.

"Besides, you may be unaware of your own faults because you think so highly of yourself. Your mistress, on the other hand, knows them well. If she sees someone wiser, more capable, better educated, and more perfect than you (even though you may believe yourself worth more), she will prefer to have that other one near her. Moreover, if you peer honestly into your conscience and examine your actions, perhaps you will find you deserved this for something you have done. Maybe certain things you said were reported which angered her. If, indeed, somehow you are at fault, your mistress might like you less for it; another might have expelled you or exiled you. So you have no cause to be annoyed. Maybe you were too easy-going, too proud; maybe you thought nothing could harm you. Accept what you have! Complain only to yourself. Anyway, what do you really know about the one who is now in such great favor even though you believe her unworthy of it. Has she some special merit, or has she performed some special service for God? Why should He want to reward her in such a manner in this world? You know that God's ways are mysterious, so it is unwise for you to judge what He sees, however surprising it may seem. For this same reason, you should not stand in the way of someone else's position or advancement.

"Think of your soul. Governing yourself wisely, always doing your duty well, for God will know it. He is the Master whom it is good to serve. He is entirely wise, wholly good, and all powerful. All other service is mere wind and vanity. Beware of any misdeeds you commit against Him by injuring another in word or action. Do not damn yourself. Even if someone else has done you a disservice, God does not permit us to avenge ourselves. If you have even thought of such a thing, beg mercy from God. Do not worry who goes before and who after, who is in favor and who is not. Whatever happens, you will not be the less worthy. Furthermore, those who observe you graciously bearing the pride and arrogance of others, saying not a word and showing not a sign, will value and love you the more for it. If you want to keep your rightful place among the others, keep it graciously. Do not wish to surpass them. Protect your conscience against envious nonsense, lest you give others cause for trouble. The blame will fall upon you." These and similar remedies are advice for the wise lady or maid-in-waiting at court to apply against the pricks and punctures of envy.

Concerning this ugly sin which must be shunned, a wise man has said: "I do not know why any reasonable creature does not cast out from herself the sin of envy before all others. Consider the quality of all other sins. In each one, the act entails some pleasure: the glow of pride in vanity, the pleasure of eating in gluttony, the delights of the flesh in carnality. These pleasures might tempt one to adore them even though they are forbidden to the soul, but the diabolical sin of envy does not offer the person dominated by it any pleasure whatsoever. It produces only sorrowful thoughts; a diminution of courage; a sorrowful, altered face; torments which pierce the soul; and every sort of miserable displeasure. In brief, it inclines one to all felonies without doing anyone any good. Also, the one who is envious is hated." Another wise man has railed against them saying: "Please God, let the envious man have such large eyes that he can see all prosperity and joy scattered among others throughout the world; thus, he will have all the more reason for torment."

6. Which speaks of the fourth point, the second of those to be avoided. It tells how women of the court should be careful to avoid telling falsehoods; whence these falsehoods come; and for what reason.

Slander is the second vice any lady of the court must protect herself from committing. First of all, slander cannot be excused for any good reason. To come to terms with slander quickly, I will speak of its three common causes, all of which are prevalent at court, sometimes all three at once. One such cause is hatred; the second is opinion; the third, pure envy. All three causes are reprehensible; slander which envy causes is least easy to excuse. All three must be avoided, for slander never is permissible. In fact, it is a mortal sin which violates God's commandments, namely, "Do unto others as you would have them do unto you," and also, "Love thy neighbor as thyself." These are protective remedies for ladies.

First, that first cause, hatred. Four principal reasons govern why one never should slander another out of hatred, no matter what the injury which has caused it. The burning passion of hatred usually is sparked by a deep hurt received from someone else. Rightly or wrongly, the person who is injured, or considers herself injured, is very readily inclined to slander the one she thinks has offended her. Frequently at court, one lady or another will know that a certain person or people would like to harm her or to create difficulties between herself and her mistress or lord or her friends; or they will try to have her dismissed. The woman or demoiselle might, indeed, lose her appointment, her property, and her job. Because of all this, even her honor might be damaged without cause. Even if the cause were just, nevertheless she will hate the person who has done this to her and, no doubt, will slander her in private and in public unless the person in question is so powerful that she does not dare. Even so, it would be unusual if she did not whisper just a bit. Her heart will be broken. Naturally, she will speak ill of the person who has injured her, telling both what she knows and what she does not know at all. This kind of slander, springing from hatred inspired by injury, may seem justifiable to some. Nevertheless, it is not.

Why not? God expressly commands us to love our enemies and to return good for evil. Whoever acts against God's commandment damns himself and gains nothing by it. For this reason it would be more profitable to restrain the impulse to slander. Likewise, and secondly, the slanderer acts against his or her own honor. How so? A person of great courage never slanders her enemy, because malicious words are the weapons of people with little power. To use them is to admit cowardice. Thirdly, those who hear slander about an adversary or enemy scarcely will believe it. They will say this person is speaking out of hatred and should not be believed. The fourth reason is: the person who first caused the damage, or threatened to cause it, will be even more indignant when she hears the rumors you circulate. So she may aggravate the initial injury or do even worse. It is not quite as bad to receive one injury as two. An apt illustration of the folly of slander is the person who wanted to make war on the heavens and pointed his bow toward the clouds. The arrows fell back on his head and wounded him severely. Likewise as these four reasons clearly show, the slander a hateful person speaks against her adversary turns against the slanderer, wounding both soul and honor.

7. Concerning the same, and how women at court should guard against speaking ill of their mistress.

The second cause from which slander arises is erroneous opinion: the opinion that another is bad or deficient in some certain respect or in everything, or that she does not conduct herself properly either in general or in particular. Without the truth being known, she will be misjudged and slandered abundantly and inconsiderately. People everywhere are in the habit of slandering without certain knowledge, and do so without hesitation. There is hardly a court without such conceited slanderers, who spare no one, not even their master or mistress. Despite the great harm in defaming another person, especially the one who supports and nourishes, nonetheless at many courts servants malign their masters. If either men or women see, or imagine they see, in their master or mistress some small sign of a particular vice, immediately they make charges against him or her, with great elaboration, saying the thing they imagined has in fact happened. Our point here is addressed to women, but it might well benefit men, too.

Too many women who frequent courts in various countries seem predisposed to misinterpret simple actions. Servants merely may see their lady or mistress speaking in a low voice to the same person once or twice, or showing some small sign of intimacy or friendship. Or they may overhear some slight laughter or a pleasantry made by chance, or by youth or innocence, and quite without evil intent. If the mistress is ever so slightly flamboyant or charming or meticulous in her dress, all of which are quite natural for certain people, immediately someone will leap to misjudge her. Every trivial justification leads them rashly to form a poor opinion of the mistress. Misjudgment, however, is the least of it, for they will do worse, even though she is their mistress and feeds them and supports them with good wages from her wealth. They pretend to be obedient, on bended knee, very respectful, with abundant flattery. However, they do not keep their peace. They pass along unfounded opinions to each other and whisper suggestions which spread around the court, just as the unhealthy sheep spreads its mange to others in the flock. Of course, they will see to it their mistress does not notice or overhear their words, although it will please them if she alone is ignorant of their gossip. Even those who themselves have encouraged her by saying that it is a good idea to do thus and such, will make fun of her, talking behind her back, adding details that warp the truth. Many servants do this. Ladies, demoiselles, and other women at court who so act not only misbehave badly but commit a worse sin than if they slandered one another. Five reasons make this true.

First, the greater their mistress, the better known her honor or dishonor throughout the country. Far more than for any ordinary woman, she could suffer from the slander, because talk might travel through several countries. Second, they are betraying the one to whom they owe the most loyalty and obedience. In the third place, they are acting contrary to their sworn oaths, in which they promised to protect her honor. Fourthly, they repay good with evil by harming the one who sustains, nourishes, and provides them their situation in life. Fifth, they judge others. That is against God's commandment: "Judge not lest ye be judged."

Suppose now that they will know that their mistress is a wicked, perverse creature. Even so, they should not talk against her, either among themselves or elsewhere. No words ever are spoken so discreetly that they are not repeated. People committed to protecting their lady's honor also are committed to covering her shame. If they hear others slandering her they should try to silence such remarks. Those who do not, contribute to their own dishonor and should be held accountable because of it. Certainly they must not be excused. You might say to us, "I have very good reasons to talk about my mistress and to slander her. Working in her service is neither good nor attractive!" We reply: "Leave if you are not pleased! If you cannot leave and must serve, then avoid your own great prejudice. Keep still and pretend you do not see anything. Notice nothing, because there is nothing you can do about what you notice. It is not your affair. Do well and loyally what is expected of you and involve yourself in nothing else. Pray God that He may correct your mistress and give her knowledge, if you think she requires it. When hearing others speaking of it silence their words if you can. If not, at least be quiet so that you yourself will be more highly respected."

Reality usually is quite different. God knows that many who talk ill of their mistress do so from spite, perhaps because they are not taken into her confidence or from envy because others know her better. Few who slander can pretend to any more noble cause. However, the good, loyal lady, demoiselle, or other courtier, wishing to preserve a good conscience and loving the welfare and honor of her mistress, will act in this manner if she sees her lady's honor diminished or endangered: If she does not dare to speak with her directly or admonish her for her own good, she will go only to her mistress's <u>confessor</u>. There, secretly, in confession, she can tell what is being said about her mistress, the peril in which she is placing herself, and the harm which might come of it. Then she will beg the confessor for God's sake to point out all this to her mistress and not say anything more about it.

8. Which tells how unsuitable it is for women at court to talk about each other and to say unkind things.

Women of the court must not slander or malign one another. Not only is it sinful and wrong because of the pertinent reasons already mentioned, but also, she who speaks ill of another deserves the same fate. The woman who knows others are maligning her will tend to combat gossip with gossip. No one, however, is sufficiently righteous to be able to say: "I do not fear a soul. What could anyone say about me? I am pure. And so, I boldly can speak of others." This is foolishness. Everyone has something that can be criticized. As the Scriptures say: "<u>No man is without crime</u>

which means without sin." If you don't have a particular vice, you may actually discover you have a worse one, or two or three. If you examine your conscience well, you will find faults aplenty. Sins hidden from the world are known to God, who alone knows who is a good pilgrim.

Women of the court bicker; it is said around the town that the women of the court speak ill of one another. The court of a princess should resemble a well-run abbey, where the monks are under oath not to speak to lay-people or to others about what goes on in their midst in secret. Similarly, women of a court should love and support one another like sisters. They should not quarrel with each other in the ladies' quarters, nor talk behind each others' backs like fishwives. Unsuitable for the court of a princess, such behavior should not be permitted.

Envy, the third cause inspiring slander, is the least excusable, most wicked, and farthest removed from right reason. If the hate-filled person slanders the one who has wronged her, it is natural retribution for injury. If God did not forbid it, such slander would be understandable. Likewise, she who slanders because of opinion at least can base her accusations upon some vague appearances and misunderstandings. On the other hand, speaking ill from envy has no cause but sheer wickedness dwelling and flourishing in the human heart. This wickedness poisons the slanderous speaker and imperils the one slandered. Not the bite of a serpent, nor the blow of a sword, nor any other sharp thrust was ever as dangerous as the tongue of an envious person. This pointed barb strikes and kills aggressor and victim alike in both body and soul. If we were to count, good Lord, how many kingdoms, countries, and good people have been destroyed by false reports founded on envy, our sum would be staggering. But for brevity, we will omit these examples.

Envious slander also comes from pure malice, without another motive. How does the person who is good, or who has been blessed with certain gifts of grace or fortune, deserve to have anyone speak evil of him or to cause him difficulties? Good things surely may have come to him rightfully. He may be particularly happy or fortunate. Thus, slander coming from no reasonable cause must derive from sheer perniciousness, and for this reason it is most damnable. Since we already have spoken of this envy in the fourth and fifth chapters of this second part, we will say no more. Let this suffice as a warning to ladies, noblewomen, and others at court.

9. Which speaks of the lady baronesses and the sort of knowledge which may be useful to them.

Now it is time to speak to the ladies and demoiselles who live in castles or other sorts of manors on their own lands, in walled cities, or in smaller market towns. For them this advice should be helpful. Because their estates and powers vary, we must differentiate among them in our discussions of certain things: their status and their style of living. As for their morals and good deeds on God's behalf, certainly they can profit from our advice in the earlier chapters to princesses and women living at court. All women can learn to cultivate virtue and avoid vice. However, the women I address now are powerful women: baronesses and great land owners who nevertheless are not called princesses. Technically, the name "princess" should not be applied to any but empresses, queens, and duchesses. Yet in Italy and elsewhere, wives of men who because of their land holdings are called princes, after the names of their territories, may be called princesses. Although countesses are not universally called princesses, because they follow duchesses in rank according to the importance of their lands, nonetheless we have included them among the princesses. First we address these baronesses of whom there are many in France, in Brittany, and elsewhere.

These baronesses surpass in honor and power many countesses, even though their titles are not as distinguished. Certain barons have enormous power because of their land, domains, and the nobility that goes with them. Thereby, their wives have considerable status. These women must be highly knowledgeable about government, and wise—in fact, far wiser than most other such women in power. The knowledge of a baroness must be so comprehensive that she can understand everything. Of her a philosopher might have said: "No one is wise who does not know some part of everything." Moreover, she must have the courage of a <u>man</u>. This means that she should not be brought up overmuch among women nor should she be indulged in extensive and feminine pampering. Why do I say that? If <u>barons</u> wish to be honored as they deserve, they spend very little time in their manors and on their own lands. Going to war, attending their prince's court, and traveling are the three primary duties of such a lord. So the lady, his companion, must represent him at home during his absences. Although her husband is served by bailiffs, provosts, <u>rent collectors,</u> and land governors, she must govern them all. To do this according to her right she must conduct herself with such wisdom that she will be both feared and loved. As we have said before, the best possible fear comes from love.

When wronged, her men must be able to turn to her for refuge. She must be so skilled and flexible that in each case she can respond suitably. Therefore, she must be knowledgeable in the mores of her locality and instructed in its usages, rights, and customs. She must be a good speaker, proud when pride is needed; circumspect with the scornful, surly, or rebellious; and charitably gentle and humble toward her good, obedient subjects. With the counsellors of her lord and with the advice of elder wise men, she ought to work directly with her people. No one should ever be able to say of her that she acts merely to have her own way. Again, she should have a man's heart. She must know the laws of arms and all things pertaining to warfare, ever prepared to command her men if there is need of it. She has to know both assault and <u>defense</u> tactics to insure that her fortresses are well defended, if she has any expectation of attack or believes she must initiate military action. Testing her men, she will discover their qualities of courage and determination before overly trusting them. She must know the number and strength of her men to gauge accurately her resources, so that she never will have to trust vain or feeble promises. Calculating what force she is capable of providing before her lord arrives with reinforcements, she also must know the financial resources she could call upon to sustain military action.

She should avoid oppressing her men, since this is the surest way to incur their hatred. She can best cultivate their loyalty by speaking boldly and consistently to them, according to her council, not giving one reason today and another tomorrow. Speaking words of good courage to her men-at-arms as well as to her other retainers, she will urge them to loyalty and their best efforts.

Such courses of action are suitable for the wise baroness whose absent husband has given her the responsibility and commission to take his place. This advice would be useful if an aggressor or some baron or powerful man should defy her. So, also, the baroness will find particularly expedient the advice in the chapter on widowed princesses. For if during a baron's lifetime his wife knows everything about the management of his affairs, then if left a widow, she will not be ignorant of her rights if anyone dares to try to take advantage of her and make away with her inheritance.

10. Which explains how ladies and demoiselles who live on their lands should conduct themselves with respect to their households.

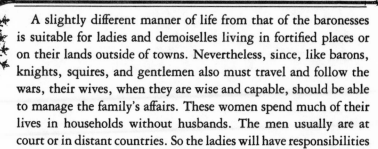

A slightly different manner of life from that of the baronesses is suitable for ladies and demoiselles living in fortified places or on their lands outside of towns. Nevertheless, since, like barons, knights, squires, and gentlemen also must travel and follow the wars, their wives, when they are wise and capable, should be able to manage the family's affairs. These women spend much of their lives in households without husbands. The men usually are at court or in distant countries. So the ladies will have responsibilities for managing their property, their revenues, and their lands. In order for such a woman to act with good judgment, she must know the yearly income from her estate. She must manage it so well that by conferring with her husband, her gentle words and good counsel will lead to their agreement to follow a plan for the estate that their revenues permit. This plan must not be so ambitious that at year's end they find themselves in debt to their retainers or other creditors. Surely there is no disgrace in living within one's income, however small it may be. But it is shameful to live so extravagantly that creditors daily shout and bellow outside the door, some even raising clubs and threatening violence. It is also terrible to have to resort to extortion from one's own men and tenants. The lady or demoiselle must be well informed about the rights of domain of fiefs and secondary fiefs, about contributions, the lord's rights of harvest, shared crops, and all other rights of possession, and the customs both local and foreign. The world is full of governors of lord's lands and jurisdictions who are intentionally dishonest. Aware of this, the lady must be knowledgeable enough to protect her interests so that she cannot be deceived. She should know how to manage accounts and should attend to them often, also superintending her agents' treatment of her tenants and men. If they are being deceived or harassed beyond reasonable bounds, both she and her husband would suffer. As for penalties against poor people, she should be more compassionate than rigorous.

Farming also is this good housekeeper's domain. In what weather and in what season the fields should be fertilized; whether the land is moist or dry; the best way to have furrows run according to the lay of the land; their proper depth, straightness, and parallel layout; and the favorable time for sowing with seed suited to the land—all these she must know. Likewise, she must know about vineyards if the land lies in a region where there are grapes. She requires good laborers and supervisors in these activities, and she should not hire people who change masters from season to season. It is a bad sign if workers are always on the move. Nor should she hire workers who are too old, for they will be lazy and feeble, nor too young, for they will be frivolous.

She will insist that her laborers get up early. If she is a good manager she won't depend on anyone else to see to this but will arise early herself, put on a cloak, go to the window, and watch there until she sees them go out, for laborers usually are inclined to laziness. She should often take her recreation in the fields to see just how they are working, for many willingly stop raking the ground beyond scratching the surface if they think nobody notices. There are plenty of workers capable of sleeping in the shade of a willow tree in the field, leaving the workhorses or the oxen to graze by themselves, caring only that by evening they can say they have put in their day. The good housekeeper must keep her eyes wide open.

She will not wait for the season when labor is in short supply to hire her workers. Rather, when the grain is ripening, even as early as the month of May, she will engage her workers for August, selecting good, strong, diligent fellows. She will agree to pay them either in money or grain. At harvest time she will supervise, or have others make sure that the workers do not leave grain sheaves behind them or try any of the other deceptions farm workers commonly practice on unsuspecting landholders. Just as she watched the other workers, the lady in charge at harvest time should arise early daily. Things rarely go well in a household where the mistress lies abed late. Keeping an eye on her entire domestic enterprise will give her plenty to oversee. For indifference reigns where supervision won't.

<u>Sheep</u> must be put out to pasture on schedule. Noting how the shepherd cares for them, she will make sure that he knows his business. Arrogant shepherds allow their flocks to die when they want to, in spite of master or mistress. Therefore, she must make sure the sheep are kept clean, protected from too much sun and from rain, and cured of mange. If she is wise, she and one of her women will go up to the manor-house roof to observe how the sheep are looked after. Knowing of this scrutiny, the shepherd

will be more careful to avoid complaints. She will insist that he plan carefully when the lambs should be born, thereafter attentively caring for them, for lambs often die for lack of foresight. Just as she superintends the raising of proper food for her sheep, she also will be present at their shearing, seeing to it that it is done properly in the right season.

If her lands are in a warm, humid country with abundant meadows, she will keep many horned animals. If she harvests more oats than she can sell well, she will fatten oxen at the manger to sell later for considerable profit. If she has woods, she will have a breeding stable there which can be a profitable venture for those who manage it well. During the winter when labor is cheap, she will have her workers cut her willow and hazel groves to make stakes for vineyards to be sold in due season. Then she will set her men to cutting wood to be stored for heating the house, or she will order them to clear some field. If the weather is too cold outside, she will put them to work inside the granary, never leaving them idle. Nothing is more wasteful in a household than a lazy staff.

Furthermore, she will instruct her maids to look after the animals, prepare food for the workers, take care of the milk, weed the gardens, or hunt for herbs, even though it may muddy them to the knees. It is their duty. She, her daughters, and attendants will make cloth, separating the wool, sorting it out, and putting the fine strands aside to make cloth for her husband and herself or to sell. The thick strands will be used for the small children, her servingwomen, and the workmen. She will stuff bedcovers with the large balls of wool. And she will have hemp grown by the farmers. During the long winter evenings, her maids will work and spin it into coarse linen. Many more such tasks as these would take too long to describe here.

In the lowlands, women take pride in their skill in household management. No matter how important her status, the most diligent woman is the proudest and most highly praised. The excellent keeper of the household sometimes brings in more profit than derives from the rents and income of the land itself. Such was the case with that wise, prudent housekeeper, the <u>Countess of Eu</u>, whose son, the young count, died in Hungary. Not ashamed to devote herself to all honest work of the household, she generated such profit from it that this income was greater than from all other revenues of her land. Of such a woman one well can repeat the Book of <u>Solomon's praise for the wise woman.</u>

11. Which speaks of those who are extravagant in their dress, headgear, and other ornaments.

Ladies and demoiselles living on their estates ought to consult with their husbands about their economic situation, meaning that they must not attempt a finer style of living than their revenues permit. It seems to us useful to advise those wishing to live prudently and following our doctrine that they should strive to avoid <u>extravagance</u> and the outrageous habits in which some women indulge. Two problems—both associated with pride—are particularly troublesome and indeed are common enough, but because our present concern involves them and such vices and shortcomings are capable of damaging their souls and are not even good or attractive for their bodies, we speak of them. First are the ludicrous ornaments and clothes they choose; second is the pretentiousness of whoever takes <u>precedence</u> when they are together.

Those who take too much pleasure in clothing clearly are in error. In the good old days, duchesses would not dare to put on the costume of queens, nor countesses wear duchesses' robes, nor simple ladies dress in the clothes of countesses, nor demoiselles wear the garb of ladies. Now, however, all is in chaos where before there was decorum. No order is observed either in clothing or in ornaments. Whoever can wear the most of the best, whatever her station in life demands it, and one follows the other, like sheep. If any man or woman sees another indulge in some ridiculous, unsuitable clothing, straightaway each follows the other, insisting that the fashionable must imitate one another. They tell the truth—one extravagant creature emulates another. But if most people could moderate their behavior they would not lead one another to outrages, rather they would disdain the one who started the style and who would stand alone in such folly.

I do not know what pleasure people derive from these fantastic fashions. Only poor judgment makes creatures behave this way. People are less rather than more admired for such excesses by those of good taste. Nothing is more ridiculous than to see a woman pretending to a great, exaggerated status when one knows it is not really her own and that she does not even possess the means for maintaining it. Nowadays, one rarely sees anything else but this. If such people become poor because of their extravagances, they invite their troubles and we should not pity them. They relegate themselves to poverty by indulgences in such follies. Had they been willing to live moderately, they could have been reasonably well off. Certain people incur even greater shame by running up huge debts with dressmakers, tailors, and goldsmiths to whom they owe money all at the same time. Often they have to pawn one gown in order to buy another. Only God knows if they ever extricate themselves from creditors. Merchandise costs them double in the end. We say these things in warning for those who believe that in this way they can outshine their neighbors.

Remember, all this comes from abundance of overweening pride, which reigns today more than ever before. Nobody accepts his true station in life but pretends to resemble a king. I would not be surprised if God punishes such people severely; He cannot endure this. Outrageous superfluity in clothes was illustrated recently by a Parisian dressmaker who had made for a simple lady living in Gastinois a tunic which required five ells of wide Brussels material trailing three-quarters on the ground, replete with bombard sleeves hanging to the feet. With such a costume one must wear a wide headdress with high horns, truly a particularly ugly and unbecoming style. Anyone with taste knows that moderation is the more attractive, agreeable quality. French ladies in particular ought to know this.

In other countries it is customary to maintain styles of men's and women's clothing for a longer period of time than here, not changing as we do from year to year, going from one extravagance to another. Italian costumes in particular, as well as those of certain other places, are more admirable. Although more impressive to look at, covered with pearls, gold, and precious stones, still they are not extravagant. Those ornaments last. They are put on one robe after another. Our French excesses in materials and trailing panels too soon wear out, requiring replacement by others. So too with the headdresses. Surely their heads are more attractive. Nothing, after all, is a more beautiful headdress for a woman than fine blond hair, as St. Paul bears witness when he says: "Hair is a woman's capital ornament."

12. Which speaks against the pride of certain women.

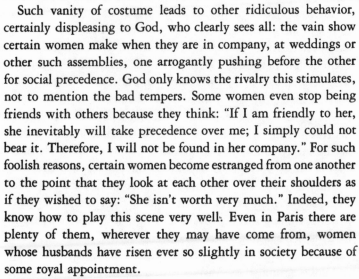

Such vanity of costume leads to other ridiculous behavior, certainly displeasing to God, who clearly sees all: the vain show certain women make when they are in company, at weddings or other such assemblies, one arrogantly pushing before the other for social precedence. God only knows the rivalry this stimulates, not to mention the bad tempers. Some women even stop being friends with others because they think: "If I am friendly to her, she inevitably will take precedence over me; I simply could not bear it. Therefore, I will not be found in her company." For such foolish reasons, certain women become estranged from one another to the point that they look at each other over their shoulders as if they wished to say: "She isn't worth very much." Indeed, they know how to play this scene very well. Even in Paris there are plenty of them, wherever they may have come from, women whose husbands have risen ever so slightly in society because of some royal appointment.

Even worse is the behavior of such ladies, demoiselles, and

other women in God's church, the very place where one must especially eschew all sin. Unsuitable thoughts or acts are all the more distressing there, the place of prayer and services dedicated to the Creator. The ceremony that these women make of preceding one another to the Offering is incredible. (The custom is even worse in Picardy and Brittany than in France.) Certain bold women even have come to blows in the church itself, doing and saying shocking things. This charade is repeated during the offering of the Peace.

But worse yet, the wretched husbands abet and even encourage their wives in this display. If their wives did not behave in this manner, the husbands would be annoyed with them, thinking: "I am more a gentleman than he, so my wife should precede his." The other will think: "But I am richer," or "I hold more important office," or "I have greater pretensions to grandeur; so I will not allow his wife to be honored before mine."

Thus, these foolish men themselves sometimes come to blows. What outrageous behavior! What lack of common sense! Certainly such acts should not be allowed among Christians. The curates, the priests, or the bishops who are powerful enough, even if a single priest might not dare, should forbid such words to be spoken in their jurisdictions, and especially in the churches. Truth to tell, such women would be better off remaining in their own houses than committing sacrilege in church.

Priests who see these women advancing to the altar so ludicrously, seemingly making and offering to God (though truly offering to the Prince of Hell, who is the Prince of Pride) should turn aside and not accept their donations. Likewise with the Peace; that object should be attached to a nail on the wall so that those who wish could go up and kiss it. Those of whom we speak do not "take the Peace," but merely kiss the object so named; they rather "take war," for their hearts are spiteful from Pride. Certainly it is a very vile and ugly custom to hand the Peace from person to person as is now done and a disruption and hindrance to prayer. Some pass it to others plainly displeased to receive it.

What is the value of such ceremonies? As accepting the Peace should signify the communion of peace among Christians, it belongs as much to the humble as to the great. What comes from God belongs to all people and nobody who receives such gifts should refuse to share them with others. Such customs are to be deplored among Christians. And since diagnosing the malady without recommending the remedy to cure it is inadequate medicine: eliminating the passing of the Peace would reduce that swelling of Pride, and, so doing, achieve great charity and benefit many souls. Bishops should attempt to discard these ugly customs by excommunicating after due warning all those wishing to preserve them. It would be a great benefit to everyone.

As for People who arrogantly think to elevate themselves through such nonsensical customs, they are inspired by folly. Human beings, contemplating the misery of your beginning, where now you are, and where you are going will not give you great cause for Pride. If you insist that gentility leads you to seek honors in church, know that no matter who you are, neither nobility nor hypocritical though virtuous behavior will make you a gentle person but only virtue and good instincts. Folly deceives you if you imagine such things, no matter who you may be. All holy doctors who have spoken of this have said that the greatest is not always from the highest estate but rather whoever is the most virtuous. In *The Book of Our Lord's Words,* St. Augustine speaking to you who believe blood alone makes you noble, not virtue, said: "People deceived by illusion! You delight in grandeur and your own importance. You try to raise yourself up; but since you do not know the way well enough, you go astray. You who think you are climbing in truth are descending, for the first step where you place your foot is Pride, a deep, awful ditch. I will show you a better step to rise by, if you will believe me. Humility is that first step, followed by all other virtues. Climbing that way you will be most noble and will ascend as high as you wish without danger of misfortune."

Hereafter we must speak of ladies and demoiselles living in

the good towns and walled cities so that in our distinguishing differences among them we may say what is useful for advancing their prosperity and honor.

Often, gentlemen marry their daughters to wealthy men living in cities and large towns. Some of these men are clerks and officials of kings and princes, others are bourgeois or important merchants. These women are not necessarily badly married, if they accept their fortune and are not led astray by opinion. But some lacking sense or suffering from a surfeit of pride are not content, considering their husbands beneath them. This is ridiculous, for as already pointed out, nobody is vile if he is not base, nor noble if not virtuous.

Therefore, truly noble and gentle women should show it by their excellent manners and good works. As the *Book of Ecclesiastes* says: "If you who are great humble yourself, by just so much will your greatness and honor increase. You will be the more praised." Likewise, however far such women honor, obey, and revere their husbands and show the faith marriage requires, so much will their honor increase. Though all women are expected to do this, these will be prized even more than the others. Furthermore, they will set a fine example to other women if they are viewed as courteous, humble, not excessively domineering in their own households nor insisting overmuch on domestic service, and as well are amiable, kindly, poised, and dressed without extravagance. They will exemplify the common proverb: What is good is in good odor.

13. Which speaks of the manners suitable to women in religious orders.

We have spoken about the doctrine suitable for ladies and demoiselles. Religious women belong to this noble estate no matter who they may have been at birth, because of reverence to God, to whom they have given themselves in marriage, most surely they walk before all others. The honor due to their Husband

and the religious life according to God is among the world's very high estates. To generalize our doctrine to all classes of women, we will speak to the religious, recalling to them their manner of life, which truly is founded on the three principal virtues. We will speak according to the words of Jesus Christ and the witness of the Doctors of the Church. Through the praise of virtues, vices are corrected. Just as it is good to do good and bad to do evil, so it is a pleasure to hear good spoken rather than evil. Therefore, it is pleasing to describe this vocation and so honor this holy order.

So, women in religious life, although you know all this well enough—because of the statues and rules your houses' founders have established—do not be displeased to hear again from us, your friends, the major virtues you ought to practice. Seven are principal: first is obedience, the foundation of all others; second, humility; third, sobriety; fourth, patience; fifth, solicitude; sixth, chastity; seventh, benevolence and concord. While of course we address our words to you, religious women, all women might lend an ear to hear whatever might be to their profit. For if a drop or crumb should fall before people, let them not turn away in disdain or cast it aside: good doctrine can be compared to a good, faithful friend who, when he cannot help, at least does no harm.

The virtue of obedience, on which religious life is founded, can be no better praised than by what the Holy Scriptures say of Our Lord. He Himself proved it by example when He was obedient even unto death. Obedience is best understood in three principal ways. First is obedience to God in keeping his commandments; nothing should be put before this. Second is obedience to the established laws, and third, to one's sovereign. So, a woman in religious life above all should keep God's commandments. Afterward, she must obey the laws established by her Order, namely its regulations. And lastly, she must obey her abbess or prioress.

Everyone knows that whoever breaks God's commandments sins mortally. But, since the religious life is more worthy than other estates, a Brother or Sister sins more grievously than another who falls into sin. There are several reasons for this. One, as has just been mentioned, is their more holy estate, just as it would be worse for the king's chamberlain to commit some crime against his majesty than for someone with no responsibility or official duty to the king. Moreover, religious people who sin act against their vows, in which they had expressed their will to serve God alone with all their might. She who sins does not serve. Quite the contrary. Take care, ladies, to not break any rules of your Order. If you do, you sin grievously. Certain acts that would not be sins for laypersons are sins for you because you would be disobeying your institution. Therefore, commandments of your superior should not offend you if you consider the great merit you gain by obeying them humbly.

Humility is the second virtue. Without it, you could not please God, even if you had all the other virtues. The Holy Scriptures bear witness that this virtue pleases God, because the humility of the Virgin Mary delighted Our Lord more than her virginity, as expressed in her song of the *Magnificat:* "He beheld the humility of His handmaiden." Anyone wishing to collect and catalogue the praise of the virtue of humility in the Holy Scriptures would have an endless task.

The third virtue is sobriety, which includes abstinence. To show its merit, St. Augustine, in the *Book of the Holy Virgins,* says that sobriety is the guard and protector of thought, of the senses, and, indeed, of the whole body. It is the custodian of charity, the neighbor of shame, the companion of peace and friendship, and the banisher of all vice. Also, Origen says on the same subject that, just as intoxication gives birth to all vices, so sobriety is the mother of all virtues.

Patience is the fourth virtue. Who could tell the great qualities of this? They are best exemplified by the life of Our Lord. He is the very source of patience. The patient can call themselves Children of God. Therefore, the Scriptures call them blessed, for theirs is the Kingdom of Heaven.

Fifth of the virtues suitable for a nun is solicitude or diligence.

To explain its goodness without seeking other proof, Saint Jerome says in his sermon on the *Psalter:* "Conquer and overcome nature by virtuous diligence." So that the greatest good shall not be denied you strive to overcome bodily sleep and all the senses. This you can accomplish by diligence, for that virtue can overcome and dominate even human nature. By great will power, the spirit can control the body; that is a necessary skill for a good nun.

Chastity is the sixth virtue, which includes honesty in habit, veil, words, and bearing. If you observe this virtue properly, it forbids you all vestments and headdresses with even the slightest degree of worldliness or vanity. Rather, all should be simple and unadorned, according to the individual Order. Let this be a warning against those who wish to be pretty in their habits and coifs, wearing them tight-fitting and handsomely pinned. Such indulgence is very ugly and quite indecent for a religious person. Even more inappropriate is a nun with a sloppy habit. Yet worse is the religious who wants to dance, caper, or play improper games. Nothing is more unattractive or distasteful than words which transgress the bounds of purity and honesty. Those of you who are guilty of this behave as if the devil himself were among you. In God's name, my dear friends, vigorously avoid these sins against chastity, for you are mingling a terrible poison with honey for your damnation. Instead, delight in the beautiful virtue of chastity of which Saint Ambrose says, in the *Book of Virginity:* "Chastity makes one an angel. Who observes chastity is like an angel; who loses it is a devil; who preserves it is a citizen and dweller in Paradise." Saint Bernard says that just as balsam protects flesh from decay, so chastity keeps the soul from corruption, maintaining it in cleanliness and keeping its renown for good odor. Because of this, it was said of the saintly Judith, praised by all her people: "You are the glory of Jerusalem; you are the joy of Israel. You are the honor of your people. God gave you the strength of a man, with which you have labored because you have loved chastity."

The seventh virtue is concord or benevolence. That is necessary in your midst. You should love concord and cherish it in your convents as the proper bond of peace. Hear what <u>Saint Ambrose</u> says in the first book *Of Offices:* "Benevolence is like the mother of us all. It binds and joins people together so that they are like brothers faithfully loving one another's good. She makes them rejoice at the prosperity of others and feel sad at the contrary. Whoever removes benevolence from a group of people might just as well take away the sun." Then he says: "Benevolence is like a fountain which refreshes the thirsty. Benevolence is like a light which shines on itself as well as upon others. It engenders peace and breaks the sword of wrath. It joins together the many into the one. Altogether it is such a great force it can triumph over nature."

By all these things you can understand, dear ladies, that you should live and abide together in true, loyal love as sisters united in peace.

Let this suffice for the second part of this book.

END OF BOOK II

BOOK III

1. The first chapter explains how all that has already been said can apply to some women as well as to others, and it speaks of the kind of management a woman of position should observe in her household.

At the beginning of this third part, having followed the path of the princesses, and the ladies and demoiselles both at court, and away from it we will speak to the women of importance in cities: those who are married to <u>clerks</u>, to the <u>counsellors</u> of kings or princes, or to guardians of justice and other officials, as well as to women married to the <u>burghers</u> who live in cities and large towns and are considered, in certain countries, to be noble if they belong to ancient families. Thereafter, we will speak to other women, so that all may hear our doctrine.

As we have repeatedly stated, whatever we have said regarding virtues and the proper manner of life can pertain to any woman, whatever her estate. On these subjects, what is specifically suitable for some may also be suitable for others. Each can take from our teachings whatever she finds useful. Do not imitate certain foolish people, who only listen to a sermon when the preacher speaks of subjects or situations in which they have no stake. These they note well, saying his words are true and well-expressed. But when it comes to what really affects them or pertains directly to their own lives, they lower their heads and close their ears. As if their own imperfections were too trivial to mention, they ignore them and concentrate only on the foibles of others. For this reason, the wise preacher should know what sort of people are present at his sermon. If he speaks directly to some, he should touch the others in such way that they will neither mock one another nor murmur against each other.

Once again then, we Three Virtues recommend to women of high position who are inhabitants of cities and towns—presupposing that you are good and devoted to God—that you listen carefully to any of our previous teachings which might apply to you, specifically our four major points which we have mentioned elsewhere. As for what concerns Worldly Prudence, the first of these pertains to the love and faith you owe your husband and your conduct with him. The second concerns the management of your household. The third describes your clothing and ornaments. And the fourth explains how you can protect yourself from blame and from falling into disrepute.

We need not repeat the justifications for your affection and fidelity to your partner, be he old or young, good or wicked, peaceable or quarrelsome, faithless or gentlemanly. Rather, please read chapter 13 of the first part of this book, where this is discussed at length. But if you need encouragement to maintain your relationship as we recommend, remember the rewards of conducting yourself well and wisely with your husband, whoever he may be, preserving your vows of fidelity and loyalty, keeping the peace, and performing your duty. You will acquire three benefits: great merit for your soul, great honor in this world, and great riches. Experience demonstrates that although certain rich men (among others) often mistreat and mistrust their wives, in the end when death approaches, their consciences smite them, forcing them to realize how good their wives have been and how patiently they have put up with them despite the wrongs done, and so they leave them mistresses of all their worldly possessions.

The second point of our instruction pertains to your household. You should carefully, diligently, wisely, and profitably distribute the property and goods which your husband acquires through his own efforts, his position, or his income. It is the man's role to acquire and bring in the provisions and his wife's role to organize and disperse them suitably, discreetly, and without parsimony. She should avoid extravagance, for that empties the purse and causes penury. To insure no wastefulness in any part of the household, she should supervise everything, rather then delegating everything to servants, and often oversee the accounts. The wise <u>housekeeper</u> should know all aspects of her household, even how to prepare the food, so that she will capably direct and order her servants and so that her husband will not worry if he invites guests to dinner at home. She should herself go into the kitchen, if necessary, to make appropriate arrangements for their service.

Her house must be well kept, everything in its place, and in good order. She will supervise the raising of her children and make sure they are neither coddled nor allowed to be too boisterous while they are young. The children must be kept clean and mannerly. Nor should their belongings nor the nurses' belongings be strewn about the house. All of her husband's clothes and materials must be properly cared for; the husband's neat appearance honors his wife. He should be served well and his peace and quiet protected. When he comes home for his meals, all should be ready, the tables and sideboards in order and well set. If she is prudent and wants to have her husband's good will and the praise of the world, a wife will always preserve a cheerful countenance.

Responsibilities and various things that men are expected to accomplish sometimes cause them great displeasure. By her gracious welcome, the prudent wife should be able to help her husband forget his troubles. When a man returns home burdened by daily worry and distress, it is a great relaxation to find his wife there to receive him wisely and graciously. It is only right that it should be so for the provider who sustains the trouble and difficulty of providing should at least have a warm welcome in his own home. Therefore, his wife should not quarrel, complain, or revile her household during meals. Anything the servants do badly should be reproved in few words without unpleasantness. Mealtime should be a happy occasion with no wrangling. If the husband is overwrought and ill-tempered, she should soothe him as best she can with soft words, rather than harassing him further with her own problems. Neither should she mention confidential matters at table in front of the servants, but rather save these for their private discussion.

This wise mistress of the household will arise early; having heard mass, said prayers, and returned home, she will give orders to the servants according to the requirements of the day. Then she will do some useful work such as spinning or sewing. When her chambermaids have finished their tasks, she will expect them to do the same, for neither she nor her serving-women should spend any hour in idleness. After buying flax at the market at a good price, she will have it spun by poor women in the town. However, she must never exploit their labor by any sort of trick or stratagem, since exploitation is damnable and would only discredit her. The women will make linen, both coarse and fine, tablecloths as well as towels. Having smoothly-woven, fine linens is a well-earned, honest pleasure for any woman who is careful and provident. She can take great pleasure in white, sweet-smelling linens stored in her coffers. These may be used for any special guests her husband invites to stay with them at the house, for which she will be highly praised.

The wise housewife will waste nothing the poor could use. Before leftovers spoil and clothes become moth-eaten, she will give them away. For the good of her soul and the virtue of charity, she will not limit her gifts to only these castoffs, but often will give wine and meat from her own table to poor women in childbed, to invalids, and to her poorer neighbors. Wisely, as her resources permit, she will realize that the virtue of this almsgiving is the only treasure she can take with her from this world. She will not be the poorer for it; however, she must use discretion in choosing the recipients of her charity.

In all this, the wife will be wisely gracious, with a pleasant and honest countenance. Receiving and welcoming her husband's friends and associates courteously, she will speak gently to everyone. Her neighbors will appreciate her as provider of good company, small necessary trifles, and friendship in need. Never ill-tempered with her servants, nor speaking to them rudely or harassing them all day over nothing, she will reprove them straightforwardly when they misbehave and threaten to expel them if they do not improve, but do all this without shouting or commotion the neighbors can hear. Some foolish creatures believe that to be considered good housekeepers they must be disagreeable and make trouble for their husbands and households over nothing. So they make great disturbances over trivialities, criticizing everything and chattering unceasingly. That sort of household violates our doctrine. Our disciples are to be wise in all actions, never intemperate, never malicious, never evil-intentioned, nor babbling, which is most unbecoming to a woman.

2. How women of property and city women should be suitably dressed, and how they should protect themselves against those who would deceive them.

The third point necessary for you women of property in the good towns, as well as women of the bourgeoisie, concerns your clothing and apparel. Do not go to extremes either in expense or in style. Five principal reasons should influence you to avoid extravagance. First of all, it is sinful and displeasing to God to pay too much attention to the body. Secondly, one really never is more admired for pompous, vulgar behavior, but rather less. Thirdly, it wastes money. It impoverishes and empties the purse. Fourth, one sets a bad example for others, encouraging them to the same or worse. The mature woman imitating a young girl's airs and the bourgeois woman who feels she must inflate her own status encourage frivolity and ostentation to grow and multiply daily. Each woman is tempted to outdo the other. Therefore, many people are harmed and impoverished, in France and elsewhere. Fifth and finally, unseemly, exaggerated costume prompts others to sin by envious murmuring or unbridled covetousness, both of which greatly displease God.

So, dear friends, since extravagance is worthless and potentially so harmful, do not take great pleasure in such frivolities. Wear such costumes as are suitable for yourself and your husband. She who belongs to the bourgeoisie and wears garments appropriate for a gentlewoman, and the demoiselle who sports what a lady should wear, and so on up the steps on society's ladder, clearly overstep the bounds of propriety. Custom well regulated in any country restrains ostentation.

Now to the fourth point, namely, protecting yourself from blame and ill-repute because of appearance, cost, or style of your clothing. Even though a woman may be inspired only by good will and has neither a wicked act nor thought in her body, the world will never believe it if she is indiscreet about her clothes. False opinions will be formed no matter how good she is in reality. Thus any woman wishing to preserve her good name should cultivate unpretentiousness in her dress and accoutrements. She should avoid clothes that are too tight, too low-cut, or have other details in bad taste. She should especially avoid styles that are too flashy, too costly, or too suggestive.

Besides all this, a woman must have poise and restraint in her bearing and countenance. Nothing is more unbecoming than a loud and undisciplined manner. Similarly, nothing is more pleasant in a woman than a handsome face and graceful speech. Even though young, a woman should be temperate, not disorderly, in laughter and games. Knowing how to take everything in her stride, she must act suitably, never speaking coyly but rather elegantly, gently, and without affectation. Her look should be reticent, attentive, and as joyful as the occasion warrants.

A women's exaggerated clothes and ill-considered manners can lead to evil gossip and even more dangerous results. Evil men may think she is trying to attract their attention, so they will feel free to make improper advances. She may never have contemplated such an idea but only acted on her own natural inclination for her own pleasure. Yet men of various sorts will pursue such women and devise ways to attract their love.

What should a wise young woman do to avoid the blame, harm, and dishonor which are the only possible results of such love affairs? Never listen to such men-about-town. Do not behave like certain idlers who are only too pleased to be pursued with grandiose gestures. They think it fine to say, "I am loved by everyone—a sure sign I am attractive and have considerable merit. I won't love any one but will please them all. I will keep the world guessing." That is no way to protect your honor. Indeed, no woman can maintain this state of affairs for long. Her reputation will plummet, whoever she is. Therefore, the moment the wise woman notices any sign that a man has designs upon her, she should give him every opportunity to withdraw. Persistently discouraging him by her words and her manner, she must persevere until he realizes he does not attract her. Yet, if he challenges her, she should reply in this fashion:

"Sire, if you have any romantic thoughts about me, kindly stop thinking them. I swear to you I have no interest in such a love affair, nor ever will I any day of my life. No man nor anything in creation will be capable of changing my mind. Take it for certain that I will persevere in this idea throughout my life. You waste your time if you give it another thought. Control yourself. Don't look at me that way. Don't say such things to me. On my word, I will be greatly displeased and try never to go near you. I tell you this now, once and for all, nor will I ever have anything more to say on this subject. Now, good-bye!"

Thus briefly, without lingering at length, the good, wise young woman who cherishes her honor will reply to every man who makes propositions to her. Her looks must be in keeping with her words. Her glances and bodily signs must not give any encouragement to a man who for any moment might think he has a chance of success.

If he sends her any gift whatsoever she must refuse it definitively. She who accepts a gift sells herself. If anyone gives her a message from a man, she must say pointedly and with a severe expression that she does not want to hear another word about him. If any household maid or servant dares to speak of this matter to her, she must dismiss that person from her service. Such an imprudent servant is not dependable. Therefore, she must find some pretext for eliminating this servant without disrupting her household and, above all, without her husband hearing of it. For, despite her good intentions, such information might provoke him to some rash fury of action which, no matter how she might try to calm him, would be dangerous and unnecessary. She must protect herself prudently, keep her peace, and be persistent: In the long run, there is no man who will not give up.

For the same reasons, she should not discuss this with a neighbor or anyone else. Gossip always is repeated. A spiteful man who cannot bear a woman's rejection will devise ways to avenge himself if he hears that his exploits are being discussed among the women. To soothe himself, he will boast of the affair among the men, there being no point in his not speaking of it. This reflects poorly upon the woman.

Moreover, women wishing to protect themselves from blame should avoid bad or dishonest company. Clerics, lords, and other people often arrange gatherings in such places as gardens, using the pretext of entertaining a group of people to conceal some machination or personal love affair. If a woman knows perfectly well that such a gathering is not what it appears to be, she must not provide the cover for someone else's intention and thus contribute to evil and sin. She should not attend if she knows or even has any suspicion of this. Before going anywhere, the wise woman will consider with whom, by what means, and who will be where she is going.

Some women travel on pilgrimages away from town in order to frolic and kick up their heels in jolly company. But this is only sin and folly. It is a sin to use God as excuse and shelter for frivolity. Such pilgrimages are entirely without merit.

Nor should a young woman go trotting about town, as is the custom—on Monday to St. Avoye; on Tuesday, to who knows where; on Friday to St. Catherine, and elsewhere on the other days. Even if some do it, there is no need for it. Of course, we do not wish to prevent anyone from doing good works. But considering a woman's youth and exuberance, plus men's desire to seduce women, as well as the fact that words so often are spoken so readily and so rashly, the surest thing for the soul's profit and the body's honor is to avoid the habit of trotting here and there. God is everywhere to hear the prayers of his devout believers, wherever they happen to be, and He wishes all things done discreetly and not necessarily at will. Bathing establishments, public baths, and other such gatherings which women too often frequent are needless convivialities and superfluous expenditures which lead to no good. For all these and similar reasons, a wise woman who loves honor and wishes to avoid censure should exercise great caution.

3. Wherein it speaks of the wives of merchants.

Now we speak of merchants' wives, namely, women married to men occupied with commerce, of whom there are many very rich ones in Paris and elsewhere. The wives of these men maintain great and costly establishments. This is even more true in other cities and countries than in Paris, notably in Venice, Genoa, Florence, Lucca, and Avignon. However, even though extravagance never is a virtue, in those places the women are more to be excused than in these parts of France, because differences among the upper class are fewer than in Paris and hereabouts. That is, here the social differences are more marked among queens, duchesses, countesses, ladies, and demoiselles. Therefore, in France, the noblest realm in the world, everything should be most orderly—as the ancient customs of France have established, no matter what exists elsewhere. As I have said several times, the wife of a laborer in the Low Countries has equal status with the wife of an ordinary artisan in Paris; but the ordinary artisan's wife does not have the importance of a burgher's wife, nor does that woman, in turn, have the social status of a demoiselle. The demoiselle is unlike a lady, the lady dissimilar to a countess or duchess, and neither of these is comparable to a queen. Each ought to maintain her proper place in society and, along with this, her particular lifestyle. But these rules are not at all well observed today in France, nor, regrettably, are many of the other old, good, once typical customs.

The unfortunate results are pride and snobbery never so outrageous as they are now among all classes of people, from the great to the low. The chronicles and histories of the past suggest the changes between then and now. In Italy, as we have stated, women still make a greater display, though I admit it is not as costly to maintain elegance there as here, where to judge by the company they keep and the follies they commit, they try to surpass one another by conduct as much as by clothes.

Since we are speaking of merchants' wives, let me remind you of one truly outrageous woman who lived not at all like the merchants' wives of Venice or Genoa. Those merchants travel overseas, having their representatives in other countries; they buy at wholesale and conduct a large-scale business, and likewise transport large bales of their merchandise to other countries, thus earning their wealth. Such as these are called noble merchants. But the merchants of whom we now speak buy at wholesale and sell at retail for four crowns worth of merchandise. They can undersell or oversell even if they are wealthy. Yet they put on the airs of nobility; plenty of them do it.

Anyway, this particular woman made a huge display at her lying-in for her recently-born child. Before entering her room, one passed through two other very fine chambers; in each one was a large ornamental bed, richly curtained; in the second was a large dresser decorated like an altar, all covered with silver vessels. Only then did one enter the woman's own bedchamber. Large and handsome, it was hung all round with tapestries marked with her coat-of-arms richly worked in fine gold thread from Cyprus. The bed, large and beautifully curtained with a single hanging, and the rug surrounding the bed, on which one could walk, were likewise embroidered with gold. The great, wide display sheets beneath the coverlet were of such fine toile from Rheims that they were valued at three hundred francs. Over the coverlet, woven in thread of gold, was yet another great coverlet of linen fine as silk, all in one piece without seams—something newly invented and very expensive—which one might estimate to be worth two hundred francs or more. Besides, it was so long and so wide that it covered the large bed completely, hanging over the border of the other coverlet, touching the floor on all sides.

In that room was a great sideboard displaying a panoply of gilded vessels. Sitting in the bed was the woman herself, dressed in crimson silk, propped up against large pillows covered in the same silk and decorated with pearl buttons, wearing the headdress of a lady. God knows what other superfluous expenses there were for that celebration. She immoderately surpassed the ritual baths, refreshments, customary in Paris for gatherings of women friends and relatives celebrating the birth of a child.

Although there have been other displays, this one surpasses them all and so is worth describing in this book. The affair indeed was reported in the queen's chamber, whereupon some remarked that Parisians have too much blood, the abundance of which sometimes brings on particular maladies (that is, great riches are capable of corrupting). Therefore, it would be better if the king were to impose upon these merchants some additional tax or tithe, or obtain from them a large loan, so that their wives would not be tempted to try to rival the queen of France, who could scarcely have done more. Such displays are out of all proportion, coming from presumption rather than good judgment. They gain scorn rather than admiration, for though these women take upon themselves the status of great ladies or princesses, by no means are they really such, and they cannot be called so. Certainly, they do not lose the name "merchant's wife."

Indeed, in Lombardy such commercial venturers are not called "merchants," but rather "retailers," since they sell in small lots. Theirs is great folly to dress up in other people's costumes when all know who they really are, or to take on another's estate rather than being content with their own. If such people who indulge in exaggerated costume or status were to give up their commerce and take on the nobleman's many horses and estates, their manner of life would follow naturally. But it is ridiculous to feel no shame in selling one's merchandise and carrying on business, and yet to feel shame at wearing the corresponding costume. It has its own luster for those who wear it appropriately; the merchant's place is good and honorable in France and in every other country. Those pretending to finery must be considered disguised. We do not say this to diminish their honor, for, again, the merchant's place is excellent and good for anyone who fulfills it properly. Our good intent is to offer counsel and advice to merchants' wives to avoid ostentation. Not only is it not good for either soul or body, but it can cause new taxes for their husbands. So, no matter how great their wealth, it is better for them to wear suitable clothes—which can be handsome, rich, and decorous—well adapted to their lives, without any pretentions to being something other than what they are.

Good Lord, what can such people do with their possessions? They would be well advised to lay up treasure in Heaven according to the admonition of the Scriptures, for this earthly journey is short and that other is eternal. So it would be profitable, as well as good provision for the future, if they were to share their riches with the poor in true charity. No doubt some of them do, and a good thing it is. By that noble and worthy virtue of charity, so pleasing to God, they can buy the field mentioned in the parable, where the greatest <u>treasure</u> is hidden. This is a joy of Paradise.

<u>Pope Leo</u> describes that holy virtue in his *Sermon on the Apparition*, saying, "So great is the virtue of charitable mercy that without it other virtues cannot flourish. However much a human being may be abstinent, devout, avoiding sin, and having all other virtues, without this one to enhance the others, all is vain. On Judgment Day, it will carry the banner before all those who have practiced it and loved it in this world, leading them to the place where the Lord will receive them into Paradise, condemning those who have lacked it with a definitive sentence to Hell." The Scriptures bear witness to this. So, rich women, you can save

yourselves by avoiding frauds and trickery in your business dealings and your behavior with other human beings.

4. Which speaks of widows young and old.

In order for this work to be more completely profitable to
women of all classes, we will speak now to <u>widows</u> among the
more common people, having already discussed the case of
widowed princesses.

Dear friends, we pity each one of you in the state of widowhood
because death has deprived you of your husbands, whoever they
may have been. Moreover, much anguish and many trying problems afflict you, affecting the rich in one manner and those not
rich in another. The rich are troubled because unscrupulous people
commonly try to despoil them of their inheritance. The poor, or
at least, those not at all rich, are distressed because they find no
pity from anyone for their problems. Along with the grief of
having lost your mate, which is quite enough, you also must
suffer three trials in particular, which assault you whether you
are rich or poor.

First is that, undoubtedly, you will find harshness and lack of
consideration or sympathy everywhere. Those who honored you
during the lifetime of your husbands, who may well have been
officials or men of importance, now will pay little attention to
you and barely even bother to be friendly. The second distress
facing you is the variety of lawsuits and demands of certain people
regarding debts, claims on your property, and income. Third is
the evil talk of people who are all too willing to attack you, so
that you hardly know what you can do that will not be criticized.
In order to arm you with the sensible advice to protect yourself
against these, as well as other overpowering plagues, we wish to
suggest some things you may find useful. Though some of them
we have already spoken of elsewhere, nevertheless they also fit
particularly well here.

Against the coldness you undoubtedly will find in everyone—

the first of the three tribulations of widowhood—there are three possible remedies. Turn toward God, who was willing to suffer so much for human creatures. Reflecting on this will teach you patience, a quality you will need greatly. It will bring you to the point where you will place little value on the rewards and honors of this world. First of all, you will learn how undependable all earthly things are.

The second remedy is to turn your heart to gentleness and kindliness in word and courtesy to everyone. You will overcome the hardhearted and bend them to your will by gentle prayers and humble requests.

Third, in spite of what we just said about quiet humility in words, apparel, and countenance, nevertheless you must learn the judgment and behavior necessary to protect yourself against those only too willing to get the better of you. You must avoid their company, having nothing to do with them if you can help it. Rather, stay quietly in your own house, not involving yourself in an argument with a neighbor, not even with a servingman or maid. By always speaking quietly while protecting your own interests, as well as by mingling little with miscellaneous people if you don't need to, you will avoid anyone taking advantage of you or ruining you.

Concerning the lawsuits which may stalk you, learn well how to avoid all sorts. They damage a widow in many ways. First of all, if she is not informed, but on the contrary is ignorant in legal affairs, then it will be necessary for her to place herself in the power of someone else to solicit on behalf of her needs. Those others generally lack diligence in the affairs of women, willingly deceiving them and charging them eight crowns for six. Another problem is that women cannot always come and go at all hours, as a man would do, and therefore, if it is not too damaging for her, it may be better to let go some part of what is her due rather than involve herself in contention. She should consider circumspectly any reasonable demands made against her; or if she finds herself obliged to be the plaintiff, she should pursue her rights courteously and should attempt alternatives for achieving her ends. If assailed by debts, she must inform herself of what rights her creditors have and make an appropriate plan of action. Even presupposing there is no official "owing" letter or witness, if her conscience tells her that something is owing, she must not keep anything that really belongs to another. That would burden her husband's soul as well as her own, and God indeed might send her so many additional, expensive misfortunes that her original losses would be doubled.

But if she protects herself wisely from deceitful people who make demands without cause, she is behaving as she should. If, in spite of all this, she is obliged to go to court, she should understand three things necessary for all who take action. One is to act on the advice of wise specialists in customary law and clerks who are well versed in legal sciences and in the law. Next is to prepare the case for trial with great care and diligence. Third is to have enough money to afford all this. Certainly if one of these things is lacking, no matter how worthy the cause, there is every danger the case will be lost.

Therefore, a widow in such a situation necessarily must look for older specialists in customary law, those most experienced in various sorts of cases, rather than depending on younger men. She should explain her case to them, showing them her letters and her titles, listening carefully to what they say without concealing anything which pertains to the case, whether in her favor or against her. Counsel can utilize in her behalf only what she tells him. According to his advice, either she must plead steadfastly or accede to her adversaries. If ever she goes to court, she must plead diligently and pay well. Her case will so benefit.

If it is necessary for her to do these things, and if she wishes to avoid further trouble and bring her case to a successful conclusion, she must take on the heart of a man. She must be constant, strong, and wise in judging and pursuing her advantage, not crouching in tears, defenseless, like some simple woman or like a poor dog who retreats into a corner while all the other dogs jump on him. If you do that, dear woman, you will find most people so lacking in pity that they would take the bread from your hand because they consider you either ignorant or simple-minded, nor would you find additional pity elsewhere because they took it. So, do not work on your own or depend on your own judgment, but hire always the best advice, particularly on important matters you do not understand.

Thus, your affairs should be well managed among those of you widows who have reached a certain age and do not intend to remarry. Young widows must be guided by their relatives or friends until they have married again, conducting themselves particularly gently and simply so as not to acquire a doubtful reputation that might cause them to lose their prospects and their advantage.

The remedy against the third of the three misfortunes pursuing a widow—being at the mercy of evil tongues—is that she must be careful in every way possible not to give anyone reason to talk against her because of appearance, bearing, or clothing. All these should be simple and seemly, and the woman's manners quiet and discreet regarding her body, thus giving no cause for gossip. Nor should the widow be too friendly or seemingly intimate with any man who may be observed frequenting her house, unless he is a relative. Even then discretion should be observed, including the presence of a father-in-law, brother, or priest, who should be permitted few visits or none at all. For no matter how devout a woman herself may be, the world is inclined to speak evil. She should also maintain a household where there is no suspicion of any great intimacy or familiarity, however fine she knows her staff to be and despite the innocence of her own thoughts. Nor should her household expenses give people opportunity for slandering her. Moreover, to protect her property better, she should make no ostentatious display of servants, clothing, or foods, for it better suits a widow to be inconspicuous and without any extravagance whatsoever.

Because widowhood truly provides so many hardships for

women, some people might think it best for all widows to remarry. This argument can be answered by saying that if it were true that the married state consisted entirely of peace and repose, this indeed would be so. That one almost always sees the contrary in marriages should be a warning to all widows. However, it might be necessary or desirable for the young ones to remarry. But for all those who have passed their youth and who are sufficiently comfortable financially so that poverty does not oblige them, remarriage is complete folly. Though some who want to remarry say there is nothing in life for a woman alone, they have so little confidence in their own good sense that they will claim that they don't know how to manage their own lives. But the height of folly and the greatest of all absurdities is the old woman who takes a young husband: There a joyful song rarely is heard for long. Although many pay dearly for their foolishness, nobody will sympathize with them—for good reason.

5. Which concerns unmarried girls.

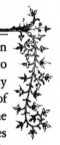

Certainly it is not right to forget one important group: women or young girls who are still virgins. Let us speak of them in two different categories: those intending to maintain their virginity all their lives, for love of God; and those awaiting the time of their marriage, arranged according to their parents' wishes. The differences in their intentions should be paralleled by differences in their apparel, their speech, and their style of life even in this world.

A devout, solitary life is most suitable for those disposed to piety and solitude. Although such a life benefits everyone, more pious behavior suits some of them more than other women. If they are obliged to work to earn their livelihood, or if they enter service in a household, after their daily chores are done, they must observe their obligations in God's service: devout prayers, fasting, and discreet abstinence. These deprivations must not be so severe as to make them impossible to endure or to continue, nor troubling to their minds, for nothing excessively rigorous should be attempted beyond reason. The good that they do in keeping themselves free from sin in both thought and word will be equalled by their actions. After all, there would be little merit in being poor, chaste, devoted, and abstinent and simultaneously a great sinner. Everyone striving to the good should make a clean offering to God. To present the king with a fine, savory food mixed with disgusting filth would give Him no pleasure. Rightfully, He would refuse it. Moreover, the maidens' language should be good, simple, and devout, neither excessive nor prolix. Their clothes should be modest without coquetry, their demanor humbly quiet, with lowered eyes and diffident speech. Their joy should be in hearing God's word and frequenting His church. Those chosing this life were born in a good hour, for they have selected the better part.

Maidens awaiting marriage can be altogether different. Nonetheless, in bearing, behavior, and speech they should be temperate and honest. Especially in church they must be decorously quiet, looking at their books with eyes lowered; in the street or in public they should seem modest and calm; in the house, never idle but always busy with some domestic task; in their clothing, wearing garments and dresses well made, graceful, and in good taste, as well as clean and neat; in their grooming, their hair must be well combed, not hanging over their cheeks or in any way ill-kempt; in their manner of speaking, agreeable and courteous to everyone, humble, and not too talkative.

At social gatherings, dances, and assemblies, they especially should be on their best behavior, for more people will have their eyes on them than upon other women. Dancing modestly and singing in a low voice, their glances should not vaguely wander here and there. They should not be overly bold among the men, but rather ought to stay close to their mothers and the other women. Young girls also should avoid becoming embroiled in debates or arguments with servants or maids, or anyone else, for insolence and combativeness are not only unattractive but possibly damaging to their futures, because servants tend to spread evil or false reports with little provocation. Young women should never be bold, skittish, or ribald, especially in the presence of any men whatsoever, whether clerks in the household, servingmen, or retainers attached to the family, and under no circumstances should they allow any man to touch them, fondle them, or be too playful. This would damage both decorum and their good name.

A maiden also ought to be devout, especially toward Our Lady, St. Catherine, and all the virgin saints. She should willingly read their lives and <u>fast</u> on holy days. Food and drink require special sobriety. She should content herself to eat small quantities of meat with dilute wines, for gluttony in food and drink is very unattractive in young girls. She must also be careful never to be seen affected by too much wine, for she who has such a fault would be expected to have no other good. Therefore, all maidens should water their wine and make it a habit to drink little.

Beyond the good manners normally expected of young women, they should be humble and obedient to their fathers and mothers, diligently serving them and depending upon their judgment exclusively for their prospective marriage arrangements, never considering marriage without their consent. Such well-instructed young women are very attractive to men who wish to marry.

6. Which discusses how older women should conduct themselves toward younger women and what customs they should observe.

All too frequently, debate and discord spoil the association between old people and young. In opinions as well as language, they differ enough to dislike one another as if they were two different species. Age differences cause divergencies in morals and life conditions. In order to make peace in the war among women of varying stages in life, let us consider certain things useful to that end.

First of all, let us examine the habits suitable to the older ones. All older women should be wise in their actions, clothing, appearance, and speech. Wisdom in action should come from the knowledge based on experience and remembrance of things seen in their time. Therefore, a woman should act upon past example. If she knows good or evil will result from a particular behavior, she will understand that similar situations will turn out the same way. Thus, old people commonly are thought wiser than young ones for two reasons. Their understanding is greater, based upon deeper reflection. Second, having seen more in the past, they can profit by example.

Expected to be wiser, old people are all the more to be censured if they are not. It is reprehensible or simply ridiculous when old women behave without judgment or simplemindedly, or commit follies which mere youth suggests to the young. For that they are reproved. Therefore, the older woman should avoid things considered foolish. She should not dance, caper, nor laugh raucously. However, if she is joyous by nature—as some are more than others, and exuberance itself surely is not a bad thing—she should express her vivacity suitably, not in the manner of young people but by amusing herself without excessive playfulness.

Though wise and poised, she should not be ill-natured, sharp-tongued, or ungracious, giving the impression that she is all good sense. Her good sense and wise discretion will keep her from those passions ordinarily ascribed to older people, such as being petulant, querulous, and quarrelsome. When inclined to complain or to quarrel, the wise old woman will say to herself: "Good Lord, what is the matter with you! What do you expect? Is this the behavior of a wise woman to carry on in this manner? Why are you so disturbed? Things badly done you simply cannot change. Calm down. Stop speaking so arrogantly. If you could only see how unattractive your face is when you are agitated, you would be horrified! Be more agreeable and kinder to your servants and to those whose behavior you must correct. Reprove them more courteously. Avoid such anger, for behavior of this sort is displeasing to God. Your body is the worse for it; and, it makes you less liked. Have patience!" Thus the wise older woman should speak to herself when moved to anger.

With equal good judgment, the older woman should clothe herself in ample, suitable garments. Machaut said truly: Old women's coy coquetry is a subject for mockery. The old woman's face should be composed and venerable. For, in truth, no matter what anyone says, it is a great ornament and object of honor and reverence and well reflects the nature of an elderly person, man or woman, who is wise and honorable in all things. Her words always should be dictated by discretion; false, dishonest, or disordered remarks should never come from her mouth. Nothing is more ridiculous than silly or indecorous words from the old, who ought to set a good example.

To return to the contentiousness and lack of agreement commonly found between older people and younger ones: The older woman should be sufficiently aware of this problem. When she feels any antipathy to young people because of their youth itself, which really she cannot endure, here is how she should counsel herself: "Good Lord! You were once young yourself! Remember what things you did then. Would you have wanted to be spoken of this way? Why are you so hard on them? Consider the great tribulations of youth! You should pity them, for you have passed that way yourself. Of course one must reprove and scold young people for their follies, but certainly not hate them nor speak ill of them, for they neither know what they are doing nor do they know themselves. Therefore, you should treat them kindly, and correct by good example those for whom you still have some responsibility. Rather than blaming or defaming them, as others do, excuse them through pity, taking into account youth's ignorance, which interferes with better judgment.

"Dear God! Examine your own thoughts. Don't you still have the feelings that youth gives to young people? If you do not still enjoy such indulgences, it is because that same age which has matured you has chilled you. Still you are not blameless, but

perhaps have greater and worse sins than you ever had at that age
or, indeed, than many young people have ever had. If youth's
vices have left you, worse ones may have replaced them, such as
envy, greed, anger, impatience, and gluttony, especially for wines.
Because of these you often commit great indiscretions. You who
should be wise do not have the strength of character to resist the
inclinations of age, which attract you, tempt you, and urge you
on. Yet you expect young people to be wiser than you are and
to resist the temptations which youth makes them covet, thereby
doing what you yourself cannot do. So leave young people in
peace. Don't whisper slander against them, for if you look carefully
at yourself, you will have enough to reform. The vices of youth
have left you not because of your virtue but simply because nature
no longer inclines you in that direction, and that is the reason
they seem so terrible to you."

7. How young women should conduct themselves toward their elders.

Now we come to the teachings which protect young people
from disputing, offending, or despising the elderly but rather
encourage them to revere their elders.

Dear children and young people who are able to learn and
remember: This lesson will instruct you profitably in the habits
and customs you should observe toward the honorable elderly.
Five principal points comprise it. First is the respect you should
bear them; the second considers obedience; the third, fear; the
fourth considers the aid and comfort you owe them; and the fifth
points out the good they can do you and the benefit you can
receive from them.

Reverence is the first quality you owe them, through due
gratitude. There is a story that once there was a king of Greece
named Lycurgus, who established many fine laws. Among these
was a law that young people should honor and revere their elders.
It happened that one time that king (or perhaps one of his succes-

sors) sent his ambassadors into a foreign country, and with them went young noblemen of their own country to protect, serve, and bear them company. When the time came for the ambassadors to state publicly their diplomatic mission, the crowd was very large in the place where they were to be seated. People had assembled there to hear what they were going to say, and all places were taken. Then there came an elderly man to listen with the others. He went groping about trying to find a place to sit, but found none of his countrymen courteous enough to offer him a place. When he came to the seats of the young foreigners, immediately, in keeping with the law of their country, they arose and made a place for the old man. That act was widely noted, praised, and in every way esteemed.

The Romans had the same custom when they were governed by sovereign laws. Therefore, children and young people, let this be an example among you, for right and reason dictate that the elderly must be honored. Even the Holy Scriptures testify to that. Know also that doing this will be to your great credit, for the merit is reflected not on the object of the respect but on those who show it. If, in fact, you owe them honor, it follows that you ought to avoid mocking them or saying or doing disrespectful things. Certainly you must not do anything that might harm, outrage, or aggrieve them. Nor should you argue with them like badly behaved children who in reproach call "old men" or "old women" those for whom this should be a true compliment if they were honorable.

The second point on obedience insists that you sincerely ought to believe that elders are wiser than you are. So you must respect older people's opinions more than your own—at least those of the wise. Use their advice, and guide yourself by their counsel in your most important affairs. Then you cannot be blamed for what you do.

Third, although your elders may not be powerful enough in body to overcome you, and you need never fear their physical force, still you should stand in awe of them as if they were your fathers and mothers. Through their good sense and their knowledge, the old have inherent in themselves the rod of correction which you need; demands your respect in their presence, for they note improper behavior immediately.

The fourth point: When elders need your comp should aid and comfort them by the strength of your own bo. and also with your possessions. Pity their illnesses and infirmities, remembering that if you live long enough, you yourself will become helpless and feeble and will wish for someone to comfort you. You should lavish this care also because it represents very great charity and alms for God. There is no greater infirmity than old age.

The fifth item concerns the benefit which you receive from the old, which above all should encourage you to support them with compassion. They established the sciences and likewise the laws which teach you and govern you. You can never altogether return the great benefits you have received from them. Moreover, in all lands, countries, and kingdoms, these same benefits continually support the worthy rules and ordinances of the world. In spite of the strength of the young, if it weren't for the wisdom of the ancient sages, the world would fall into confusion. The Scriptures demonstrate this: "Woe unto the kingdom where the king or lord is a child." That refers to someone young in morals. So, young people, conduct yourselves with your elders by these rules so that your good fortune and reputation may increase, for opinions of good renown coming from the mouths of ancient, wise people have great authority and elicit considerable attention. The young desiring such good names are well advised to keep their elders' good will so that they will praise them. (All this, of course, applies as much to young men as to young women.)

However, let us return to the instruction of women. Goodness and wisdom come from elderly people, notably those who are honorable and wise. We will not speak of certain wretched old people hardened in their sins and vices, in whom there is no sense or kindness. These are to be avoided like the plague. But a young woman desiring a good reputation should seek out the ones who are fine and honest. She should go to public gatherings more willingly in their company than with young people. First, she will be more greatly praised for it. Besides, she will have greater security. If any misadventure occurs, the blame and ill repute would scarcely fall on anyone there in the honorable company of a well-respected, elderly woman.

Thus, the young woman should serve, respect, and revere the older one, tolerating correction with good grace if she should do anything wrong or imprudent. Never should she answer disrespectfully, but rather hold her peace, avoiding what she knows will displease. In so doing, she greatly will be praised. Therefore, if the old treat the young considerately and the young reciprocate to the old, peace will be preserved among those often in great contention, and it will endure.

8. Which speaks of artisans' wives and how they should conduct themselves.

Now we must speak of the lifestyle of women married to the artisans who live in the cities and good towns, both in Paris and elsewhere. Of course, these women will find valuable the good advice already given to others if they so wish. However, although certain trades are more highly regarded than others (for instance, goldsmiths, embroiderers, armorers, and tapestry weavers are thought more distinguished than masons and shoemakers), we address the wives of all craftsmen. All of them should be attentive and diligent.

If they wish to earn money honorably, they should urge their husbands and their workmen to take up their trade early in the morning and leave it late. No trade is so good that if one is not hard-working one barely lives from one crust of bread to the next. Urging the others to action, she herself should put her hand to the task, making sure that she knows the craft so well that she can direct the workmen if her husband is not there and reprove them if they do not work well. She must admonish them against laziness; a master often is deserted by irresponsible, lethargic workmen. When her husband gets a commission for some difficult and unusual task, she firmly must convince him not to accept any work through which he might suffer a loss. If he does not personally know his client, she should advise him to produce as little work as possible on <u>credit</u>. Several already have been ruined by this. Sometimes greed to earn more or the importance of the tendered offer tempts one to such risks.

The artisan's wife should keep her husband attracted to her by love, so that he will stay at home the more willingly, not tempted to join those foolish bands of <u>young men in taverns</u> and not likely to dissipate his earnings with superfluous, outrageous expenses, as many young artisans do, especially in Paris. Rather, treating him with tenderness, she should keep him nearby. Common wisdom has it that three things drive a man from his home: a quarrelsome wife, a smoking hearth, and a leaking roof.

Furthermore, she should be willing to stay home, not running here and there every day, gossiping in the neighborhood to find out what everybody else is doing, nor frequenting her cronies. All this makes for poor housekeeping. Neither is it good for her to go to so many gatherings across town, nor to go traveling off needlessly on pilgrimages, which invariably would cause unnecessary expense.

She also should encourage her husband to let them live within their income so that their expenses will not be greater than their earnings, which would force them into debt at the year's end. If she has children, she first should have them taught at school so that they will better know how to serve God; then she ought to have them apprenticed to some trade so that they can earn their living. For a great gift to one's child is knowledge, a skill, or a trade. Beyond these, the mother above all must protect the child from affectation and indulgence. These greatly discredit children of the good towns—and reflect badly on their fathers and mothers, otherwise expected to be the source of virtue and good habits. Sometimes, however, parents so spoil their children by pampering them during their years of growing up that they cause their offsprings' ultimate misfortune and ruination.

9. Which speaks to women servants and chambermaids.

Now follows advice on living well dedicated to the many women servants and chambermaids of Paris and other places. Young women needing to earn their living often are placed in household service when young. Therefore, they may have been prevented from learning much about salvation and from serving God by hearing Masses and sermons and by saying *Pater Nosters* and other prayers. Though this may grieve the pious ones, demands of service do not allow the possibility. Therefore, it is a good idea to consider actions, deeds, and attitudes useful for these women's salvation, as well as some things they must carefully avoid.

All women servants ought to be excused if they cannot do certain things on God's behalf. Their mistresses and other women in easier circumstances would not similarly be excused from devotions. That is, someone in service, because she must earn her living, necessarily works very hard in this service, getting up early, going to bed late, having very little leisure, dining and supping only after others have finished eating, grabbing a bite here and there as she keeps on working, perhaps not even having enough food to sustain her but only eating eagerly and meagerly. If she does not fast on all the days the church requires, certainly she must be forgiven. Indeed, she may believe she cannot fast at all without damaging her body, which otherwise might fail her altogether.

However, such a servantwoman should not break her fast through gluttony, nor should she say, with foolish presumption: "I am a servant so I should not have to fast." Discretion and good conscience should guide her judgment. Some chambermaids, after all, are better off in every respect than some mistresses of households who fast and observe abstinences for the love of God. We do not speak, however, for the benefit of such paragons as these. What can the good servant do to be worthy to be saved? Rightfully, she should go often to church and there say her prayers. But certainly she must remember that God, who knows and sees all, asks only for the heart. And whoever gives her heart to Him will not fail to prosper. But even the one whose heart is imperfect still can save herself by avoiding all ugly, damaging sins; by remaining loyal in deed and word to her master and mistress; by serving them with diligent care; and by saying her *Pater Noster* and other prayers, even while performing her duties. Therefore, she who cannot be in church in person can have her heart there through her good intentions. Nevertheless, hardly anyone is so busy that if she really wants to arise early she will not have time to hear a Mass on most days, commending herself to God, then returning to her household tasks. By so conducting herself, and with other good works, a good servant certainly will assure her own salvation.

Following the habits of the Goliards and other such dubious characters, however, is a sure road to damnation. Servants imitating their wicked, foolish ways surely merit reproof. Certain false, greedy servants provide good service to flatter better in the great houses of the bourgeoisie and other rich people. There they are given considerable authority because they know how to appear to be good housekeepers. Supposed to buy meat, they go to the butcher cart, where they know all too well how to play both ends against the middle. They pretend that a certain cut costs more than in fact it does, and they keep the change. So, a quarter of mutton which they say costs them four gold crowns they buy for a mere ten silver crowns or less. So it is with other things. In this way, in the course of the year they do a lot of damage to the household budget.

On some days they do even more. They bring back from the butcher shop a tempting morsel which they have a baker bake into a meat pie at their master's expense. Then, when the master is at the law courts and their mistress at High Mass, they spread a luncheon in the kitchen with abundant good cheer because there is no shortage of drink—of course, they drink only of the house's best vintage. They invite in other maids from the street and still other cronies to join their joyous band; and then they proceed to stuff themselves. (Sometimes the brazen one even carries a big pastry to the room she keeps in town, and there her fine admirer comes for their mutual amusement.) Women who come to the main house to help with the laundry and scour the pots also are in the maid's band. These women do the heavy work around the place while she goes off to play. When the master and mistress return, they will find everything in order. The maid, of course, will have sent her companions away in good time and fully besotted with food and wine.

These cronies are useful to the housemaid for yet other purposes. While the mistress who herself is very busy will assume that her good servant is at the river washing the clothes, in reality, the servant is off at the baths in peace and quiet while her friends are doing her work. Certainly she is not paying them for it out of her own pocket. And if she also has cousins and friends who frequently visit her at the house, this raft of relatives and jolly company cost the establishment many a bottle of wine.

If such a woman serves in a household where the mistress is young, newly married, and a little naive, she finds herself in luck. She will flatter the master, speaking to him as a woman of experience and offering a lot of nonsense so that he will put her in charge of his wife as well as everything else. However, she will not stop at leading only the master around by the nose. She also will flatter the young woman. Therefore, through her wiles she will get the better of both of them until they do not believe in any other god but her. Then she will supervise wine and meat, candles, bread, fat and salt, and all expenses for the household. If the master sometimes complains that supplies disappear too fast, straightaway she will have her answer ready, saying that it is because of all the dinners the master gives and the friends he invites to drink with him. If some gallant promises, or actually gives her, a bonnet or new gown for delivering a message to her mistress, if she doesn't do it freely and willingly, then let her be burned!

Such greedy serving-maids are a great danger in a household. By the fine service they skillfully perform, with all of their flatteries and the good meals they prepare, keeping all things neatly and in orderly fashion, they blind people completely. Their fine talk and clever answers so confuse all hearers that nobody notices their great craftiness as they mix in devotion better to cover up their activities, even going to church with all of their loud prayers. There is the great peril. So you who are served beware of the danger and take care lest you be deceived. We speak also to you who serve so that you will abhor and avoid such things as these, for those who do them damn themselves into deserving death of both body and soul. Burning or burial alive have been the rewards for lesser evils.

10. Which speaks of the instruction of women of light morals.

Just as the sun shines on both the good and the wicked, let us extend our doctrine even to the frivolous, light-moraled, and dissolute. For even though they may be reprehensible, we should not forget that the most worthy person, Jesus Christ, was not displeased to associate with whores while converting them. So, if they chance to hear these words, with charity and the good intent that some of these women might gain and retain something from our teachings to enable them to withdraw from their foolish life (for no greater good work can be done than to turn the sinner from wickedness and sin), we will speak directly to them.

Open your eyes to the truth! Sinning, wretched women, withdraw while you have the light of day, before the night overtakes you. While life still breathes in your bodies, repent, lest death assail you and surprise you while you are in sin that will lead you straight to Hell. Nobody knows her final hour.

Note the filth of your despicable way of living. Not only have you incurred God's wrath, but also you are profoundly despised by the world. Every honest person avoids you as contaminated and in the streets averts his gaze in order not to look upon you. Why does your blind courage persist in plunging you into this swamp of abomination? How is it possible for a woman who by very nature and condition is honest, simple, and modest to fall so low that she can endure such baseness, perpetually living, drinking, and eating among men worse than swine? How do you endure men who beat you, drag you about, and threaten you, and because of whom you find yourself daily in danger of death? Alas, why are womanly decency and goodness transformed to such wantonness in you?

For Heaven's sake, you who bear the name of Christians and convert it to such baseness, get up and leave the dreadful muck. Do not allow your poor soul to be so burdened with the filth your vile bodies have reveled in. For merciful God will receive you if you wish to repent and cry for His mercy in great contrition. Consider the example of blessed Mary the Egyptian, who repented her frivolous life and was converted to God and now is a glorious saint in Paradise. Similarly, consider blessed Saint Affre, who offered in martyrdom her body, with which she had sinned, for love of Our Lord. Others in like manner also have been saved.

Any of you might make excuses for yourselves by saying that you would repent willingly except that three things discourage you. First, the dishonest men you frequent would not permit it. Then, the world which holds you in scorn would throw you out, pursuing you from all sides, shaming you so that never would you dare to be seen among good people. Finally, you would have nothing to live on because you have no craft or trade. We maintain that these reasons are not valid, because a remedy exists for each of them.

First, no matter how common a woman is or how familiar with large numbers of customers, if she determines to withdraw from sin no matter what happens, and if she cries mercy to God in repentance and draws near to Him with a firm intent never to backslide, He will protect her from all who would dissuade her. But if she wants to protect herself in fact and in behavior, she should at once give up her suggestive clothing and dress herself in a long, modest, simple gown. She should avoid her accustomed haunts, drawing close to a convent or a church in sincere prayer, attending sermons, devoutly and contritely confessing her sins to a wise confessor. She ought to answer plainly to all who would encourage her to sin that she would offer her body to martyrdom before she would indulge in sex. For since God has given her grace to repent and withdraw from her sinful life, she will not return to it while living, but would prefer to die first.

By firmly maintaining this resolution and calling God to her aid, she would protect herself from any wandering goliard. If she finds any man so wicked that she cannot escape from him, she should take her complaint to the law, which would pity her and protect her.

That the world would scorn her is the next invalid reason. She should not believe this because, in fact, the world will treat her very differently from what she expects. Good creatures who see her contrite and converted from her sinful, frivolous life would have great pity. They would call her to them, speaking words of encouragement to her, giving her occasion to persevere and to do good. When they observe her to be of such forthright devotion, gentleness, and humility, where earlier she had been shunned by everyone now she would be received and welcomed by all good people. So, through her efforts and God's mercy, she would have exchanged shame for honor. Why should this not be? When God has forgiven her and received her in His grace, should the world then cast her out? Any woman wallowing in shame and sin should desire an ascent to that state of virtue which she could attain if she wished.

That she would have no way of earning her living—the third reason—also is untrue. If her body is strong enough to perform evil and suffer bad nights, blows, and numerous other misfortunes, she should be strong enough to earn her wages otherwise. If she were willing, people eagerly would take her in to help with the laundry in the great houses, pity her, and gladly offer her work. Of course, she would have to be careful that they saw no trashiness or immorality in her behavior, nor any form of evil-doing.

She could spin; care for women lying-in; or tend the sick. She would live in a little room on a respectable street among good people. Living simply and soberly, never would she be seen drunk or gorged, ill-tempered or quarrelsome, or gossiping. No unseemly or dishonest words would come from her mouth, but rather she would always be courteous, humble, gentle, and would willingly perform good works for all people. Likewise, she should be sure that she did not attract men, for then she would lose everything. In so living to serve God and to earn her own support, she would profit more from one cent honestly earned than from one hundred received in sin.

11. Which speaks in praise of honest and chaste women.

Just as black differs from white and the difference best is perceived when they are set side by side, let us call greater attention to honest, chaste women by praising them. This is not to make them proud but to encourage their perseverance in doing good, making it seem more pleasurable to them, and so to stimulate all women to want to join their ranks. Just as fallen women can, with God's grace, raise themselves up to conversion and salvation, so good ones, through temptation of the devil and their own human frailty, can be perverted and lost. The good pilgrim's true steadfastness is not really known until the end of the pilgrimage. Since human frailty inclines us to falter, no one should assume that she is more steadfast than St. Peter, David, Solomon, or any of those others of great knowledge who fell into evil ways.

Honorable women of chaste lives! All praise to you for your desire for good! Dear friends, the radiant glow of chastity should illuminate for us its noble properties along with the praises accorded it. Just as the good workman praised for a fine piece of work is pleased to work with ever greater skill, do likewise yourselves. Although all of chastity's properties are difficult to describe adequately, still let us celebrate certain ones particularly good and beautiful.

Chastity makes a person in whom it dwells agreeable to God; without it, nobody is thoroughly pleasing to Him. St. Ambrose shows this when he says that it turns the human creature into an angel. St. Bernard expresses the same idea: "What a fine thing Chastity is; it makes a human creature, conceived in sin and foul insemination, a clean and pleasing habitation for God." Chastity, he says, is the only virtue which even in this mortal world represents the immortality to come. Creatures who practice it are comparable to the blessed spirits in Heaven. The praiseworthy qualities that Holy Scripture records concerning this virtue are infinite.

Experience shows that in addition to chastity's high position in God's grace, it is praised in this world. No creature is so full of defects that, if she has a reputation for chastity, she will not be revered. The opposite also is true; whatever other good she may do, without chastity she has no true virtue. She will be mocked behind her back and never respected.

Gentle ladies, if you wish to delight in this virtue, do not hint or pretend you are chaste when the hidden truth is quite the contrary. God, before whom nothing is hidden, will know it well and will punish you for it. Let conscience guide you to truth. Do not imitate those foolish creatures who think that by talking about others' sins they will conceal their own, and who pretend they are honorable and hold certain behaviors in abomination. Such action deserves only contempt. However good a woman may be, she is all the better for keeping quiet about it, because she ought to assume others are equally good. Finding fault with others is no indication of virtue.

So do not put on airs, boasting of your chastity and despising or mocking others even if you know truly about their vices. Nor should you speak ill of them to your own advantage to show yourself the better. Two important reasons justify this advice. First, you do not know what might happen to you in the future nor whether you might fall to temptation. The common proverb says: "When the sheep is old, sometimes the wolf steals it away." The second reason is that even if you don't have this particular defect, perhaps you possess others worse and more displeasing to God, even if they may not seem particularly disreputable in this world.

Therefore pity the weak and pray for them, giving them opportunity to reform. Thank God that He preserved you from this sin, and beg Him for strength to avoid temptation to sin. Remain humble before God and do not be overconfident, but rather apprehensive. In this way we will be able to <u>conduct your chariot</u> to the end of your road of life and to the goal of glory God has promised you.

⚡ 12. Which speaks to the wives of laborers.

Now drawing close to the end of our discussion—for which the time has come—we will speak to the simple wives of village workers. For them it is hardly necessary to forbid expensive ornaments and extravagant clothes; for they are well protected from all that. Nevertheless, though commonly they are nourished with black bread, milk, bacon, and soup, their thirst quenched with water, and though they have heavy enough burdens to bear, still their lives often are more secure and better nourished than the lives of those seated in high places. Because all creatures, no matter what their estate, need instruction in living well, we wish these women to participate in our lessons.

Humble women living in the village, on the plains, or in the mountains! You often cannot hear what the church preaches about salvation except from your priest or chaplain in his brief Sunday instruction. If our lesson should reach your ears, remember it so that the ignorance which could mislead you will not hinder your salvation.

Know, first of all, that there is a single God: all powerful, completely good, just, wise, from whom nothing is hidden, and who rewards every being for good or evil according to what she deserves. He alone should be perfectly loved and served. Because He is so good, He holds agreeable all the service laid before Him with good heart. Because He is so wise, He recognizes everyone's potentialities; if the heart is in it, it is enough for each to do for Him with pure devotion whatever she is able. Some among you, by whose labor the world gains its sustenance and nourishment, have neither leisure nor ability to serve Him through fasting, saying prayers, or attending church, as do the women in the larger towns. Yet you have as great a need of salvation as they. You must serve Him in another manner.

Whole-heartedly and willingly, as you love Him, you must be sure that you do not do unto your neighbors or others what you would not have them do unto you. You must admonish your husbands to do likewise. If working the land for others, they must do it well and loyally, as if for yourselves. At harvest time, they should pay the master with wheat that has been grown on the land, if such is the agreement, and not mix in oats, pretending that nothing else was grown there, not hide the good ewes or the best rams at their neighbor's in order to pay the master with inferior animals, and not pretend that his best ones are dead by showing him the skins of other animals, nor pay him with the worst fleeces. Nor should they give the master a dishonest accounting of his carts or other property, nor of his poultry.

Furthermore, they should not cut wood from another's property without permission to build houses. When they take responsibility for the vineyards, they should be diligent and thorough, and work at the proper season. When the master commissions them to hire helpers, if they are hired at four groats a day, they should not pretend they cost seven. In all such matters, good wives must encourage their husbands to prudence; otherwise they will damn themselves. Working with loyalty not only will make all your tasks more agreeable but also will assure your salvation by living a life pleasing to God.

You women, yourselves, should do what you can to help your husbands, neither breaking down hedges nor allowing the children to; not stealing grapes, fruit, vegetables, or anything else from someone else's garden either by night or day; not putting animals to graze in a neighbor's seeded fields or meadows; not stealing from anyone else or letting anyone else steal from you. Go to church whenever possible, pay <u>tithes</u> to God faithfully (and not with the worst things), and say *Pater Nosters*. Live in peace with the neighbors, without perpetual <u>lawsuits</u> over trifles—as has become the habit of many villagers who seem never happy unless they are in court. Believe in God, and pity those in trouble. By following these paths, all good people can ensure their salvation, men as well as women.

⚡ 13. Which speaks of the situation of the poor.

We began with the rich, subsequently speaking to all classes of women; now we will end our work by addressing the poor, beloved by God yet despised by the world. We urge them to patience in hope of the promised crown after life.

<u>Blessed poor</u>, so called by the word of God in the Scriptures, awaiting the possession of Heaven merited by poverty patiently borne! Rejoice in that mighty promise of all-surpassing joy to which no other can compare. It is not promised to kings or princes or to the rich unless they can equal you in spirit, that is, if they are voluntarily poor, disdaining all riches and all worldly vanities.

Dear friends, beloved of God: Let our admonitions enter your understanding to remind you to protect yourselves against the arrows of impatience. They may prick you because of your various, overwhelming afflictions such as hunger, thirst, cold poor lodgings, helplessness, friendlessness, old age, illness without comfort, and, topping all, the world's deprecation, unkindness, and rejection of you as if you were not Christians at all but some other species of being.

When the pricks of impatience assail you, help will come to prevent your loss of the very great treasures which have been promised you. Lady Hope comes, armed by Patience and her shield of Faith, who strives valiantly against these pricks of impatience until she vanquishes them and her victory is won.

Patience attacks with five darts. The first she throws is this: "Poor sinner, why should you complain of poverty? Isn't any man or woman in this world well clothed if dressed in the King's robes and in His livery? O Good Creator, all-powerful King of Kings. I, Your poor servant, though clothed in these royal robes in soul and body, am insufficient in spirit. You have created me in Your image. In body I am of human flesh, such as You were willing to put on, and I, too, am clothed in poverty, the cloak You chose to wear all Your life. You clearly showed that You gave more importance to perfection through poverty when You Yourself chose it. Who in the world ever was poorer than You, when it pleased You to be born in a poor, isolated stable among dumb animals in winter; to be wrapped in ragged swaddling clothes; and to live Your whole life in such poverty that never did You have anything of Your own except what was given You in alms. You suffered hunger, thirst, and terrible discomforts; yet it pleased You to die naked in torment, and so poor that You did not have even a little pillow on which to rest Your wounded, sacred Head. And I, miserable creature, why should I complain at being Your follower? Rather, I thank You that You deigned to so greatly honor me that I can count myself among them. Your wish, dear sweet Lord, is that after this transitory hunger I now suffer, I will be fed at Your holy table forevermore. Pleased and willing, I ask that your holy will be done."

Here is the second dart Dame Hope flings: "If now you are ill and have little comfort, that is what God wishes. Through your patience, your merit will be increased."

Third: "If now you are old and have no friends, consider what difference these friends might really make. What can they do for you? Certainly they can neither take away your old age nor increase your heavenly merit. The older the better, for you are nearer the end of your voyage and closer to God. In His mercy, if you are patient, He will heal you with the strength and youth of His Glory."

The fourth dart is aimed at that little pile of filth upon which you sleep, which will last but for a little while. Or it is aimed at that wretched lodging in which you have no comfort. But however can those harm you? The blessed, beautiful, and delightful lodging of Paradise will reward your persistence.

Of course you are wounded by the fifth dart: the world's despising you and casting you out. But for God's sake, consider how trivial are honors given to kings and rich men, now dead, in their lifetime. Such temporal rewards have caused the damnation of many who would have been far better off in your situation.

For you, poor, indigent people, five darts can vanquish and nullify the assaults of impatience. Those impatient barbs are not negligible, coming from the force of necessity. But if you accept your poverty, firmly trusting in God and not coveting things other than those which please Him, you can acquire more noble possessions and greater riches than a hundred thousand worlds can hold and these can endure forever. All things considered, if you know how to benefit from it, you have reason to praise God for the estate to which He has called you.

Good poor women, you should comfort your husbands with our advice and help one another. Poor widows, you must take comfort in God, awaiting the endless joy God will grant you. And we three queens—Reason, Rectitude, and Justice—recommend the same to you, Christine, dear friend, as we take our leave from this work.

14. Conclusion and end of this present book.

The three ladies stopped speaking and suddenly vanished. I, Christine, remained there, somewhat weary from writing for so long a time, but overjoyed at seeing the fine work which had come from their worthy lessons. Afterward, having summarized, reviewed, and revised it, I think it is better than ever now, and extremely useful for the improvement of virtuous habits intended to increase the honor of ladies and all women now living and to be born. This advice will endure wherever this work may circulate and be read.

I, their servant, though in no way adequate to the task, intend, as always has been my habit, to devote myself to promoting their welfare. Therefore, I thought I would multiply this work throughout the world in various copies, whatever the cost might be, and present it in particular places to queens, princesses, and noble ladies. Through their efforts, it will be the more honored and praised, as is fitting, and better circulated among other women. I already have started this process; so that this book will be examined, read, and published in all countries, although it is written in the French language.

Since French is a more common and universal language than any other, this work will not remain unknown and useless but will endure in its many copies throughout the world. Seen and heard by many valiant ladies and women of authority, both at the present time and in times to come, they will pray to God on behalf of their faithful servant, Christine, wishing that her life in this world had been at the same time as theirs so that they might have known her. May those who now see me and my work keep me in their grace and memory as long as I live, praying to God that in His mercy He will increasingly favor my understanding, granting me such light of knowledge and true wisdom that I may employ these to continue the noble labor of study, in behalf of the praise and promotion of virtue through good example to every human being. After my soul has left my body, may these good women recognizing and rewarding me for my services offer to God on my behalf *Pater Nosters,* oblations, and other devotions for alleviating such pains as I may suffer for my shortcomings, so that I may be presented before God in the World Without End, which reward also is promised to you. Amen.

Here ends the Book of the Three Virtues for the instruction of women.

GLOSSARY

Abbey—A monastic religious community of monks or nuns. Usually operating as a self-contained economic unit, the community was involved in practical as well as spiritual concerns. Its members—mindful of their strict religious vows of obedience to Church, Order, and presiding abbott or abbess—would be sufficiently well-disciplined to keep their affairs to themselves.

Accustomed haunts of whores—Prostitutes worked in special districts, and wore gowns, capes, and hats which were uniforms signaling their geographic origin and sexual specialty. They were examined routinely for venereal disease and treated with mercurial inunctions if infected. An institutionalized profession with legal and political protections, prostitution for entrepreneurial women was not only a palliative against poverty but highly lucrative. [See Leah L. Otis, *Prostitution in Medieval Society* (Chicago, 1985); her "Prostitution and Repentance in Late Medieval Perpignan," in *Women of the Medieval World,* ed. Julius Kirshner and Suzanne Wemple (Oxford, 1985); and Christine Fell's *Women in Anglo Saxon England* (Bloomington, 1984).]

Advocates of Parliament—The most prestigious lawyers who pleaded cases at the highest royal courts, these university-trained attorneys worked in fifteenth-century Paris to effect "efficiency and equity" in the individual cases they litigated and the rules and laws ultimately based upon their precedents.

Antiochus of Persia—Reigned 175 to c. 163 B.C. and was despised as a tyrant. His attempt to Hellenize Judea resulted in the rebellion of the Maccabees. The unhappy tale is told in Daniel, 11:25–30; I Maccabees 1:10–25, 43–53; II Maccabees 9. Christine already had mentioned him in her *Mutacion de Fortune* (III, pp. 238–241).

Authority given to women—Although Isabeau de Bavière acted as her husband's representative during his spells of insanity, it is doubtful that Christine was speaking of her in Chapter 21. But among ladies who did enjoy considerable authority were two duchesses of Burgundy, whose stories would have been well known to Christine: Margaret of Flanders, who often governed for Philip the Bold when he was absent from his territories [R. Vaughan, *Philip the Bold,* pp. 114–118], and Margaret of Bavaria, who governed for John the Fearless, first in Flanders and then in Burgundy [R. Vaughan, *John the Fearless,* pp. 173–192]. Earlier, Flanders had been ruled by women for more than sixty-five years, first by Johanna and then by her sister Margaret, who rehabilitated the country after a devastating war [see F. Heer, *The Medieval World,* p. 262].

Bailiff—an important administrator (from Latin *bajulus,* a guardian) who served as tax collector, magistrate, estate manager, or landlord's steward, taking responsibility for executing the ruler's authority.

Barons—Such noblemen were subject to the king and owed him military service as well as service at court. A baron might leave home for extended periods for wars, crusades, or pilgrimages. Christine's contemporary, the Marshall Boucicaut, for instance, fought the Hussites in Prussia and the Turks in the Middle East. Ghillebert de Lannoy, whom Christine would have known when he was the squire to the Senechal of Hainaut, was also a great traveler, recording his observations for the Duke of Burgundy. While the barons were absent, their wives were expected to manage affairs at home.

Bearing, maidenly—Advice similar to Christine's was given by the Chevalier de la Tour Landry to his daughters at the end of the fourteenth century in his *Livre du Chevalier de la Tour.*

Bedroom—Not merely a room for sleeping, the bedroom of a woman in power often was an audience chamber in which she held court while seated propped by pillows in an elaborate, high-backed, canopied and curtained bed. At other times, the room also would serve as a bathing chamber in which a large, portable, curtained tub would be placed near the fireplace and filled with warmed, herb-fragrant water prepared for the leader's hygiene, relaxation, and pleasure.

Bend the twig—Christine's ideas on discipline, permissiveness, and influences in education were advanced for her time. She preceded even the Italian humanistic educator Guarino da Verona (d. 1460), who is considered a true pioneer. He believed in training students by reasoning with them rather than resorting to physical force. He also taught arithmetic by using games and emphasized the need to study the child's personality and to teach each according to his or her own nature. Christine had had practical experience with her own three children, but it would be interesting to know more about the sources of her pedagogical ideas. [See F.B. Artz, *The Mind of the Middle Ages* p. 311; and M.P. Cosman, *The Education of the Hero in Arthurian Romance* (Chapel Hill and Oxford, 1965).]

Blessed are the poor—Luke 6:20.

Blessed poor—The beginning of the fifteenth century saw a new interest in and an exaggerated celebration of the poor and humble in literature and art, particularly in tapestries and manuscript illustrations. Perhaps generated by the miseries brought on by war and epidemic, this interest may have been stimulated by the guilt of those indulging in excessive luxury, and by the complaints of the poor themselves [see J.-L. Goglin, *Les Miserables dans l'Occident Medieval* (Paris, 1976), pp. 193–195]. Though charity was expected to be provided by the wealthy, it was thought that the poor were to be rewarded in heaven rather than to be helped out of their situation in this world. This reasoning was set forth by Jean Gerson in his treatise *Le Mendicité Spirituelle (Oeuvres Complètes*, Vol. 7, pp. 220–280), in which Man admonishes his Soul to beg grace in the manner of beggars.

Blind woman—The parable about the blind leading the blind can be found in Matthew 15:14, although it had also become a popular proverb in Christine's time. [See J.W. Hassel Jr., *Middle French Proverbs, Sentences and Proverbial Phrases*, p. 45.]

Bombard sleeves—Voluminous hanging sleeves which often swept the ground. They had come into fashion around 1385.

Bouchart, the Count of Corbeil—In Book I, Chapter 9 Christine refers to the rebellion of this Count; she also refers to the three Montlhéry brothers who were successively Viscounts of Troyes during the reign of Philip I (1060–1108). Philip's son, Louis VI (1108–1137), subdued the rebellious and overly independent barons, which both increased the power of the Capetian monarchy and suppressed other noblemen who were terrorizing the countryside. [See *Les Grandes Chroniques de France*, Vol. V, pp. 102, 191.]

Brussels material—Brussels was becoming a center for the production of luxurious articles, fabricated by tapestry weavers; the fabric referred to in Book II, Chapter 11, is an elegant brocade, shot through with gold thread.

Burghers—Citizens of the towns who frequently enjoyed special privileges. "Bourgs" originally were suburbs that developed around towns.

Camel and the eye of a needle—Matthew 19:24; Mark 10:25; Luke 18:25.

Chastity—St. Ambrose's quotation in Book II, Chapter 13, probably from his *De Virginitate,* appears with the quotation from Saint Bernard in the *Manipulus Florum* under "Castitas." The quotations in Book III, Chapter 11, are from the same source.

Cherish good repute—Ecclesiasticus (Sirach) 41:12–13.

Children, care and upbringing of—Royal children easily might be influenced adversely or corrupted by unscrupulous servants or courtiers acting in their own interests. Louis of Guyenne, for instance, spent most of his life as the pawn of political factions trying to dominate the government of his insane father. If he had lived long enough for Marguerite to bear him an heir to the French throne, protecting such a child would have been a serious problem. [For a review of instruction manuals for noble children see Madeleine Pelner Cosman's *The Education of the Hero in Arthurian Romance*].

The Chronicles of France—Also known as the *Chronicles of Saint Denis,* this work is a vast compilation of French history from that country's mythic Trojan origins to the death of Philip-Augustus, with a prolongation up to 1350. Continuations after 1350, were composed by writers attached to the French royal court, not by the monks of the Abbey of Saint Denis who were the original authors.

Chrysostom, Saint John (c. 350–407)—A Church Father and Patriarch of Constantinople, Chrysostom was the most prolific of early Christian authors. He was called "the Golden Mouth" because of his eloquence; his most significant writings, commentaries on the Scriptures, stress literal interpretation. P. G. C. Campbell (*L'Epitre d'Othéa: Etude sur les Sources de Christine de Pisan* pp. 166–167) points out that all of Christine's quotations from the Church Fathers come from the *Manipulus Florum*. Rouse calls attention to 182 extracts from Chrysostom's commentary on Matthew in that collection [Richard H. and Mary A. Rouse, *Preachers, Florilegia and Sermons: Studies on the Manipulus Florum of Thomas of Ireland,* p. 423].

The City of Ladies—A woman's utopia, this fictional ideal city, constructed as a dwelling place for worthy women, was used as a literary device in Christine's history of women. She had finished writing that book shortly before beginning the present one. [See the Translator's Introduction, and *The Book of the City of Ladies,* translated by Earl Jeffrey Richards.]

Claiming what should be hers—According to French law from the time of Charlemagne onward, a widow had a right to either a half or a third of her husband's household possessions and such treasures as jewels. However, after the death of Louis de Guyenne at the end of 1415, when the Duke of Burgundy demanded that his daughter be returned to her family and that her dowry be remanded along with half of her husband's possessions, the daughter returned without either. [M. Laigle, *Le Livre des Trois Vertus,* p. 337.]

Clerks and counsellors—These officials of either local or royal government—literate and sometimes well-educated men—were already beginning their rise in society, a movement which would ultimately lead to the French Revolution in the eighteenth century.

College and Court of Paradise—Christine's reference in Book I, Chapter 5 might be a recollection of Dante's *Divine Comedy,* in this case the end of the *Paradiso.* However, since the first descriptions of the Court of Heaven date at least from the fourth century, Christine may have drawn upon other sources. The heavenly choirs were traditionally nine in number, symbolizing the Trinity repeated three times. Of these choirs, the angels represented the lowest order of pure spirits. Then, in ascending order, came the archangels and principalities, then the powers, virtues, and dominations or dominions, and, finally, the thrones, cherubim, and seraphim. All revolved perpetually around God's throne.

College of Women—This could refer to a group of persons engaged in a common pursuit or to a religious community. However, in Book I, Chapter 1, Christine uses it to mean the women, regardless of class, who have gathered to learn by hearing the lessons given by the three Virtues and by Wisdom and Worldly Prudence.

Come and go at all hours—Certainly a woman alone on fifteenth-century Paris streets at night would not have been safe from robbery or attack, but her reasons for being there could also be suspect. Respectable women simply did not go about unattended.

Complaint to the law—In spite of severe restrictions, the law seems to have been willing to help prostitutes if they showed any inclination to reform. [See G. Truc, *Histoire Illustrée de la Femme*, p. 179.]

Conduct your chariot—This expression suggests an image from Petrarch's Triumph of Chastity. Although his *I Triumphi (The Triumphs)*, finished by 1374, was not yet well known in France, it is quite possible that Christine knew it in Italian.

Confessor—A Princess was usually provided with her own personal spiritual counsellor, who took charge of her private chapel and was responsible for seeing that she carried out her religious obligations. He would normally have the confidence of the princess and would be in a position to admonish her about any shortcomings.

Contribution, or cens—A tax paid by a tenant to the landowner, either in money or in crops.

Counsellors—Christine elaborated on the importance of such officers in the *Livre du Corps de Policie*, which she wrote for Marguerite's husband, Louis de Guyenne. [See *Le Livre de Corps de Policie*. Ed. R.H. Lucas, pp. 64–66, 72–75).

The Countess of Eu—Eu was a county on the border between Normandy and Picardy, in the region of Dieppe. Christine refers in Book I, Chapter 10 to Isabelle de Melun (d. 1389), whose second husband was Jean d'Artois, Count of Eu. The Countess's son was one of the victims of the Turks at the French defeat of Nicopolis (1396). The young count's widow was Marie de Berry, one of Christine's patronesses, who in 1400 married Jean, Count of Clermont. The tomb of Countess Isabelle de Melun can still be seen in the crypt of the Church of Our Lady and Saint Lawrence in the town of Eu.

Courtly Love—(See Service of Love).

Credit—Certain noblemen were notorious for spending more than they could afford on luxuries, a well-known example being the Duke of Berry; works of art and other treasures had to be sold after his death in 1416 to pay his creditors.

Damnation—Hell's torments are forbiddingly described in various scriptural passages, notably the Book of Revelation 14:9–11 and 20:1–5, 9–15. In addition to these descriptions, Christine undoubledly was familiar with Dante's *Inferno*. We know that *The Divine Comedy* served as the inspiration for her *Chemin de Long Estude*. Those who lived during the Middle Ages did not question the literal truth of punishment in Hell.

Defense—The lady of the castle might be required to resist an attack by some other lord. Attackers might be rapacious neighbors, aggrieved complainants using extralegal means to gain redress, or bands of freebooters who roamed the countryside at certain periods. Some ladies were very successful leaders. Sometimes, the best military men would have gone to war with the husband; therefore, the lady would depend on remaining vassals who owed military service in return for their land. Provisioning a castle with food, supplies, and arms was as important as providing fighting men because siege was a common means of warfare. Materials would have to last as long as possible, until the husband or other help arrived. Thus, it was most important not to be taken by surprise.

Dependable priest—An educated priest, serving as the lady's secretary or confidante, might be the person in whom she could confide delicate matters. For details about literacy among medieval women, noble and otherwise, see R. Pernoud, *La Femme au Temps des Cathédrals,* pp. 75–91.

Ecclesiasticus—Book of Ecclesiasticus (Sirach) 10:14–15.

Ell—According to the Paris measure, an ell was usually the length equal to the distance between the extended middle finger and the elbow, or a length slightly longer than a meter or 39 inches.

Envy—Passages on envy derive from the section entitled "Invidia" in the *Manipulus Florum*. Christine's contemporary Jean Gerson made use of the second quotation in a sermon against Envy [Jean Gerson, *Oeuvres Complètes*. Ed. P. Glorieux, Vol. 7, p. 915].

Evil men—The problem Christine describes in Book III, Chapter 2, was not merely a literary one. Records from her time mention kidnappings, assaults on women, and numerous other irregularities. Two members of the Parisian Court of Love, founded in 1401 for the praise of women, were later accused of unseemly behavior toward them. [See C. Commeaux, *La Vie Quotidienne en Bourgogne au Temps des Ducs Valois 1364–1477*, pp. 82–84.] Both the *Quinze Joyes de Mariage* and *Les Cent Nouvelles Nouvelles* bear witness to the schemes men employed to take advantage of women in the fifteenth century.

Extravagance in clothing—The relative simplicity of style which had characterized women's clothing during the reign of Charles V was exchanged toward the end of the fourteenth century for a flurry of new styles for women, perhaps intended to compete with the variety of clothes already worn by men. This new passion for boldness apparently reflected the manners of the royal court dominated by Queen Isabeau, who loved elaborate clothes and jewels and encouraged extravagant styles, although she did not necessarily invent them. [See I. Brook, *Western European Costume: Thirteenth to Seventeenth Century*, Vol. I, pp. 85–90; J. Verdon, *Isabeau de Bavière*, p. 99.]

Regulations called sumptuary laws were passed by civic and religious authorities at the time in both England and France, governing ostentatious display in clothing and other articles. By limiting the use of certain furs, silks, and other fabrics to specific classes or nationalities, the laws attempted, unsuccessfully, to maintain traditional class distinctions in costume. As the bourgeoisie became increasingly wealthy, they could not be restrained from displaying their wealth, especially when they were actually lending money to noblemen. [See P. Contamine, *La Vie Quotidienne pendant la Guerre de Cent Ans*, pp. 205–206.]

Farming—Christine's knowledge of agricultural matters undoubtedly comes in large measure from the translation of the *Livre des Prouffits Ruraux (The Book of Rural Profits)* by the Bolognese Pietro de Creszenzi (Petrus Crescentius), which gives advice on the management of an estate. The translation was made at the request of

Charles V, which bears witness to the French king's interest in improving agriculture in France.

Fast—Fasting served as many purposes as its opposite, feasting. A requirement of the church calendar, fasting also served as an indicator of faith, a form of penance, a type of punishment, a reaffirmation of the mind's (or spirit's) control over bodily demands. Physicians recommended fasting as adjuvant to medication or surgery and often alternated fast with the medicinal feast. Abstinence from almost all food was the severest form of food deprivation, often thought to be an indicator of sainthood. [See Rudolph M. Bell, *Holy Anorexia* (Chicago, 1985); and Bridget Ann Herisch, *Fast and Feast: Food in Medieval Society* (Philadelphia; 1976).]

Feast—Serving multiple purposes beyond sustenance, the medieval feast alternated numerous courses with entertainments: a meat dish, then vocal music; a fish followed by jugglers and jesters; a fowl such as flamboyant peacock, then magicians; a sculptured "illusion food" such as a ship-shaped cake with "pirate mariners" hidden within to leap out, amaze and amuse the guests. A form of ostentatious display, the fabulous feast also reaffirmed a leader's political control. Menus were crafted for medical and physiological effects of foods and wines. [See Madeleine Pelner Cosman, *Fabulous Feasts: Medieval Cookery and Ceremony* (New York, 1978), and her entries in the Scribner *Dictionary of the Middle Ages* (New York, 1982–7): "Feasts"; "Herbs"; "Pharmacopoeia."]

Fief—Land granted by a lord in return for a vassal's service. A secondary fief was land granted by a vassal in turn to a third person; effectively, a sublease.

Flatterer—The quotation in Book II, Chapter 2 is from the *Manipulus Florum* in the section entitled "Adulatio."

For fear of the children—A woman leader's children were a patent threat of "preventive retribution." An aggressor against the mother could expect a daughter's or son's vengeance later on, or immediately if the child had knights and barons already owing allegiance, as many titled children did.

Gastinois—Modern Gätinoi; in Christine's day this referred to the region around Orleans, effectively "the provinces" or "the sticks." The ridiculous vanity of ordinary women in matters of fashion is mocked in *Les Quinze Joyes de Mariage* (Ed. J. Crow, p. 6). For example, in the First Joy, the wife extracts a fanciful new dress from her husband who cannot afford it. This book too was probably written early in the fifteenth century.

Gatherings in such places as gardens—Although there is no known literary instance of such a deception, it is a worthy setting for a fabliau. Both the *Quinze Joyes de Mariage,* where a wife arranges assignations with her lovers, and the *Cent Nouvelles Nouvelles,* in which the clergy are scarcely notable for their virtue, suggest that such gatherings were a reality.

Gesines—Traditional rituals associated with the birth of a child. Only women were allowed to be present at a birth, which was supervised by women obstetricians and midwives and attended by friends and relatives. During the period of lying-in, the mother received her friends and guests, accepting symbolic gifts and entertaining them with symbolic foods and a considerable display of luxury. Compare the description in Book III, Chapter 3 of this book with the *gesine* of Isabelle de Bourbon at the birth of Mary of Burgundy, described by Alienor de Poitiers in *Les Honneurs de la Cour* (pp. 238–243), and with the expenses for the lying-in of Jeanne de Saint-Pol, the Duke of Burgundy's daughter-in-law, in 1403 (*Itineraires de Philippe le Hardi et de Jean sans Peur,* E. Petit, ed. (Paris, 1888), pp. 568–573). [See also La Curne de Sainte-Palaye, *Memoire sur l'ancienne chevalerie* (Paris, 1759), II, pp. 216–225.] Late medieval paintings of the birth of the Virgin, the birth of Jesus, and the celebrated scene of the birth of St. John from the *Milan-Turin Hours* depict this custom. See E. Panofsky, *Early Netherlandish Painting* (Cambridge, MA, 1953), Plate 164.

Goliards—Originally the term applied to wandering poets: some were serious, itinerant students making their way between universities; some were greedy, half-starved reprobates who traveled the roads with threadbare coats and scraps of Latin they could turn into verse. Since many were students who had left church schools and cloisters for some reason, they were a considerable problem for the church. By the thirteenth century they had become such pests that a series of councils tried to suppress them. Thus the goliards became social outcasts, commonly linked with jugglers, buffoons and other itinerant entertainers. By the fourteenth century they existed only in a term of reproach, one used by Chaucer in describing the miller of *The Canterbury Tales*. Christine obviously regarded the scheming maid in Book III, Chapter 9 in the same light. Christine's descriptive powers are at their best in depicting these scenes of domestic corruption.

Hair—In Book II, Chapter 12, Christine may be referring to I Corinthians 11:15, where St. Paul alludes to a woman's hair.

Headdress, horned—One of the various styles of headdress, many rather wild, extravagant, and fanciful, which marked the end of the fourteenth and the beginning of the fifteenth centuries. In this case the material of the headdress was wired on both sides of the head to stand up in a fashion resembling horns. Christine herself is seen wearing such a headdress in the miniature in which she presents a manuscript of her works to Isabeau de Bavière (London, British Library, Harley Ms. 4431, fol. 3).

Homage to knowledgeable people—The idea of moral and practical benefits resulting from honoring the most intelligent had been developed previously by Christine in her biography of Charles V (*Fais et Bonnes Meurs,* ed. Solente, Vol. II, pp. 46–49).

Hospitals—In a profoundly pious medieval society, hospitals aroused considerable interest among all classes of the populace. Most such institutions were founded by religious organizations; the Hôtel-Dieu in Paris, however, was a royal foundation of long standing, with contributions for its maintenance coming from ordinary people as well as from royalty. It was during a charitable visit to the Hôtel-Dieu that Marguerite's sister, Anne, Duchess of Bedford, caught a contagious disease from which she died in 1432.

Hours—The Book of Hours was the personal prayer book of the laity, although its contents were derived from the official liturgical books of the Catholic Church. In Book I, Chapter 12, "Hours" refers to the first of the eight Canonical Hours of the day. These were ritual prayer periods, named Matins, Prime, Terce, Sext, Nones, Vespers, Compline, and Lauds, which, in the most observant communities, divided each day's activities. A Book of Hours permitted an individual to follow in her or his own manner the Church's program of daily devotion. Toward the end of the Middle

Ages, such books became very elaborate and ostentatious in their decoration. [See J. Hartman, *The Book of Hours.*]

Saying one's Hours also had a purely pedagogical function, as a young girl often learned to read from her Book of Hours. An idea of what was involved in such a spiritual exercise can be gathered from Jean Gerson's *A.B.C. des Simples Gens (Oeuvres Complètes,* ed. P. Glorieux, Vol. 7, pp. 154–157).

Household mirrors the spirit of master or mistress—The proverb quoted in Book I, Chapter 18 is one of Christine's favorites, which she used as the refrain to a ballade dedicated to the Duke of Burgundy in 1403 (*Oeuvres Poétiques.* Ed. Roy. Vol. I, pp. 251–252), in her biography of Charles V (Ed. Solente, Vol. I, p. 243), and in her *Livre de la Paix* (Ed. Willard, p. 80), as well as in Book II, Chapter 3 of this volume.

Housekeeper—Christine's advice on running a household should be compared with that given in the late fourteenth century *Ménagier de Paris,* ed. G.M. Brereton and J.M. Ferrier and translated into English by E. Power.

Humble shall be exalted—Matthew 23:12; Luke 14:11, 18:14.

Husband's relatives—Chapter 14 highlights the relative insecurity of a princess in a strange and possibly hostile court to which she had been sent for purely political motives. For instance, if the marriage had been arranged to formalize a treaty, as was the case with Isabelle of France's marriage to Richard II of England, a princess might find herself enduring rivalries, political realignments, or reawakened antagonisms.

Husbands—A queen or royal princess always would have her own household and thus essentially would lead a life independent of her husband. Since it was customary for the king or prince to visit the lady in her apartments rather than the reverse, she would need to consult his attendants for information about his well-being.

Instruction—Education of both women and men leaders was a subject of political as well as practical importance from the days of the classical Isocrates's *Ad Nicoclem* (374 B.C.) This instruction book for the powerful was the first in an unbroken tradition of admonition which culminated in Renaissance humanist education treatises. The education of children to develop wisdom, morality, and practical skills of leadership generally had three phases: first with women; then with tutors; finally a period of apprenticeship in chivalry and courtliness as a member of a court. Noble children served in neighboring or distant castles' chambers, banquet halls, and armories to learn the habits, the etiquette, and the skills, observing while acting. [For a review of historical documents and literary educations, see Madeleine Pelner Cosman, *The Education of the Hero in Arthurian Romance* and F. B. Artz, *The Mind of the Middle Ages,* pp. 180–202.]

Christine developed her humanistic ideals for educating the young in her *Livre du Corps de Policie* and her *Livre de la Paix,* both of which she wrote for Louis of Guyenne. These treatises follow the tradition of the *miroirs de princes,* the mirrors of princes or mirrors of princesses, in which an ideal figure of a ruler combines prowess of mind *(sapientia)* with power of body *(fortitudo)* through a prescribed course of study with tutors and mentors and by practice.

Jealous hatred—In writing Book I, Chapter 16, Christine may well have had in mind the situation of Valentina Visconti, the Duchess of Orleans, who, too much admired by the king, was exiled from the court after 1396 through the jealous machinations of the queen, Isabeau de Bavière. The duchess's exile left her husband, the duke, free to indulge in a series of adventures, notably with the queen herself. While a common human condition, jealousy also was a predictable expectation in *courtly love* (see its definition, above).

John of Salisbury (c. 1115–1180)—Born in England, he went to France as a student and was involved in many important events of his day. At one point he was the secretary of Thomas Becket, and later he became Bishop of Chartres. His *Polycraticus,* inspired by his observations of court life, was written after the murder of Becket in 1170. Its text was translated from Latin into French by Denis Follechat in 1372 at the request of Charles V.

Judith—Judith 15:9–10. Christine retells the story of Judith in *The Book of the City of Ladies* (Part II, Chapter 31), and also holds her up as an example to Isabeau de Bavière in a letter written October 5, 1405 asking Isabeau to be a peacemaker in the quarrel between the Dukes of Burgundy and Orléans. Christine further compares Judith to Joan of Arc in a poem written in July 1429.

King Clovis's queen—Clotilda (c. 475–545). Daughter of Chilperic, king of the Burgundians, Clotilda is credited with an important role in her husband's conversion to Christianity; after his death she devoted herself to the poor. Christine already had written of her accomplishments in *The Book of the City of Ladies* (Part II, Chapter 35).

Madame de La Tour,—In *The Book of the Duke of True Lovers,* the name of the governess is Sebille de Monthault, Dame de la Tour, a name which Christine retains here. There was a de la Tour family in northern France connected to the Counts of Boulogne, but it is doubtful that any historical allusion is intended in Book I, Chapter 27, even though Christine knew something about the region through her husband's family, which came from Picardy in northern France.

Laurel crown—Woven of evergreen twigs, in classical tradition it was placed on a hero's head to symbolize victory and immortality. Christian iconography adopted laurel as a sign of triumph over worldly temptations.

Lawsuits—The proliferation of lawyers toward the end of the Middle Ages undoubtedly encouraged lawsuits in the towns and on the seigneurial lands, which often had their own lawcourts. Boundary disputes were quite common. See the well-known case of the scheming shepherd Agnelet, who got the better of both his master and his lawyer in the farce of Maitre Pathelin [*La Farce de Maitre Pathelin.* Ed., R. T. Holbrook (Paris, 1937)].

Lay up treasures in Heaven—Matthew 6:19–20.

Letter written by the governess—As Christine notes, the letter in Book I, Chapter 27 is repeated from an earlier work, the *Livre du Duc des Vrais Amants (The Book of the Duke of True Lovers)* [*Oeuvres Poétiques,* Vol. III, pp. 162–171]. It quite effectively sums up Christine's views on the snares of so-called courtly love, which she had attacked in earlier works, beginning with the *Epitre au Dieu d'Amour (Cupid's Letter),* written in 1399.

Low-cut necklines—The changing styles evoked much criticism from preachers and writers, notably Eustache Deschamps in his

Miroir de Mariage (*Oeuvres*. Ed. G. Raynaud, Vol. IX, pp. 3292–3319, pp. 110–111). From miniatures of the time, one sees that the previously stylish, discreet, round necks were being replaced by gowns with collars and necklines open nearly to the waist. Although modest ladies wore a garment under these gowns, it appears from comments by Christine and others that not everyone did. [See also note on **Extravagance** in clothing.]

Lucifer—Known as the "light-bearing" angel, Lucifer was cast out of Heaven because he pridefully thought himself to be the equal of God (Isaiah 14:12–15).

Lycurgus—Lycurgus is considered to be the traditional founder of the Spartan constitution, although a considerable diversity of opinion exists as to when or whether he really lived. He was first mentioned by Herodotus, and later by Plutarch. Christine, who had mentioned Lycurgus in her biography of Charles V (Part I, Chapter 7), apparently knew of him from the anonymous French translation of Bernard Gui's *Flores Chronicorum,* originally written at the end of the thirteenth or the beginning of the fourteenth century.

Machaut, Guillaume de—Christine's indebtedness to the older poet was considerable and has been studied in detail by J.C. Schilperoort, *Guillaume de Machaut et Christine de Pisan (Etude Comparative)* (The Hague, 1936).

The Magnificat—Luke 1:46–55.

Major-domo—A nobleman or high-ranking official who would be put in charge of the household of a princess, overseeing all the stewards and other serving-people. Usually several people would alternate service in this office for specific periods in the course of a year.

Man, heart of or courage of—Christine repeatedly admonished women to stand on their own feet and to act with courage, a lesson she undoubtedly learned from her own experiences. This is the source of her allegory of having been changed by Fortune into a man in *La Mutacion de Fortune.* Furthermore, Christine maintained that if a woman can be independent, she need not remarry if she does not choose to. Women of a later generation, such as Louise of Savoy, Margaret of Austria, and Mary of Hungary, all of whom owned and read Christine's book, never remarried.

Managing their property—A generation after Christine, Margaret Paston in England showed, through her letters, that she had to contend with many of the problems discussed here. [See H.S. Bennett, *The Pastons and their England* (Cambridge, 1970); *Paston Letters and Papers of the Fifteenth Century,* ed. N. Davis (Oxford, 1971); and D. Bornstein, "The Ideal Lady of the Manor as Reflected in Christine de Pizan's *Livre des Trois Vertus,*" in *Ideals for Women,* pp., 117–128.]

Manor—A territory ruled by a lady and lord, it consisted of the manor house, lands, farms, mills, waterways, forests, and other perquisites in which peasants and other tenants paid rents and fees in money, goods, and service in return for protection and rights to the use of property. Large manors resembled towns, with local manorial control over jurisprudence, husbandry, public health and safety.

Martre—A game of chance played with small bones from sheep.

Mary and Martha—Their story is told in Luke 10:38–42. The two came to be the representatives of the contemplative and active lives, notably among the late medieval mystics, followers of Meister Eckhart. [See J.A. Bizet, *Mystiques Allemands du XIVe Siècle,* pp. 64–65.] Sisters of Lazarus, according to John 11:1, they supposedly voyaged with him by boat to the south of France and there founded churches at Aix, Marseilles, and Avignon. Mary most likely is Mary of Bethany, who during Jesus's last days anointed his feet and wiped them with the "hair of her head"; she may be identical to Mary Magdalene whom Christ freed from "seven devils," and who faithfully attended Him at the Crucifixion (Mark 15:40) and the Resurrection (Mark 16:1, Matthew 28:9, John 20:14).

Mary the Egyptian—(Feast Day, April 2) Admired as a penitent. According to popular legend, she left home at the age of twelve to live in Alexandria, where she worked as a prostitute for seventeen years. Led by curiosity to join a pilgrimage to Jerusalem, she was miraculously directed to cross over the Jordan. She then lived in the desert, where she was divinely instructed in the Christian faith. A monk met her by chance, heard her story, and promised to bring her communion on Maundy Thursday, but when he returned, he found her dead. Her life was written in the thirteenth century by the poet Rutebeuf, and she was often depicted in carvings, paintings, and stained glass in French churches and cathedrals.

Mass—The Christian service celebrating with music the basic tenets of belief; it is named from the last words spoken by the priest in the service, the dismissal: "Ita Missa Est." The choir or congregants sing songs or chants interspersed with scripture readings and sermons which on particular holidays had special texts called the Propers (including formulaic prayers such as the Introit, Gradual, Offertory, Allelujah, Tract, and Sequences). These were added to the more invariable sections, called collectively the Ordinary of the Mass (including the Kyrie, Gloria, Credo, Sanctus, Benedictus, Agnus Dei, Ita Missa Est).

A lady normally would be expected to attend Mass daily, so Christine's view that this was not invariably necessary was distinctly liberal.

Merchants—Venice and Lucca undoubtedly were the Italian cities best known to Christine, beause of her father's relations with Venetian merchants even after he moved to France and because of the large colony of Lucchese merchants who carried on trading and international banking in Paris. Venetian wealth came from trade with the Middle East; both Venice and Lucca were important centers of the medieval silk trade. Both cities also had connections with Avignon, where the papal court served as an important market for imported luxuries.

Class distinctions were traditionally assumed to have been ordained by divine law, but the rise of a wealthy merchant class and prosperous weavers in northern France and the Netherlands upset the traditional balance, in part due to the progressive secularization of society in the late Middle Ages. At the same time, the distinctions continued to exist, along with a certain amount of animosity between international bankers and merchants and the purely local merchants who operated on a much more limited scale.

Minor regent—Both medieval England and France had recently experienced trying times before an heir to the crown attained his majority. Richard II (who became King of England in 1377 at age 10) and Charles VI (who became King of France in 1380 at age 12) both had been objects of the ambitions of uncles. On the other hand, Christine already has mentioned Blanche of Castille, who successfully protected France against the rapacious barons who attempted to exploit the minority of her son, Louis IX.

Moralia *(Morals on the Book of Job)*—The quotation in Book I, Chapter 8, also is taken from the *Manipulus Florum*, where it is found under the heading "Paciencia." [See also Glossary entry on "Saint Gregory."]

Mournful costume—Christine disagrees with Aliénor de Poitiers who, later in the fifteenth century, wrote in *Les Honneurs de la Cour* (p. 258) that a queen of France should remain in her bedroom for a year after the death of the king and that the whole apartment should be draped in black.

My Father's sheep—It is impossible to find in the Bible the exact quotation used in Book I, Chapter 2, but there are several similar passages in John 10. Christine often paraphrased or quoted her sources from memory.

No man is without crime—I John 1:8.

Nebuchadnezzar (d. 562 B.C.)—The king credited by classical historians with making Babylon one of the wonders of the world. Christine already had noted his overweening pride in her biography of Charles V, *Fais et Bonnes Meurs* (Vol. I, pp. 75–76). However, the person of this name described in the Book of Daniel, Chapters 1–4, is a fictitious king.

Obliged to live and die with him—Divorce was difficult and annulments were rare, granted more for political than personal reasons. No lady wanted to be repudiated by her husband and sent home in disgrace. That was the fate of Marguerite's sister Catherine who, betrothed to a prince of the House of Anjou in 1407, was sent home when his family changed sides in the civil war in 1413. The young woman died, ostensibly of chagrin, before another marriage could be arranged for her.

Offering—In the Church ritual of the period, the faithful went in ordered procession to make an individual offering to the celebrant.

This was an ideal opportunity for ostentatious display and jockeying for precedence, especially among those who had no real status.

Origen (185–254)—An Alexandrian theologian famous for allegorical interpretations of the Bible. Although the quotation in Book II, Chapter 13, can be found under "Sobrietas" in the *Manipulus Florum*, it is not attributed to Origen there.

Pardoners—Like Chaucer's character in the *Canterbury Tales*, pardoners dispensed or sold pardons, which were official documents granting absolution from sin.

Parisians have too much blood—In medieval medicine, high blood pressure or "excess blood" were relieved by bloodletting or phlebotomy; the harshest warfare, or punitive taxes, by analogy were called "bloodletting." In Christine's day, Parisians were plagued by taxes, which went to support the extravagant life of the French court. Merchants or lesser nobles foolish enough to flaunt their wealth soon lost it; for a rapacious ruler gladly would relieve any citizen of Paris of "excess blood" in order to maintain "health."

Pater Noster—(Latin "Our Father") The beginning of the Lord's Prayer, which is set forth in Matthew 6:9–15, and in Luke 11:2–4.

Patient, the—Matthew 5:10. This verse really refers to the persecuted.

The Peace (pax)—A handsomely fashioned object, usually a bronze plaque depicting a Biblical scene, with a handle at its back allowing a clergyman to hold it aloft for admiration and veneration during processions and for the faithful to kiss at the time of the Offering. Other writers of the period, notably Eustache Deschamps in his *Miroir de Mariage (The Mirror of Marriage)* and the anonymous author of the *Quinze Joyes de Mariage,* mention the disgraceful behavior of some women during and because of this ceremony.

Pilgrim—Christine might have in mind (Book II, Chapter 8) Philippe de Mézière's idea of a pilgrim in his *Songe du Vieil Pelerin (The Dream of the Old Pilgrim),* written in 1389 for the moral instruction of the youthful Charles VI.

Pilgrimage—The Book II, Chapter 5 image is almost certainly a reference to the popular poem of Guillaume de Digulleville, *Le Pélerinage de vie humaine (The Pilgrimage of Human Life, 1330–1332),* although Christine may have been thinking, too, of the beginning of Dante's *Divine Comedy.* Pilgrimages were familiar in the fourteenth and fifteenth centuries as journeys to holy places, undertaken for a religious reason, such as doing penance.

Pilgrimages away from town—From Chaucer's *Canterbury Tales* we know that pilgrimages were often used for more than spiritual purposes. In the *Quinze Joyes de Mariage,* the wife makes a pilgrimage to Le Puy as a sort of vacation from domestic responsibilities; in the "Ninety-Third Tale" of the *Cent Nouvelles Nouvelles,* a woman tells her husband she has gone on a pilgrimage so that she can keep a rendezvous with the village priest.

Pity the sinner—Those who have accused Christine of prudery (D. W. Robertson Jr., *A Preface to Chaucer in Medieval Perspective,* pp. 361–362; J. V. Fleming, "Hoccleve's 'Letter to Cupid' and the 'Quarrel' over the *Roman de la Rose,*" pp. 21–40) were surely not familiar with her recommendations in this book. In keeping with her contemporaries, notably Jean Gerson, Christine distinguishes the willingness to commit sinful deeds from the act of compassionately aiding a sinner.

Plague—The bubonic plague (The Great, or Black, Plague) first struck Europe as an epidemic in 1348, sweeping the continent at intervals thereafter. The disease was frequently characterized in the early stages by swollen lymph glands, or buboes, such as Boccaccio described at the beginning of the *Decameron:* "In men and women alike it first betrayed itself by the emergence of certain tumors in the groin or the armpits, some of which grew as large as the common apple, others as an egg, some more, some less, which the common folk called 'gavocciolo.'" (Quoted by P. Ziegler in *The Black Death,* pp. 18–19.)

Pope Leo—Christine quotes a particular *Sermon on the Apparition* in Book III, Chapter 3, found in the *Manipulus Florum* under "Miseracordia."

Precedence—In a society where social status followed distinct lines of demarcation, rank determined seating at table, in court, and in church and precedence took on great literal and metaphorical importance. The struggle for upward mobility, which would become accentuated in the sixteenth century, was already evident in the late Middle Ages, as we can see from Christine's comments.

Royal officials were especially ambitious. They had the opportunity to rise in society through royal favor, notably during the reign of Charles V, and tensions between new rank and old rank were always at boiling point. The situation deteriorated unpleasantly during the reign of the mentally incapacitated Charles VI.

Pride—Generally accepted as the worst among the Seven Deadly Sins (the others were covetousness, lust, envy, gluttony, anger and sloth), pride was the arrogant error of Adam and Eve in Eden and of the fallen angels. However, in medieval thought, pride generated the opposite humility, a virtue in humankind as well as an attribute of Jesus Christ. Were it not for Adam and Eve's fall from God's grace in the Garden of Eden, there would have been no necessity for Jesus's coming and ultimate offer of salvation to sinners. Thus, pride caused a fortunate fall, a *felix culpa.*

Christine's description of this common allegorical and pedagogical subject in Book II, Chapter 11, is reminiscent of the Lenten Sermon (the second of two) preached by Jean Gerson on March 11, 1403.

Princess—Throughout this book, Christine uses "princess" in its broader sense of a woman with sovereign power. In various parts of Europe, the term "princess" might have been used in the fifteenth century to refer to any of a number of titled women, including queens, empresses, duchesses, countesses, and—in some areas, especially Italy—wives of men with very large land-holdings who were loosely called "princes."

Conversely, Christine suggests in Book II, Chapter 9 that titles do not always correspond exactly to the extent and importance of a lady's domains. The wife of Philip the Bold, Duke of Burgundy, for instance, held important territories in her own right as the Countess of Flanders, although she never would be called a princess.

At several points in this book, Christine alludes to specific princesses of her time. The picture of the lazy and self-seeking princess in Book I, Chapter 3, could be seen as a veiled criticism of the French Queen, Isabeau de Bavière, who by the summer of 1405 was being denounced by preachers for her dissolute life. [See L. Mourin, *Jean Gerson, Predicateur Francais,* p. 169; *Chronique du Religieux de Saint-Denis,* ed. L.F. Bellaguet, Vol. III, p. 268;

and J. Verdon, *Isabeau de Bavière,* especially Chapt. 3.]

In Book I, Chapter 12, Christine must have been thinking of Charles V's queen, Jeanne de Bourbon. She already had spoken of this queen's virtuous life in her biography of Charles V, *Fais et Bonnes Meurs* (Vol. I, p. 57 n.).

Protocol—Guests at meals were always seated according to social rank. On saints' days and other festivals, the lady and her honored guests would sit at a high table, raised on a dais, at one end of the great hall. Other tables were set up extending from this high table so that the honored ones were always visible to the rest of the court. The lowest ranking persons sat the farthest away from the dais. [See also the Glossary entry on "Precedence," and M. P. Cosman, *Fabulous Feasts: Medieval Cookery and Ceremony.*]

Provost—A magistrate or other legal officer. The Provost of Paris, for example, controlled military service, the police, and upheld justice within the limits of Paris. At the time Christine was writing this book, the office was held by Guillaume de Tignonville, with whom Christine had at least a literary acquaintance: in 1402 she had sent him a copy of her letters about the *Romance of the Rose.* [See Hicks, *Le Débat sur le Roman de la Rose,* pp. 7–8.]

Noblemen who owned large domains had their own system of courts and hired their own provosts.

Public baths—Literary descriptions of Roman baths contributed to the popularity of fifteenth century establishments, as can be seen from illustrations of copies of Valerius Maximus made during that period, notably Anthony of Burgundy's copy, now in Breslau. The bathhouse keeper provided food and drink and rented out rooms when requested.

Published—Christine died well before William Caxton, the first English printer, published one of her books in 1475–6 as among the first from his printing presses at Westminster and Bruges. However, publication during Christine's lifetime had two efficient forms: hand-copying of manuscripts by scribes in writing factories called "scriptoria," and public readings as a form of entertainment, instruction, and mealtime accompaniment. Books handlettered on parchment, vellum, or paper were very expensive: one illuminated volume might equal in cost two townhouses in a fifteenth-century English city. About twenty million remarkably cheaper books were printed in the last decades of the fifteenth century, the so-called *incunabula* or "infancy" (literally, "cradle") period of publishing. [See Susan O. Thompson, "Paper Manufacturing and Early Books," in *Machaut's World: Science and Art in the Fourteenth Century*. Ed. Madeleine Pelner Cosman (New York, 1978).]

We know that Christine's books were copied in England and translated into Portuguese before the end of the century. Records from medieval libraries indicate that French was read in these countries, as well as in Spain and Northern Italy.

Queen Blanche of Castille—As Louis IX was only twelve at the time of his father's death, his mother was appointed regent. A little-known foreign woman, she immediately faced the seemingly impossible task of putting down a revolt of barons, some of them princes of the royal blood. However, partly because of divisiveness among her opponents and partly through the support of the towns of the realm, she triumphantly overcame the dangers to herself and her son. Thus, in 1234, she was able to turn over to Louis an undiminished inheritance. [See Glossary entry on "Saint Louis."]

Queen Esther—Though today Esther is well known as the heroine of the Old Testament book, Christine probably also knew her story from a compilation of history known as *L'Histoire Ancienne jusqu'à César*, one of the principal sources for her *Mutacion de Fortune*, where Esther's story is retold at length (Ed. Solente; Vol. II, pp. 263–271). Esther also appears in *The Book of the City of Ladies* (Part II, Chapt. 32), and is mentioned in one of Christine's letters concerning the *Romance of the Rose* and in her poem to Joan of Arc.

Queens, widowed—Jeanne of Evreux was the third wife of Charles IV. Christine already had written about her in *The Book of the City of Ladies*, Part I, Chapter 13; in the letters concerning the *Romance of the Rose*, p. 19; and in the *Fais et Bonnes Meurs*, Vol. I, pp. 54–55. Blanche of Navarre (1331–1398) was also cited in the *City of Ladies* and the *Fais et Bonnes Meurs*, Vol. I, p. 55. The Duchess of Orleans was Blanche of France (1328–1393), posthumous daughter of Charles IV and Jeanne of Evreux; she, too, was praised by Christine in the *City of Ladies*.

Reason, Rectitude, and Justice—The three Virtues are discussed in detail in the Translator's Introduction.

Reciting at meals—This custom of recounting epic poetry or exemplary tales was a major and efficient form of literary transmission in an age without printed books. Reading aloud at meals remained common until recently in religious communities.

Rent collectors—The lord or lady had agents to collect rents from tenants who farmed their estates and to keep accounts for the land. Paid to women, just as to men, rents were revenues rendered (thus "rent" from the Latin *reddita pecunia*) in money, produce, or services in return for use of a house, land, other property, or a right-of-way. For such valid purposes, "white rent" or "white mail" (silver or bright metal coin, from the French *maille* coin) was paid; whereas "black rent" or "blackmail" was paid by northern English and Scottish landholders to buy freedom from marauding pillagers and plunderers.

Repent—This admonition recalls a passage from Jean Gerson's *Doctrinal aux Simples Gens (Doctrinal for Simple Folk)* in which he urges the sinner to reform while there is still life in the body (*Oeuvres Complètes*, Vol. 10, pp. 319–320).

Revenues—Most royal princesses or wealthy noble ladies would need financial and other agents to look after rentals and other operations on lands assigned to them as part of their dowries, or as their inheritances. At the time of her first marriage, Marguerite de Guyenne was endowed with three estates, calculated to provide a certain income, and, in addition, a capital of 200,000 francs with which to buy other lands and chateaux. On the occasion of her second marriage, to Arthur de Richmont in 1423, her brother Philip the Good gave her the county of Tonnerre and eleven estates (*chastelanies*). [See M. Rey, *Les Finances Royales sous Charles VI, 1388–1413*, p. 281; and P. A. Pouquet du Haut-Jussé, "Le Connétable de Richemont, Seigneur Bourguignon," pp. 309–336.]

A competent staff was necessary to collect revenues and to make the detailed accounting that was expected. Although there is no evidence that Marguerite oversaw her own financial situation, her sister-in-law, Isabel of Portugal, did indeed appoint some of her own officers and inspect their records.

Rights of harvest—A certain percentage of the produce of a given piece of land was due to the lord. If the land was sublet, the question of how much each person involved should owe was prescribed by regional customs and laws. The lord or lady who might be administering the manor at a distance, from the other side of France, needed to know local law and have local representatives. [See G. Fourquin, *Le Paysan d'Occident au Moyen Age.*]

Robert d'Artois—Robert lived during the reign of Philip VI (1328–1350). The nephew of Mahaut, Countess of Artois, he challenged her claim to the title, even inventing false documents for the purpose. Eventually he was banished from the realm. The French king also had designs on Artois, a questionable claim which was one of the principal causes of the Hundred Years War. (*Les Grandes Chroniques de France*. Ed. R. Delachenal, Vol. IX, pp. 109–111, 123–133).

Sage—In Book I, Chapter 8, Christine summarizes a much longer passage which appears in the *Manipulus Florum* under "Caritas," where it is attributed to the *De Laude Caritatis (In Praise of Charity)* of Saint Augustine.

Saint Affra—(Feast Day, August 5.) Said to have been martyred at the time of Diocletian, c. 304, but there is some discussion about her identity. After having lived sinfully for many years, she was touched by grace and converted. Condemned by a tribunal, Affra was first asked by the judge if she would not recant. Her reply was that although she had committed many sins, that one she would not commit. She offered a final prayer as she was burned alive, asking that her death might be a compensation for her sins. Christine had already told this saint's story in *The Book of the City of Ladies*, Part III, Chapter 17.

Saint Ambrose (340?–397)—The preaching of this Doctor of the Church was so eloquent that it was instrumental in converting St. Augustine to Christianity. Many of Ambrose's surviving writings are homilies. He also arranged and wrote hymns and chants. The passage in Book II, Chapter 13 is from his *De Officiis*, cited in the *Manipulus Florum* under "Beneficia."

Saint Augustine (354–430)—Augustine embraced Christianity in 387 after fathering an illegitimate son and spending a number of years in intellectual and spiritual disquiet, studying various philosophies. Eventually named Bishop of Hippo, he came to have a tremendous influence on Christianity through his theological and philosophical writings. His *Confessions* are regarded as one of the greatest classics of Christian mysticism, and his powerful defense of Christianity, *The City of God,* has also retained its importance for centuries.

The quotation in Book I, Chapter 11 can be found in the *Manipulus Florum* under "Fama." The quotation in Book II, Chapter 13, is from the *Manipulus Florum* under "Sobrietas."

Saint Avoye—Also called Saint Avia or Aurea; Feast Day (May 6). Her story is largely legendary, but she was reputedly associated with Saint Ursula of Cologne and escaped death with her to reach Boulogne-sur-Mer in France, where she was martyred by barbarians. She was venerated in a Parisian church which preserved her relics until the time of the French Revolution (*Vie des Saints et des Bienheureux selon l'Ordre du Calendrier avec l'Historique des Fêtes,* par les R. R. P. P. Bénédictines de Paris, XIII, Vol. Paris, 1935–1959).

Saint Badour—We have not found any trace of this saint's life or attributes.

Saint Basil (c. 330–379)—After a career in the world he founded various monastic communities, for which he wrote the *Longer Rule* and *Shorter Rule* on which the lives of the monks were based. He also wrote a revision of the liturgy still used occasionally today, as well as elegant theological defenses of Catholicism. Considered one of the Fathers of the Greek Church, he later became Bishop of Caesarea in Cappadocia, heading much of the huge Asia Minor Church.

Although it has not been possible to identify the quotation in Book I, Chapter 10, it probably comes from some version of the *Manipulus Florum,* the text of which varies slightly from copy to copy.

Saint Bernard (1090?–1153)—Founded the Cistercian monastery of Clairvaux in the Champagne region of France in 1115, where he instituted strict discipline and asceticism. Bernard's activity was so indefatigable that his fame and influence spread rapidly until the spiritual center of Christendom was for a time virtually transferred from Rome to Clairvaux. His sermons on the Song of Solomon are the most important of his mystical writings. There were eighty-six in all, of exceptional eloquence, which were delivered first to the monks of Clairvaux, then later disseminated.

In his *Paradiso,* Dante hailed Saint Bernard as the supreme guide to the heavenly realm. Christine undoubtedly knew of the saint through the *Divine Comedy,* but one suspects that in Book I, Chapter 4 she was quoting Jean Gerson, who was certainly familiar with Saint Bernard's sermons (L. Mourin, *Jean Gerson,* p. 359).

Saint Catherine of Alexandria—(Feast Day, November 25.) Catherine lived under the Emperor Maximian, was imprisoned, and was finally decapitated because she resolved to remain a Christian. Her body was miraculously transported by angels to Mount Sinai. She was widely venerated during the thirteenth century, and in 1221 the French king, Saint Louis, laid the cornerstone of Saint Catherine of the Val-des-Escoliers, which received scholars coming to study at the University of Paris. She became the scholar's patron, in memory of her supposed theological disputes with the philosophers of Alexandria, and was also the patron saint of young girls.

Saint Elizabeth (1207–1231)—The daughter of King Andrew II of Hungary, she was betrothed in infancy to Louis II, Landgrave of Thuringea. In 1211 she was sent to his court to be reared in her adopted country, and at the age of fourteen she married Louis, who encouraged her in charitable works. After his death the hostility of his family and subjects obliged her to seek the protection of her uncle, the Bishop of Bamberg. Then, having provided for the futures of her three children, she became a member of a Franciscan Tertiary Community, devoting herself to contemplative life. In 1235, shortly after her death, she was canonized.

Saint Gregory (540–604)—This saint was a strong leader and set many precedents during his career as a Doctor of the Church, including the encouragement of monasticism and of clerical celibacy. He also assisted in the development of the Gregorian chant.

Although his numerous writings emphasize practicality, their popularity was enhanced by the medieval fascination for the wonderful, of which his vision of Paradise is a prime example. Christine probably knew the passage in Book I, Chapter 5 from the *Manipulus Florum,* where it occurs in the section entitled "Gloria Eterna." She also used it in *L'Avision-Christine* and in *L'Epître de la prison de vie humaine.*

Saint Jerome (c. 347–420?)—Father and Doctor of the Church, he renounced his early classical scholarship for a life of asceticism. At one time, he served as spiritual advisor to a number of noble ladies living in convents. Later, he devoted himself almost entirely to writing, including commentaries on the Scriptures, a Latin translation of the Bible, and over one hundred vivid letters, some of them correspondence with St. Augustine.

Christine's quotation in Book II, Chapter 13 is from the *Manipulus Florum* under "Nativa," where it is attributed in some manuscripts to Saint Ambrose.

Saint Louis (1214–1270)—Son of Louis VIII and Blanche of Castille, he inherited the French crown at the age of twelve. After his mother's regency, he began his personal reign in 1234. Both his contemporaries and later generations adopted him as the ideal of medieval kingship. He reigned according to a high ideal of Christian ethics, participated in two crusades, and died before the walls of Tunis on August 25, 1270, leaving the French monarchy both strong and popular. He was canonized by Pope Boniface VIII in 1297. [See also Glossary entry, "Queen Blanche of Castille."]

Saint Nicholas (died c. 350)—Bishop of Myra (in present-day Turkey), he was named patron saint of students and children, to whom he traditionally was said to bring gifts on the Eve of December 6, his feast day. Reputedly, the man generously provided dowries for poor girls, and saved three children from being murdered.

Saint Paul—I Corinthians 13:2.

Seneca—Lucius Annaeus Seneca was born in Cordoba, Spain, c. 3 B.C., son of the historian Seneca. He spent the major part of his life in Rome, where he served as Nero's tutor. Though he was a prolific writer, some of his works have disappeared. During the

Middle Ages certain texts were incorrectly attributed to him, notably the *Book of Four Virtues (De Formula Honestae Vitae)*, Christine's principal inspiration in writing *The Book of Prudence (Le Livre de Prudence)*. Seneca's moral philosophy, based on Stoic doctrine, was especially popular in medieval times. Numerous epigrams were quoted from his writings or attributed to him in such collections as *The Sayings of the Philosophers (Les Dits des Philosophes)*, translated from the Latin by Christine's contemporary, Guillaume de Tignonville. The popular medieval handbook for preachers known as the *Manipulus Florum* quoted Seneca extensively, especially in the section entitled "Labor," and that work probably served as the source of Christine's Senecan epigrams.

Service of love (Courtly Love)—Already an anachronism in Christine's time, love service was a component of the preciosity of courtly love, an "inborn suffering" of a man for a high-born, imperious woman who demanded a "service of love" from him as demonstration of devotion. Conversely, men promising service to young ladies expected sexual reward or social advancement. Courtly love was illicit and adulterous, thus secret and contrived by the necessary artifices of clandestine meetings, code names called *senjals*, fears of the jealous husband *(jelos)*, and extravagant praises of a beloved more yearned-for than accessible. Inspiring to the most astonishing feats of prowess or poetry, it also could be devastating or deadly.

A magnificent and powerful literary conceit, courtly love derived theoretically from Andreas Capellanus' twelfth century *Art of Courtly Love;* it infused the poetry of the troubadours, trouveres, and minnesingers, as well as romancers such as Chretien de Troyes, and the modern understandings of the passions of Lancelot and Guinevere, of Tristan and Isolde.

Seven Deadly Sins—Pride, Covetousness, Lust, Envy, Gluttony, Anger, and Sloth.

Seven Virtues—Faith, Hope, and Charity (the Theological Virtues), plus Justice, Prudence, Temperance, and Fortitude (the Cardinal Virtues).

She who accepts a gift sells herself—This was a common proverb. [See Hassell, *Middle French Proverbs*, F33, p. 109.]

Sheep—Christine's knowledge of sheep-raising undoubtedly is based on Jean de Brie's *Le Bon Berger (The Good Shepherd)*, which, like other agricultural texts, was translated from Latin at the request of Charles V.

Slanderers—*The Chronicle of Saint Denis* reports that in August 1405 several of Queen Isabeau de Bavière's ladies-in-waiting were dismissed or put in prison "because of slander." The queen absolutely refused to allow an investigation of the charges, despite a request for one by some of the accused women. [B. Bellaguet, ed., Vol. III, p. 290; also see M. Laigle, *Le Livre des Trois Vertus* p. 21n.]

Solomon's praise for the wise woman—Proverbs 31:10–31.

A sou—Formerly, French copper coins of small value.

Spices—Used as digestives, spices were served at feast's end in candied form, such as crystallized ginger, or, when flaked or powdered, strewn upon desserts or dried fruit, such as figs dipped in fennel and dill. Believed to help the body digest the complete meal, spices were determined by the menu, specific ones being considered appropriate for particular fish, flesh, fowl, and vegetables.

Grown locally or imported from the East, spices also served as badges of luxury and ostentation, as seasonings and preservatives for foods, as medical-nutritional substances, as important commercial products, and as ingredients in cosmetics and perfumes. [See Madeleine Pelner Cosman's "Herbs," "Pharmacopoeia," "Cookery," and "Feasting" in the Scribner *Dictionary of the Middle Ages* (New York, 1982–7).]

Stories of the saints—The powerful force of example was considered a constant in the teaching of the young, as Christine emphasizes throughout her writings. The saints were the heroines and heros of the Christian church. A popular book about saints' lives, Jacobus de Voragine's *Golden Legend,* was expanded in 1402, and various copies of it were made in Paris shortly thereafter. However, Christine's own source for the saints' lives included in *The Book of the City of Ladies* [see translation by E.J. Richards, New York, 1982] apparently was Vincent of Beauvais' *Speculum Historiale*.

Suggestive Clothing—Ordinances forbade prostitutes to wear certain articles of bourgeois clothing and insisted that they wear a distinguishing mark on their right arm.

Tithe—The Church expected one tenth of the annual production of the land, offered by the faithful in money, produce, or labor.

Titus (39–81 A.D.)—Son of the Roman emperor Vespasian, for whom he captured Jerusalem in 70 A.D. In the wake of this triumph he was promoted to virtual partnership in his father's government, and succeeded him in 79. His wealth permitted him to gain a reputation for great generosity, which, had he reigned longer than two years, probably would have caused a financial crisis. Titus was also noted for outstanding clemency, even toward his enemies.

The treasure hidden in the field—Matthew 13:44.

Trust in princes—Psalm 146:3.

Tunics—Favored by the style of the times, tunics were worn over another garment; sometimes they were made without sides. Also in fashion were gowns cut in circular form with skirts so long that they had to be gathered up in front and held in the hand for walking; trains extended behind.

Valerius Maximus (c. 49 B.C.–30 A.D.)—Wrote a nine volume compendium of "memorable deeds and sayings" that was popular for centuries as a resource for authors and orators. His Roman history had been translated in part for Charles V by Simon de Hesdin, and was finished in 1401 by Nicholas de Gonesse under the patronage of the notable bibliophile, the Duke of Berry. [For the passage cited by Christine, see Paris, B.N. Ms. fr. 282, fol. 2.]

Vespers—Evening prayer, the second of the two principal Divine Offices to be read or recited every day by clergy and laity of the Catholic Church. An important feature is the recitation or singing of the Magnificat.

Vineyard Workers—Matthew 20:1–16.

Walled cities—Communities which developed as the result of the growing independence of a middle class. Castles of the nobility might be found either within these cities or in the country. Like the castles, the cities were protected by elaborate fortifications. Manors depended on castles for protection, and in return supplied necessary commodities; a large castle might command a number of manors.

Widows, advice to—Much of Christine's advice is based on her own experience, which she describes in *The Mutacion de Fortune* and *L'Avision-Christine*. For some years after the death of her husband, she was plagued by lawsuits over property she had inherited and arising out of her efforts to collect money due her husband. *La Mutacion de Fortune*. Ed. Solente, Vol. I, pp. 46–53; *L'Avision-Christine*, ed. Towner, pp. 154–155.] It apparently was all too common for greedy acquaintances, lawyers, magistrates, and court officials to try to take advantage of widows.

Woe unto the Kingdom—Ecclesiastes 10:16.

Women attendants—In spite of her shortcomings, Isabeau de Bavière was conscientious about those chosen to take care of the royal children. Marguerite was put under the charge of three very respectable ladies, including Catherine de Villiers, Lady of Quesnoy, whose fidelity was noteworthy. In addition, there were five ladies-in-waiting and a serving maid, Marion—nine attendants in all. [See Rey, *Les Finances sous Charles VI*, p. 191.]

Women of the court—Since the court of a princess or noblewoman was an important means of preparing a young girl for a life in courtly society, and might provide the way to a suitable marriage, young women were frequently sent to grow up at the court of a kinswoman. Such courts also were frequented by the daughters of lesser (though ambitious) noblemen, and sometimes the daughters of high-ranking court officials who were not necessarily of noble rank. Inevitably, courts were the scene of a certain amount of competition. Charm and ambition played a role in social advancement, to the chagrin of less attractive and less fortunate members of a court.

Margaret of Guyenne was cast aside by her husband during his infatuation with one of his mother's ladies-in-waiting, the daughter of Guillaume Cassinelle, who was one of the king's counsellors and not of the nobility.

Xerxes—Reigned as Emperor of Persia from 486–465 B.C. Cooperating with Carthage, he fought against the Greeks. Initially successful, he was subsequently forced into retreat when Themistocles and the Greek fleet won a great victory at Salamis. Xerxes' rule was characterized by violence and intolerance; his court was weakened by intrigues, one of which resulted in his murder.

Christine had cited his tyrannical nature in the *Mutacion de Fortune* (Ed. Solente, Vol. I, pp. 242–256).

Yearly income—Although the basic purpose of the lord's and lady's manor, or manors, was to provide food, many were able to increase their revenues by improving their landholdings and their yield. The growth of the towns also provided a market for surplus crops, thus resulting in a cash income. At the same time, after the middle of the fourteenth century, epidemics and the growth of commerce reduced the number of farm workers available, greatly increasing the cost of such labor. Landowners who were not able to cope with these changing circumstances were ruined by them. Administering an estate required not only foresight, but skill in contracts, legal procedure, and accounting. [See also Glossary entry on "Revenues."]

Young men in taverns—Christine elaborates on this habit of artisans in *The Book of the Body Politic (Le Livre du Corps de Policie)*, Part III, Chapter 9 (Ed. Lucas, pp. 194–199).

BIBLIOGRAPHY

I. TRANSLATIONS OF CHRISTINE DE PIZAN'S WORKS

The Boke of the Cyte of Ladyes, Trans. Brian Anslay (London, 1521). Reprinted in *Distaves and Dames; Renaissance Treatises for and about Women.* Ed. Diane Bornstein (Delmar, N.Y., 1978).

The Book of the City of Ladies. Trans. Earl Jeffrey Richards (New York, 1982).

The Book of the Duke of True Lovers. Trans. Alice Kemp-Welch; the ballads rendered into the original meter by Lawrence Binyon and Eric D. Maclagen (London, 1908).

The Book of Fayttes of Arms and of Chyvalrye: Translated and Printed by William Caxton from the French Original by Christine de Pizan. Ed. A.T.P. Byles (London, 1932, rev. 1937).

The Fayt of Arms and of Chyvalrie. Facsimile of Caxton's 1489 edition (Amsterdam-New York, 1968).

La Ditié de Jeanne d'Arc. Ed. and trans. Angus J. Kennedy and Kenneth Varty (Oxford, 1977).

Das Buch von den Drei Tugenden in Portugiescher Ubersetzing. Ed. Dorotee Carstens-Grokenberger (Münster, 1961).

O Espelho de Cristina. Ed. Maria Manuela de Silva Nunes Ribeiro Cruzeiro. 2 vols. (Lisbon, 1965).

The Epistle of Othéa to Hector. Trans. Anthony Babington. Ed. James D. Gordon (Philadelphia, 1942).

The Epistle of Othéa. Trans. Sir Stephen Scrope. Ed. Curt F. Bühler (London, 1970).

"The Letter of Cupid" in Hoccleve's *Works: The Minor Poems.* Ed. I. Gollancz (London, 1925).

The Letter of Cupid in the Bannatyne Manuscript. Ed. W. Todd Ritchie (Edinburgh-London, 1930).

The Epistle of the Prison of Human Life, Trans. Josette Wisman (New York, 1985).

The Middle English Translation of Christine de Pisan's Livre du Corps de Policie. Ed. Diane Bornstein (Heidelberg, 1977).

Morale Proverbes of Chrystine. Facsimile of Caxton's 1478 edition of Anthony Woodville's translation. (Amsterdam-New York, 1970).

The Treasure of the City of Ladies. Trans. Sara Lawson (London, 1985).
La Querelle de la Rose: Letters and Documents. Ed. Joseph L. Baird and John R. Kane (Chapel Hill, 1978).

II. MODERN EDITIONS

L'Avision-Christine. Introduction and text. Ed. Sister Mary Louise Towner (Washington, D.C. 1932).
Ballades, Rondeaux, and Virelais. Ed. Kenneth Varty (Leicester, J.K. 1965).
Cent Ballades d'Amant et de Dame. Ed. Jacqueline Cerquiglini (Paris, 1982).
Christine de Pisan. Ed. Jeanine Moulin (Paris, 1962).
La Ditié de Jeanne d'Arc. Eds. Angus J. Kennedy and Kenneth Varty (Oxford, 1977).
Le Débat sur le Roman de la Rose. Critical edition, with introduction, translations and notes by Eric Hicks (Paris, 1977).
Epistre de la prison de vie humaine. Ed. Angus J. Kennedy (Glasgow, 1984).
La Lamentacion sur les maux de la France. In *Mélanges de Langue et Littérature Françaises du Moyen Age et de la Renaissance Offerts à Charles Foulon.* Ed. Angus J. Kennedy (Rennes, 1980), pp. 177–185.
Lettre à Isabeau de Bavière. In *Anglo-Norman Letters and Petitions from all Souls Ms. 182.* Ed. M. Dominica Legge (Oxford, 1971).
Le Livre du Chemin de Long Estude. Ed. Robert Püschel (Berlin, 1881).
Le Livre du Corps de Policie. Ed. Robert H. Lucas (Geneva, 1967).
Le Livre des Fais et Bonnes Meurs du Sage Roy Charles V. Ed. Suzanne Solente, 2 vols. (Paris, 1936–1941).
Le Livre de la Mutacion de Fortune. Ed. Suzanne Solente. 4 vols. (Paris, 1959–1966).
Le Livre de la Paix. Ed. Charity Cannon Willard (The Hague, 1958).
Oeuvres Poétiques. Ed. Maurice Roy. 3 vols. (Paris, 1886–1896).
Sept Psaumes Allegorisés. Ed. Ruth Ringland Rains (Washington, D.C., 1965).

III. BIOGRAPHICAL STUDIES

Boldingh-Goemans, W.L. *Christine de Pizan (1364–1430) Haar Tijd, Haar Leven, Haar Werken.* (Rotterdam, 1948).

Du Castel, Françoise. *Damoiselle Christine de Pizan, veuve de M. Etienne de Castel* (Paris, 1972).

———. *Ma Grand-mère Christine de Pizan* (Paris, 1936).

Favier, Marguerite. *Christine de Pisan: Muse des Cours Souveraines* (Lausanne, 1967).

Kemp-Welch, Alice. *Of Six Medieval Women*. (London, 1913).

Kennedy, Angus J. *Christine de Pizan: A Bibliographical Guide* (London, 1984).

McLeod, Enid. *The Order of the Rose. The Life and Ideals of Christine de Pizan* (London, 1976).

Nys, Ernest. *Christine de Pisan et ses Principales Oeuvres* (Brussels, 1914).

Pernoud, Régine. *Christine de Pisan* (Paris, 1982).

Pinet, Marie-Josèphe. *Christine de Pisan, (1364–1430). Etude Biographique et Littéraire* (Paris, 1927).

Solente, Suzanne. "Christine de Pizan." Extract from *L'Histoire littéraire de la France*. Vol. 40 (Paris, 1969).

Willard, Charity Cannon. *Christine de Pizan: Her Life and Works* (New York, 1984).

Yenal, Edith. *Christine de Pisan. A Bibliography of Writings of Her and About Her* (Metuchen, New Jersey and London, 1982).

IV. SPECIAL STUDIES

Bornstein, Diane, "The Ideal of the Lady of the Manor as Reflected in Christine de Pizan's *Livre des Trois Vertus*," in *Ideals for Women in the Works of Christine de Pizan*. Ed. Diane Bornstein (Michigan Consortium for Medieval and Early Modern Studies, 1981), pp. 117–128.

———. *Mirrors of Courtesy* (Hamden, Conn., 1975).

Dulac, Liliane, "Inspiration mystique et savoir politique: les conseils aux veuves chez Francesco da Barbarino et chez Christine de Pizan," in *Mélanges à la Mémoire de Franco Simone* (Geneva, 1980), pp. 113–141.

Figueiredo, A.J. de. "Espelho de Cristina," *Revista Brasileira de Folologia* III (1957), pp. 117–119.

Hindman, Sandra L. *Christine de Pizan's "Epistre d'Othéa." Painting and Politics at the Court of Charles VI* (Toronto, 1988).

Laigle, Mathilde. *Le Livre des Trois Vertus de Christine de Pisan et son milieu historique et littéraire* (Paris, 1912).

Richards, Earl Jeffrey. "Christine de Pizan and the Question of Feminist Rhetoric," *Modern Language Association Conference* 22 (1983), pp. 15–24.

Willard, Charity Cannon. "A Portuguese Translation of Christine de Pizan's *Livre des Trois Vertus*," PMLA 78 (1963), pp. 459–464.

––––––. "The Manuscript Tradition of the *Livre des Trois Vertus* and Christine de Pizan's Audience," *Journal of the History of Ideas* 27, (1966), pp. 433–444.

––––––. "A Fifteenth-Century View of Women's Role in Medieval Society: Christine de Pizan's *Livre des Trois Vertus*," in *The Role of Women in the Middle Ages*. Ed. Rosalie T. Morewedge (Albany, N.Y.-London, 1975), pp. 90–120.

––––––. "Christine de Pizan's Livre des Trois Vertus: Feminine Ideal or Practical Advice?" in Bornstein, *Ideals for Women in the Works of Christine de Pizan,* pp. 91–116.

V. GENERAL BACKGROUND

Aliénor de Poitiers, "Les Honneurs de la Cour" in *La Curne de Sainte-Palaye, Mémoires sur l'Ancienne Chevalerie,* Vol. II (Paris, 1759), pp. 161–267.

Andreas Capellanus. *The Art of Courtly Love.* Trans. and ed. J.J. Parry (New York, 1964).

Artz, Frederick B. *The Mind of the Middle Ages* (New York, 1953).

Bennet, H.S. *The Pastons and their England.* (Cambridge, England, 1921; reprinted 1970).

Bizet, J.A. *Mystiques Allemands de XIVe Siècle* (Paris, 1957).

Brook, Iris. *Western European Costume: Thirteenth to Seventeenth Century,* 2 vols. (London, 1939).

Bullough, Vern L. "Marriage in the Middle Ages: Five Medical and Scientific Views of Women," *Viator* 4 (1973), pp. 485–501.

Les Cent Nouvelles Nouvelles. Ed. Pierre Champion (Paris, 1928), 2 vols.

La Chronique du Religieux de Saint-Denis, contenant le règne de Charles VI de 1380–1422. Ed. L.F. Bellaguet (Paris, 1839–1852) 6 vols.

Commeaux, Charles. *La Vie Quotidienne en Bourgogne au Temps des Ducs Valois 1364–1477* (Paris, 1979).

Contamine, Philippe. *La Vie Quotidienne pendant la Guerre de Cent Ans* (Paris, 1976).

Cosman, Madeleine Pelner, *Fabulous Feasts: Medieval Cookery and Ceremony* (New York, 1976).

Cosneau, E. *Le Connétable Richemont (Arthur de Bretagne, 1393–1458)* (Paris, 1886).

Deschamps, Eustache. *Le Miroir de Mariage.* Vol. 9 of his *Oeuvres,* ed. G. Raynaud (Paris, 1894).

Evans, Joan. *Dress in Medieval France* (Oxford, 1952).

La Farce de Maître Pierre Pathelin. Ed. R. T. Holbrook (Paris, 1937).

Fleming, John V. "Hoccleve's 'Letter to Cupid' and the 'Quarrel' over the *Roman de la Rose,*" *Medium Aevum* 40 (1971), pp. 20–40.

Fourquin, Guy. *Le Paysan d'Occident au Moyen Age* (Paris, 1974).

Gerson, Jean. *Oeuvres Complètes.* Vol. 7: *L'Oeuvre Française, Sermons et Discours.* Ed. Mgr. Glorieux (Paris, 1968).

Gies, Frances and Joseph. *Life in a Medieval Castle* (New York, 1974).

Goglin, Jean-Louis. *Les Misérables dans l'Occident Médiéval* (Paris, 1976).

The Goodman of Paris. Trans. Eileen Power (London, 1928). (See also *Le Menagier de Paris.*)

Les Grandes Chroniques de France. Ed. Roland Delachenal (Paris, 1916–1920), 5 vols.

Hartman, John. *The Book of Hours* (London, 1977).

Hassell, James Woodrow Jr. *Middle French Proverbs, Sentences and Proverbial Phrases* (Toronto, Pontifical Institute of Medieval Studies, 1982).

Heer, Frederick. *The Medieval World* (London, 1961).

Hughes, Robert. *Heaven and Hell in Western Art* (London, 1968).

Itinéraires de Philippe le Hardi et de Jean sans Peur. Ed. Ernest Petit (Paris, 1888).

Jean de Brie. *Le Bon Bergier: Le Vrai Règlement et Gouvernement des Bergers et Bergères.* Modern version of Edition of 1542 (Paris, 1979).

Le Livre de la Chasse de Gaston Phoebus, Comte de Foix. Textes de Gabriel Bise d'après Gaston Phoebus (Fribourg-Geneva, 1984).

Le Livre du Chevalier de la Tour Landry. Ed. A. de Montaiglon (Paris, 1854).

Le Menagier de Paris. Eds. Georgine E. Brereton and Janet M. Ferrier (Oxford, 1981). (See also *The Goodman of Paris.*)

Mirot, Leon. *Etudes Lucquoises* (Nogent-le-Rotrou, 1930).

Mourin, Louis. *Jean Gerson, Prédicateur Français* (Bruges, 1952).

Paston Letters and Papers of the Fifteenth Century. Ed. N. Davis (Oxford, 1971).

Pernoud, Regine. *La Femme au Temps des Cathédrals* (Paris, 1980).

Pouquet du Haut-Jussé, B.-A. "Le Connétable de Richemont, Seigneur Bourguignon," *Annales de Bourgogne* 11 (1935), pp. 309–336.

Les Quinze Joyes de Mariage. Ed. Joan Crow (Oxford, 1969).

Rey, M. *Les Finances Royales sous Charles VI. Les Causes du Déficit 1388–1413.* (Paris, 1965).

Robertson, D. W. Jr. *A Preface to Chaucer in Medieval Perspective* (Princeton, 1962).

Rouse, Richard H. and Mary A. Preachers, *Florilegia and Sermons: Studies of the Manipulus Florum of Thomas of Ireland* (Toronto, 1979).

Sapori, A. *Le Marchand Italien au Moyen Age* (Paris, 1952).

The Secular Spirit: Life and Art at the End of the Middle Ages. The Metropolitan Museum of Art. Introduction by Timothy B. Husband and Jane Hayward (New York, 1975).

Sherman, Claire. "The Queen in Charles V's *Coronation Book:* Jeanne de Bourbon and the *Ordo ad Reginam Benedicendam,*" *Viator* 8 (1977), pp. 255–297.

Thibault, Marcel. *Isabeau de Bavière, reine de France. La Jeunesse 1370–1405* (Paris, 1903).

Truc, G. *Histoire Illustrée de la Femme* (Paris, 1940).

Vaughan, Richard. *John the Fearless* (London, 1966).

Vaughan, Richard. *Philip the Bold* (London-Cambridge, Mass., 1962).

Verdon, Jean. *Isabeau de Bavière* (Paris, 1981).

Vie des Saints et des Bienheureux selon l'Ordre du Calendrier avec l'Historique des Fêtes by the R. R. P. P. Bendictines of Paris (Paris, 1935–1959), 13 vols.

Women in the Medieval World. Ed. Julius Kirshner and Suzanne Wemple (New York, 1985).

Ziegler, Philip. *The Black Death* (London, 1969).